The
Crafts Busin
Answer Book
& Resource Guide

THE
Crafts Business Answer Book &

RESOURCE GUIDE

Answers to Hundreds of Troublesome Questions About
Starting, Marketing, and Managing a Homebased Business
Efficiently, Legally, and Profitably

Barbara Brabec

M. EVANS AND COMPANY, INC.
NEW YORK

M. Evans and Company, Inc.
216 East 49th Street
New York, NY 10017

Library of Congress Cataloging-in-Publication Data

Brabec, Barbara.
   The crafts business answer book & resource guide : answers to hundreds of troublesome questions about starting, marketing, and managing a homebased business efficiently, legally, and profitably / Barbara Brabec.
       p.   cm.
   Includes bibliographical references and index.
   ISBN 0-87131-832-6 (cloth). — ISBN 0-87131-833-4 (trade paper)
   1. Handicraft industries—Management 2. Home-based businesses—
Management. 3. Handicraft—Marketing. I. Title.
HD2341.B698   1998
745.5'068—dc21   97-35315

Design and composition by John Reinhardt Book Design

Manufactured in the United States of America

9   8

This book is dedicated to all the creative people who have read my articles and books through the years, sharing helpful information I could pass on to others through my writing.

All of the information in this book is presented to assist homebased businesspersons—those just getting started as well as those already in business. The author's goal is to familiarize readers with important areas of concern and enable them to ask the right questions if and when it is necessary to consult with an attorney, accountant, or other business adviser. Much of the material offered is in such "professional service" categories as legalities, taxes, and accounting. While this information has been carefully researched by the author and is accurate to the best of her knowledge as this book goes to press, it is not the business of either the author or publisher to render such professional services. Readers are therefore asked to exercise normal good judgment in determining when the services of a lawyer or other professional would be appropriate to their needs.

Contents

A-to-Z listings in this book are grouped here in logical business categories for easy reference.

Accounting

Advertising and Marketing

See also Pricing and Selling

Banking

See also Money Management

Business Activities

Business and Office Management

See also Insurance

Employees/Labor Issues

Insurance

Laws and Regulations

See also Legal Issues

Legal Issues

See also Laws and Regulations and Taxes

Miscellaneous Topics

Money Management

See also Banking and Insurance

Pricing and Selling

See also Advertising and Marketing

Raw Materials

Shipping and Mailing

Taxes

See also Employee/Labor Issues

Resources

Index   *273*

Alphabetical List of Articles

Introduction

Everyone feels a bit intimidated when they leave their comfort zone to step into unknown territory. In looking back over my lifetime of home-business experience, I remember all those times when I wanted to try something new but lacked specific information on how to do it. The big challenges, like how to begin the writing of my first book, launch a magazine, or publish my own books, took a lot of extra time and research to be sure, but it was the smaller, day-to-day problems that caused me the most stress and worry.

For the first few years, I had many more questions than answers and it took me a long time to work out solutions to all the little niggling problems of how to run a business at home and make a real profit from all the time and effort I was putting into my work. Although my writing and publishing work is different from your work as an artist, craftsperson, or designer, we have similar creative leanings and we certainly share common ground when it comes to the management of our homebased business and the marketing of our products. Everyone who starts a business venture at home—no matter how small—needs to know how to stay out of legal trouble, avoid costly business pitfalls, and cut expenses to the quick to make a bigger profit. More specifically, we need to know which laws or regulations affect our particular business activity. We must learn about tax and employee issues, protect ourselves with good insurance and solve problems related to technology. We strive constantly to refine our sales and marketing strategies, become better money managers, and get a tighter grip on time management. And every day, it seems, we have to find the answer to yet another question or solve another small problem never encountered before.

Experience has taught me that some small business lessons are merely frustrating while others are painfully expensive in terms of lost time, money, sales, opportunities, or ego. The less experience or information we have about a particular problem or situation, the more stressful the lesson and the more we may agonize over the outcome. Having the right information at hand when we need it enables us to "keep our cool" in the face of a new problem or predicament. This eliminates unnecessary worry and automatically lowers our stress level.

I don't pretend to know everything about running a crafts business, but this book does answer the most common questions of beginning craft sellers and offers solutions to hundreds of problems likely to affect both new and long-established craft businesses at one time or another. Its encyclopedic content is based not only on my own experience but on the experiences of hundreds of professional crafters and home business owners who have networked with me through the years. Every page offers precise and practical information to answer specific questions and help you solve small business problems as soon as they arise.

How to Use This Book

Although this is essentially a reference book, I've tried to make it interesting to read by including personal experience stories (mine and others), special tips, and "sidebar articles" on a variety of topics. An initial thumb-through of the book will reveal several topics in which you have a keen interest now. If you want to read only the articles now, look for material that has been boxed on a page or see the alphabetical list of articles at the end of the Contents section. Special tips are easy to spot—all have been screened in gray.

Tip

One of the first things you should do is check "Business Activities" and "Raw Materials" on the Contents pages to see if there are listings for your art or craft or the raw materials you normally use to make products for sale. Then check the referenced A-to-Z listings for specific laws, regulations, or warnings relative to these activities and materials.

Four ways to quickly find information in this book:

1. Check the Table of Contents to find a collection of information on a specific topic, such as business management, employees, taxes, or legal issues.

2. Check the text for alphabetical listings of specific words, phrases, or business terms that come to mind when a question or problem arises. Each listing either has a discussion of the topic or a reference to where it is discussed under a different alphabetical heading. (Unlike other books that have an index in the back that references every topic discussed, this book's index is in both the Contents listings and the text itself in the form of cross-references.)

3. Check the book's Resource Chapter for:
   a) alphabetical lists of book and periodical publishers, organizations, government agencies and suppliers, and service providers mentioned in the text.
   b) a list of recommended books, some of which have been mentioned in the text, others of which you may want to look for in your library or bookstore;

4. Check the book's Names Index to find page number references to individuals, businesses, organizations, publishers, government agencies, book titles, and laws mentioned in the text.

Why You Can Trust The Information in This Book

When I read a book, I want to know the writer's credentials so I know whether or not I can take seriously the information contained in that book. For that reason, let me give you some background information about myself that wasn't appropriate for the back cover.

Prior to my marriage to Harry Brabec in 1961, I worked for ten years in Chicago's Loop as a secretary and office manager for three different businesses. During this period, I was also a freelance musical entertainer who presented programs for women's clubs and played background music at weddings and supper clubs. Everything I learned about business and self-promotion in this period of time later proved invaluable to me as a professional writer, speaker, and publisher.

At Harry's request a few years after we were married, I left the business world to just be "Mrs. Brabec" and I practically went nuts after six weeks of not working in an office. We didn't plan to have children and I was still career-oriented, so to keep busy and earn a little extra money, I began to expand my self-employment activities. (No one called it a "homebased business" in those days.) While continuing to play club dates, I also did a few home typing jobs. One day, in response to my complaint that I didn't have enough to occupy my time, Harry said three little words that forever changed our lives: "Get a hobby." I did. I discovered the world of arts and crafts, found I had some skill as a craftsperson, began to sell my work at local shops and shows, and was no longer bored. In fact, now the days weren't long enough and I could hardly wait for Harry to leave the house so I could run down to my workbench in the basement to make things for sale.

Shortly afterward, my enthusiasm for crafts and all the questions I had about how to sell what I was making prompted Harry to suggest that we start a magazine to enable others like myself to get answers to questions while trading experiences with others. When you consider that neither Harry nor I had any writing skill, publishing know-how, or the slightest idea of how to produce and sell a magazine, it's no wonder our venture yielded a pitiful financial profit. But this five-year period was important in our lives because it positioned me to write my first book and led Harry into the production of craft expositions for major theme parks such as Silver Dollar City, Busch Gardens, and Marriott.

The sales success of my first book (*Creative Cash*) convinced me I could make a living as a writer and self-publisher. Without knowing it at the time, when I launched a home business newsletter in 1981 and followed that with a second book, *Homemade Money*, I became one of the country's home business pioneers. This book led to dozens of invitations to speak at home business conferences across the country.

In 1996, after fifteen years of newsletter publishing, I decided to cease publication, limit my speaking engagements, and focus on writing books. This is my sixth book and, God willing, there will be more. This book will be periodically updated in the future as laws or business practices change or as I learn more about everything, so

I welcome your feedback to it. Let me know what information helped you the most. If you have encountered and solved a business problem not addressed in this book (or think I've left out something important), let me know. Although I cannot correspond with all my readers or answer questions by mail, I do read every letter I receive and all mail is acknowledged with a package of information about my various books and reports. Thanks for telling others about them.

Any reader who contributes useful information for the next edition of this book will be acknowledged in the text and will receive a free copy of that edition upon publication. Direct all inquiries, questions, or comments to:

> Barbara Brabec
> "Answer Book" Feedback
> P.O. Box 2137
> Naperville, IL 60567
> Phone: (630) 717-4188
> Fax: (630) 717-5198

Accountant

Q: *How can I get the accounting and tax help I need without spending a lot of money?*

Business novices often hire a Certified Public Accountant (CPA) to do their annual tax return when only an Public Accountant is needed, or they may hire a tax preparer when what they really need is an accountant. Consider that:

• CPAs have more education than other accountants and are licensed by the state on completion of four years of college and one to two years on-the-job training. Because of their extra education, CPAs not only charge more for their services but tend to specialize in corporate work. As a result, the average CPA may be totally unfamiliar with all the allowable deductions related to a homebased business. In many cases, hiring this much power for the average homebased business would be like buying a crystal goblet when all you really need is a glass.

• Public Accountants have a good understanding of tax laws and can help you understand your total financial picture. In addition to taking care of your annual tax return, an accountant can help you make business decisions that will impact your tax return, such as whether to buy or lease a vehicle, form a partnership or incorporate your business. If you need a business loan, an accountant can prepare the financial reports your banker expects to see or stand by you in the event your tax return is audited by the IRS. (Only a CPA or IRS Enrolled Agent can *represent* you before the IRS.) If and when you decide to hire outside help or put your spouse or children on the payroll, an accountant can take care of all those aggravating tax forms and quarterly reports that must be filed. Since accountants aren't bookkeepers, they will expect you to supply all necessary figures for your tax return, which means you have to set up a good bookkeeping system right from the beginning. (Many accountants supply their clients with handy tax organizers that make it easy to pull together all needed figures at year end.)

• Tax preparers are best used for the preparation of personal tax returns only. History has shown that commercial tax-preparers often lack an understanding of the nature of homebased businesses and the deductible expenses related to their operation. Unless a tax preparer can give you the names of other homebased businesses that are clients, it would be best to look elsewhere for the help you need with your crafts business tax return.

• Enrolled Agents (ERs) may be the best solution of all. After years of hiring high-priced accountants to do my tax return and help me with employee tax forms, I finally learned about the benefits of working with an Enrolled Agent (see Enrolled Agents).

See also Accounting Methods; Employees, Family; Employees, Nonfamily; Enrolled Agents; Independent Contractors; *and* Legal Forms of Business.

Tip

Having your tax return prepared by an accountant, CPA, or Enrolled Agent does not mean it will be without error. When the tax season heats up and these people start putting in long hours to accommodate late-filing clients, mistakes may occur. You must take the responsibility for double-checking every figure on your tax return to make sure there are no typographical errors, misplaced figures, or deduction omissions.

Accounting Methods

Q: *Should I use the cash method of accounting or the accrual method?*

Some businesses are required by law to use the accrual accounting method, but an accountant can help you decide which of the following methods is best for you:

• **Cash Method**: All income is taxable in the year it's received, and expenses are generally deductible when paid, with some important exceptions an accountant can explain. Under current law, the cash method of accounting may not be used by (1) Corporations (other than S Corporations); (2) Partnerships having a corporation (other than an S Corporation) as a partner; and (3) businesses with inventories. (All sales-plus-inventory businesses must use accrual accounting for inventory.)

• **Accrual Method**: Tax is paid on earned income, whether it has been collected or not. Expenses are deducted when they are incurred, whether they have been paid or not.

• **Hybrid System**: This is a mix of the above types of accounting systems. For example, a product-oriented business might use the accrual system for inventory purchases and the cash method to record all income and expenses.

See also Bookkeeping *and* Inventory.

Accounts Payable

These are the current bills your business owes for products and services already received. Money you owe others is considered a business liability and it must be listed as such on any balance sheet prepared for your business. To keep your credit record in good shape and stay on top of the record keeping needed for tax purposes, you will need to devise a good system for paying and filing bills. For tips on how to do this, see article, "Barbara's Proven System for Paying Bills and Keeping Tax Records."

See also Balance Sheet; Credit History; *and* Liabilities.

Accounts Receivable

What customers and clients owe you are called *accounts receivable* and these are business assets that should be listed on any balance sheet prepared for your business. You will need to devise some kind of tracking system to make sure your invoices are paid according to the terms you give buyers (usually 30 days). Suggestion: File copies of all invoices due in a folder and at the beginning of each month, pull any that are overdue and send statements accordingly.

See also Balance Sheet; Invoices Not Paid; Liabilities; Statement; *and* Terms of Sale.

Barbara's Proven System for Paying Bills and Keeping Tax Records

Here is the system I have used with success for twenty-five years. At my "bill paying desk," I keep two sets of twelve 6 x 9-inch envelopes with the months written on each. One set is for personal bills, the other for business. I pay bills every Saturday so the job is never overwhelming. Each Saturday, I open all bills that have come in and note on a calendar the particular Saturday each needs to be paid. Then I drop it either in the personal or business envelope for that month, depending on which checkbook I will use to pay it. Each Saturday I pull and pay only those bills indicated on the calendar for that date.

• **Business Bills**. All paid business bills end up in one big envelope and I never handle or look at any of these paid bills again unless I need proof a certain bill has been paid. All bills are marked with check number and date paid and filed with the latest bills to the back. As each bill is paid, all pertinent information as to what I've paid for is entered on my checkbook stub, and this information is periodically posted to my accounting system on computer.

• **Personal Bills**. Any personal bill that is fully or partly tax-deductible is filed in one of several file folders that are recycled each year. These are labeled *Car Expense, Home Maintenance, Telephone, Travel, Utilities, Miscellaneous Income, Interest Earned, Donations*, and *Medical Expenses*. At year's end, the receipts and other documents in these folders will be used to figure my Home Office Deduction for Schedule C and calculate all the other figures needed for our personal tax return. When I'm through gathering figures, I store all the year's tax receipts, canceled checks, and bank statements for at least three years to meet IRS requirements.

See also Petty Cash *and article, "Solving Cash Flow Problems."*

Tip

When you hit your busy season in the fall, it's easy to get so involved producing products for sale that you let your buyers owe you money longer than they should. Remember that the people who are buying from you are just as busy as you are and may tend to overlook payment of your invoice unless you send them a timely reminder in the form of a statement. The longer you let a customer stall payment of an invoice, the harder it may be to collect payment.

Accrual Method of Accounting

See Accounting Methods.

Advertising

Q: **What's the most effective and least expensive kind of advertising I can do to promote my small business?**

Much depends on what you are trying to sell, how much money you have in your advertising budget and whether you're trying to reach retail or wholesale buyers. Most beginners in business automatically think of advertising in terms of expensive display ads in national magazines, but there are many less expensive ways to sell a line of handcrafts or build a homebased business.

• **Consumer Advertising.** If your budget is limited, the first thing you need to do is learn how to maximize word-of-mouth advertising from satisfied buyers. Then you need to learn how to write a news release that will bring you publicity—and business as well—locally or nationally. (These marketing topics are beyond the scope of this book but are discussed at length in my *Homemade Money* book and other books listed in the resource chapter.) Also explore your online advertising options on the World Wide Web. (See discussion of this topic under *Electronic Marketing.*)

If you have developed a good mail piece or catalog promoting your products, consider placing classified ads in magazines read by your kind of buyers. Here you would be using the Two-Step

Method of advertising, explained elsewhere. When you're ready to spend a few hundred dollars on an ad, consider a display ad in one of the consumer magazines that feature only handcrafts, such as *Country Sampler, Country Folk Art, Folkart Treasures* and *Better Homes and Gardens' Crafts Showcase*. All of these magazines can be found on the newsstand. (Although these magazines are aimed at consumers, many advertisers report receiving inquiries and orders from wholesale buyers who are always in search of interesting new products for their shops or mail order catalogs.)

• **Trade Advertising**. If you're trying to attract new wholesale accounts, check a periodicals directory at your library to turn up a variety of trade magazines that reach wholesale buyers likely to be interested in your products. Many trade magazines feature new products. Sometimes you can get visibility simply by sending a news release; other times, you may get a bonus mention when you place your first ad. For starters, consider an ad in *The Crafts Report,* a magazine read by many craft shop and gallery owners.

See also Business Plan; Cost of Advertising; Electronic Marketing; Federal Trade Commission Rules; Independent Contractors; Limited Editions; Mail Order Business; Printed Materials; SASE; Signs; Telephone; Testimonials; Trade Shows; Two-Step Advertising; *and* Zoning Laws.

Tip

Invest some of your advertising money into high-quality printed materials. Many craft sellers report a dramatic increase in orders when they move up to a classy catalog or start using full-color flyers that show their work at its best.

Agreements

See Author/Publisher Contract; Consignment Selling; Contracts; Lawyer; Maintenance Agreements; *and* Sales Representatives.

Air Courier Services

If you ever need to ship anything by air express, both Federal Express and Airborne Express will pick up packages at your door and bill you later if you have established an account with them. Check your local telephone book for their numbers and ask about getting a start-up supply of shipping envelopes, packages, and airbills. Airborne's service is excellent and their rates are lower than those of Federal Express because (I was told) they don't waste money on advertising but have built their company on service to customers who give them good word-of-mouth advertising.

Answering Machine

See Voice Mail vs. Answering Machine.

Apparel

See Garment Manufacturing.

Art/Craft Organizations

Hundreds of organizations cater to the hobby interests of creative people, and many are listed in library directories or have an online presence if you care to search the Internet for them. Selected national organizations that serve the business interests of professional artists or handcraft producers are listed in the resource chapter.

See also Craft Cooperative; Home Business Organizations; Inventor's Clubs and Associations; and Trade Shows.

Assets

There are two kinds of assets: Current and Fixed. Current assets of a typical homebased business would include cash on hand (in business checking account), Accounts Receivable and the value of inventory (raw materials, work in progress, and finished work ready for shipping).

Fixed assets would include the depreciated value of office equipment (computer system, fax, telephones), office furnishings (desks, filing cabinets, chairs, etc.), workshop furnishings (tools of your trade), your business reference library, and even your mail list if it happens to have value for rental purposes.

Associations

See Home Business Organizations; Organization,Formation of; *and* Trade Associations/Publications.

Attorney

See Lawyer.

Author/Publisher Contract

Q: *A publisher has expressed interest in a book I could write for them. Can you give me some pointers on negotiating a book publishing contract?*

Trade book publishers (those who sell to bookstores and libraries as opposed to the "floppy book" publishers who sell to craft and needlecraft shops) send all new authors a "standard contract" whose terms are naturally slanted to the publisher's financial interests. Every clause in a book publishing contract can be negotiated, but beginning writers don't have much power. If you are fortunate enough to find an agent who will represent you to publishers, you will probably get enough extra financial benefits to more than justify the commission he or she will take (generally fifteen percent of royalties).

I've said earlier that it's always a good idea to have an attorney check a contract before you sign it, but it won't do you much good to hire an attorney to check an author/publisher contract unless that attorney has worked with other authors before. For example, an attorney who doesn't know the book publishing industry won't understand the significance of a clause that says royalties will be cut in half for books sold at a discount greater than fifty-five percent. This may not seem important until you consider that some publishers sell mostly to book clubs and library distributors that may require discounts of sixty percent or more. Suddenly, an author's total royalties could be half the amount expected.

The average attorney is also unlikely to understand the importance of clauses that stipulate how soon rights to a book will return to the author when it goes out of print. Authors who expect to take an active role in the marketing of their books should insist on a clause that gives them the right to buy books at a considerable discount, and get publishing rights back as quickly as possible when copies are no longer available for sale from the publisher. (Some contracts stipulate that rights won't be returned for two years, which is too long if you are still marketing a title at the time a publisher lets it go out of print.) And there should be a clause stipulating that a publisher cannot remainder an author's book without first giving the author the chance to buy copies at the same price (usually pennies on the dollar).

Personal experience with six trade book publishers has given me considerable insight on this topic. If you don't have a book agent or can't find an attorney who knows the book publishing industry, I will be happy to consult with you on the telephone and give you additional tips about things you should look for in a book contract.

See also Book Copyright *and* Royalties on Books.

Bad Check Law

See article, "When You Have Evidence of Fraud."

Bad Checks

 What's the best way to collect on a check that has bounced?

Depending on why the check was returned, you will want to take different actions. Checks may bounce because of nonsufficient funds (NSF), a closed account, or no account (evidence of fraud).

• **Nonsufficient Funds.** If a check is marked "NSF" and the bank hasn't presented it twice, you can deposit it again. (Since you can only redeposit a check one time, however, you may wish to telephone the person who wrote the check to make sure there will be sufficient funds to cover it the second time around.) Many banks automatically present checks twice before returning them, and most checks presented twice will clear the second time through. If a check comes back a second time, however, you have to decide if the size of the check is large enough to be worth the trouble it will take to collect it.

• **Account Closed.** Some people move and close an account before making certain all checks have cleared while others overdraw on their account because they have incorrectly added or subtracted. While this is a sign of carelessness, it is not evidence of fraud. In writing to a customer about this problem, begin with the assumption that the bad check was unintentional. Ask the customer to honor his or her obligation with a replacement money order. Hold the bad check as evidence of the customer's indebtedness to you, returning it upon receipt of the replacement money order.

• **Customer Refuses to Honor Obligation.** If the amount owed you is large, you can't redeposit the check, and the customer has ignored your polite letter, ask your bank to try to collect the check for you. There will be a fee for this, payable only if collection is completed. (Currently banks are charging around $15 to collect a check, plus any charge the issuing bank might impose, so figure on paying around $25 for this service.) Your bank will instruct the bank on which the check is drawn to pay you as soon as funds have been deposited to the account. If no funds are deposited during the holding period (usually a month), you're out of luck.

See also Canadian Sales; Checks; COD Shipments; Collection Strategies; *and article, "When You Have Evidence of Fraud."*

Balance Sheet

A balance sheet shows what a business owns (assets) and what it owes on a specific date (liabilities). While most businesses prepare monthly balance sheets, the small homebased business whose books are done by hand and whose income and expenses have settled into a comfortable pattern may find the preparation of a quarterly Balance Sheet, Income Statement, and P&L Statement to be more than

When You Have Evidence of Fraud

If a check is marked "account closed" or "no account," this may be evidence of fraud. If the amount in question is substantial and you believe there was intent to defraud, you may wish to notify your customer that your next step will be to take legal action. Your best legal options are to:

1. Send a copy of the returned check, along with notes about your efforts to collect the money, to the District Attorney's office.

2. Contact your Sheriff or police department. Although it is not their business to act as a debt collector, it is a crime to write a bad check, and they may be willing to make a call for you. If the bad check is from an out-of-state customer in an amount of $250 or more, this makes the matter a felony instead of a misdemeanor. After making a trip to her Sheriff's office, one crafter reported she had her money within ten days. The bad-check passer was told by the Sheriff in his area either to pay up or be presented with a warrant for his arrest.

3. Consider trying to collect through Small Claims Court. Check to see if your state has a "Bad Check Law." In my state of Illinois, for example, any person who writes an NSF check can be sued in small claims court for three times the amount of the check plus the face value of the check. Just being able to quote your state's law to a delinquent account would add weight to your demands for payment. The only trouble with a bad check law is that it works only if both you and the check writer live in the same state. For more information on this, contact your Attorney General's office.

See also Bad Checks *and* Small Claims Court.

sufficient. If you use a computer software accounting package, these reports will be generated automatically as soon as you've entered all the income and expense figures for a particular month. Nearby you will find a worksheet to help you prepare a balance sheet that will be acceptable to your banker. Note that (1) Net Worth is the difference between Total Assets and Total Current Liabilities and (2) Total Assets must be the same as the figure shown for Total Net Worth and Liabilities.

See also Assets; Financial Statements; Liabilities; *and sample Balance Sheet.*

Banking

See Bank Loans; Canadian Sales; Checking Account; Checks; *and* Merchant Bank Card Services.

Bank Loans

Q: *What are my chances of getting a loan for my homebased business?*

Much depends on whether you're already established in business or just getting started. Banks do not give business loans to fledgling homebased businesses, but they will always consider making a loan to a small business that has a steady income, a good credit rating, and good financial reports. It also helps to deal with a bank you've been doing business with for some time. Most people who start homebased businesses tap their own financial resources to get started, borrowing from a savings account, insurance policy, or the equity in their home. Others generate cash by selling whatever they've got and putting that money into their business. (Check your attic or basement for salable treasures for a garage sale—you may have a gold mine there.)

See also Business Plan; Cash Flow Projection; Collateral; Credit Bureaus; Credit History; Financial Statements; Home Equity Loans; Line of Credit; Personal Loans; *and* SBA Loans.

Bar Codes

See UPC Bar Codes.

BALANCE SHEET WORKSHEET

_____(name of your business)_____

BALANCE SHEET

For Period Ending _____

A: CURRENT ASSETS

Cash in Checking	$_____
Accounts Receivable	$_____
Inventory	$_____
TOTAL CURRENT ASSETS	$_____

B: FIXED ASSETS

Tools and equipment	$_____
Office Furnishings	$_____
Computer System	$_____
(Other)_____	$_____

C: TOTAL ASSETS $_____

D: CURRENT LIABILITIES

Mscl. Bills	$_____
Unpaid taxes	$_____

E: TERM DEBT

Loans	$_____
TOTAL CURRENT LIABILITIES	$_____

F: NET WORTH $_____

G: TOTAL NET WORTH AND LIABILITIES $_____

Bedding and Upholstered Furniture Law

Q: *I've heard that some states require certain stuffed items to have a special label affixed to them. Can you provide details on this?*

If you sell items with a concealed filling or stuffing (dolls, teddy bears, quilts, pillows, soft picture frames, etc.) you should know about the Bedding and Upholstered Furniture Law. At one time all states had a bedding law, but only twenty-nine states have one today, says Morna McEver Golletz, editor of *The Professional Quilter.* In researching this topic for her readers in late 1996, she confirmed my earlier research about this being a law rarely enforced today. One of my readers said a state official told her they only check on this if and when they receive a complaint. Like zoning laws, this particular law seems only to affect those who bring attention to it or themselves, or who are turned in by others who haven't been fortunate enough to go unnoticed. (Sometimes a complaint will be registered by a disgruntled seller who has been forced to obtain the special license and affix the labels and then reports other craft sellers in his or her state who aren't complying with the law.)

Those sellers unlucky enough to get noticed by state officials may be required to purchase a license costing anywhere between twenty-five and a hundred dollars (depending on which state it is), and will have to attach printed tags that bear a special registry number. A reader in Texas reported she was required to purchase 500 one-cent bedding stamps that then had to be placed on the label of each piece of merchandise offered for sale. She was directed to a source for the labels, which had a blank space where information about the contents could be rubber-stamped.

Similar to state bedding laws are acts some states have on their books about the manufacture of stuffed toys. I have no idea how many states have such a law but a note about Pennsylvania's "stuffed toys act" came to my attention while I was writing this book. Although Pennsylvania's law is thirty years old, the state has only recently begun to enforce it.

"State officials are now visiting craft shows and inspecting merchandise to make sure it is both safe for children and properly labeled," says

Dan Engle, publisher of *Arts 'N Crafts ShowGuide*. He reported on a conversation he had with a Pennsylvania state official: "Crafters may call their items collectibles, but Pennsylvania law says it's a toy if it looks like a toy and contains any fiber, chemical, or other stuffing."

Fortunately, this law (administered by the Pennsylvania Deptartment of Labor and Industry, Division of Bedding and Upholstery in Harrison) isn't a big problem for crafters. Everyone who sells toys in this state must submit samples of each product they intend to sell in the state, buy a license that costs twenty-five dollars per year, and place an appropriately worded label on each item that bears the seller's state registration number.

See also Labels or Tags Required by Law. *If you make dolls, teddy bears, or other toys, see also* Toymaking.

Tip

The only penalty that appears to be connected with a violation of either state bedding or stuffed toy laws is removal of merchandise from store shelves or a fine if a seller refuses to comply with the law after being notified of it. For that reason, most sellers ignore this law until they are challenged by authorities.

Better Business Bureau (BBB)

Q: *If I join the Better Business Bureau, could I mention my membership in my advertisements or other printed materials?*

No, this is strictly prohibited. The BBB symbol and name are registered trademarks owned by the Council of Better Business Bureaus, Inc., and no one can legally use its name in their promotional or printed materials or even *mention* they are a member of the BBB. In my own experience with the BBB I've learned this organization is almost paranoid about anyone even mentioning its name and, if asked, they will tell you that membership or registration provides no tangible benefits. To quote the BBB, they ". . . cannot lend credibility to an individual firm as they neither recommend nor deprecate any product, service, or company."

Membership in the BBB would do nothing for a homebased business, but such businesses may *register* with the BBB if they wish. Customers who call the BBB for information about your business may think you more credible simply because you are registered, but the BBB will deny that such registration adds to your credibility. Although a consumer may get a favorable reply about you from the BBB (meaning no complaints on file), the BBB denies this is any kind of "reference" or "recommendation." However, since it costs nothing to register and may result in favorable information being passed on to customers in your area, you should consider doing this. Just don't tell anyone you've done it.

Bill of Lading

This shipping document gives evidence of a carrier's receipt of the shipment and serves as a contract between the carrier and shipper. (For air shipments, it may be called an airway bill.)

Bones, Claws, and Ivory

See Endangered Species.

Book Copyright

Q: *I have a book idea I'd like to offer to a publisher. Do I need to copyright the book before I send it to publishers for consideration?*

No, if your book is accepted for publication, the book publisher will take care of the copyright registration process for you. (Ask that the copyright be registered in your name.) Your book contract will stipulate the royalties you are to receive on your book and temporarily convey to the publisher the right to publish your work. But unless you agree to it in your contract, the publisher cannot not put your words on a recording or sell them to anyone else, such as a magazine. (Such rights are generally included in a book contract, with the author receiving half the amount the publisher receives from such extra sales of the work.) If and when your book is no longer offered for sale by the publisher and goes out of print, the copyright will revert back to you according to the terms established in your contract.

See also Author/Publisher Contract *and* LC Number.

Bookkeeping

Q: *What kind of books do I have to keep to meet IRS requirements?*

The IRS does not require any special kind of bookkeeping system, except that it must be one that clearly and accurately shows true income and expenses. You can do this with a business checkbook, a cash receipts journal, a cash disbursements ledger, and a petty cash fund. Many home businesses use single-entry bookkeeping systems that keep paperwork, figure work, and headaches to a minimum while still providing all the information needed to properly manage a business and prepare accurate tax returns. Very small businesses may find that all they need is a standard record keeping book such as the *Dome Simplified Monthly,* which can be found in any office supply store. If you have a computer, there are a variety of easy-to-use accounting packages that will make your bookkeeping fun.

P.S. Did you know that "bookkeeping" is the only word in the English language that has three double letters in a row?

See also Accounting Methods; Checking Account; Financial Statements; Petty Cash; Record Keeping; *and* Schedule C Form.

Tip

"Small business owners should keep their own books as long as possible, just to learn how to read and use the books once they've been posted," advises Bernard Kamoroff, CPA and author of *Small Time Operator—How to Start Your Own Business, Keep Your Books, Pay Your Taxes and Stay Out of Trouble* (Bell Springs Publishing). If bookkeeping is not your strong point, this small business classic (updated annually) includes all the information, ledgers, and worksheets needed to set up a good manual bookkeeping system.

Book Publishing

See Desktop Publishing; Drop-Shipping; *and article, "You Can Publish Your Own Book."*

Break-Even Point

This is the point at which total revenue equals total expenses. You can do break-even calculations for the profitability of your business, a direct mailing, an advertisement, or the profitability of a new product you've just introduced to the marketplace. By estimating the break-even point prior to making a mailing, placing an advertisement, or launching a new product, you gain valuable insight into whether the action you have planned will actually be profitable. Examples:

a) You know it will cost $810 to print and mail your new catalog to 1500 names on your prospect/customer list. If you also know that your average order is $22, you can estimate that your break-even point on this particular mailing will come after you have received 37 orders ($810 ÷ $22). However, this is only the point at which your actual cash expenditures have been recaptured. Now, to find out if you can actually make a profit on this mailing, you must take it a step farther and do another break-even analysis. Let's assume that your average $22 order has a cost-of-goods expense in it that will lower your net profit per sale to just $13. Now you can see that it will take 62 orders to break even on this particular mailing ($810 ÷ by $13). The answer to the question of whether this mailing will be profitable for you lies in the percentage of response you normally receive to a catalog mailing. If you normally receive only a 3 percent order response, you are likely to receive only 45 orders (.03 x 1500), which is not enough to even break even on this mailing. A 5 percent response, however, would be 75 orders and 75 x $13 is $975, which would cover the cost of your mailing and give you a small profit.

b) You are planning to spend $500 for a small display ad that will offer a product priced at $22.95 plus shipping. If your profit on this product is $13.95, you will break even on this ad after you have received 36 orders ($500 ÷ $13.95). Knowing this, you can estimate the likelihood of your getting this many orders based on the magazine's circulation and the percentage of people who typically respond to a display ad. (You might think that one in a thousand will order (.001 percent), but it could as easily be one in ten thousand (.0001 percent). Multiply those percentage figures times the circulation of the magazine in question and see what you come up with. Example: 225,000 circulation X .001% = 225 orders. Times .0001, however, the likely number of orders drops dramatically to just 22.5, suggesting that an ad might not be profitable. This is all a big guessing game, of course; you'll never know whether an ad will work until you try it. The trick is to never spend more for an ad than you can afford to lose.

c) You are planning to produce 100 pattern packages that will cost $1.25 each to print and package ($125 total cost). The pattern will be priced at $4.95 so the break-even point will come when 25 pattern packages have been sold ($125 ÷ $4.95). As you can see, this will be a profitable product since the remaining 75 pattern packages will yield a net profit of $3.70 each, or $277.50.

Brochure

 Q: *Do I need a brochure if I sell only at craft fairs or in malls?*

Brochures are generally distributed on a selective basis to people who request additional information about you or your products and they are valuable because they give you professional credibility. For example, if you decide to expand into wholesaling, a brochure (or the use of full-color flyers) will tell buyers you are serious about selling and will be a reliable supplier for them. Not every craft seller needs a fancy brochure, but every seller needs good printed materials of one kind or another to get initial sales and follow-up orders. (When brochures, flyers, price lists, or other printed materials are tucked into customers' bags at craft fairs, they often lead to follow-up sales by mail.)

A brochure can be something as simple as a one-page sheet that tells who you are and what you do. Standard brochures, however, measure 8½ X 11 inches or 8½ X 13 inches (legal-size), are printed on heavyweight paper or lightweight card stock, then folded (see illustration). Your local printer will be happy to provide samples.

See also Printed Materials *and* Price List.

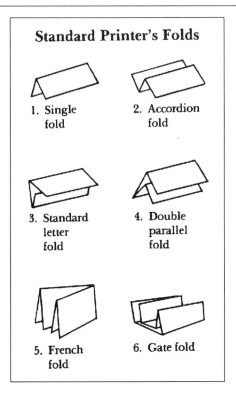

Standard Printer's Folds

1. Single fold

2. Accordion fold

3. Standard letter fold

4. Double parallel fold

5. French fold

6. Gate fold

Tip

Each time you do a new show, check your mailing list for buyers in that area and send them a brochure, postcard or even a personal note inviting them to stop by to see your newest products. One seller reported that eighty-five percent of her show sales were from customers who had received her mailings in the past.

Budget

Theoretically, a budget is a financial plan to control spending, but I like these humorous definitions better: A budget is what you stay within if you go without, and balancing the budget is when money in the bank and the days of the month run out together.

One thing is certain: putting your homebased business on a budget will force you to think more creatively, especially when you don't have money to buy advertising. Through the years I've found the less money I have to promote my business, the more innovative I become in digging up new prospects and reselling buyers already on my mail list.

Bulk Mailings

Q: **Can I save money by mailing my brochures, catalogs, or newsletters at bulk rates instead of first class?**

The postal service now calls bulk business mail "standard mail" (formerly third- and fourth-class mail). Submitted in bulk (200 pieces minimum), it can include samples, ordinary papers, and circulars.

I used to send thousands of pieces of mail at bulk rates every year because the rate was then about half the cost of a first-class stamp. In recent years, however, the cost of bulk mail has increased to the point where the difference between first and third class is only a few cents per piece. For that and other reasons, I can no longer justify mailing at bulk rates, nor can I recommend bulk mailings to others.

When the U.S. Postal Service introduced its reclassification program in mid-1996, it changed all the rules on how bulk mailings were to be sorted and bundled. Now, instead of sorting addresses in pure ZIP code order (the same way they come out of our computers), business mailers must prepare "regional bundles" that include assorted ZIP codes from several states. (If you don't have a software program that can rearrange your mailing list in this peculiar numerical order, it may take three times as long to sort and bundle a mailing.)

Furthermore, in spite of what the postal service may tell you, it still takes up to thirty days for bulk mail to be delivered, and if you ask for address corrections on this mail it can take weeks or months for some mail pieces to be returned. In comparing what I spent for address corrections ($.35 to $.50 per piece) on the last bulk mailing I ever plan to do, I figured I would have been money ahead to send the whole mailing by first-class mail. Not only would I have gotten quicker delivery, but all my address corrections would have come back free of charge.

See also Indicia; Mail, Classes of; Mail Lists, Rental of; Mail, Size Regulations; *and article; "Money-Saving Postal Tips."*

Business Cards

See Freebies; Patterns, Commercial Use of; Premiums; *and* Telephone.

Business Expenses, Tax-Deductible

Q: **What home business expenses can I deduct on my Schedule C form?**

Use the following checklist as a reminder of the many deductions available to you as a home business owner. Once you have begun your business, any expense that is *ordinary, necessary, and somehow connected with the operation and potential profit of your business* is deductible. Given the unique nature of homebased businesses, you will surely think of some items not included here.

Deductions marked with an asterisk are limited to some degree, as explained in IRS's *Tax Guide for Small Business* (Publication 334), available to you from any IRS office. See also the special notes at the end of this checklist and *Personal Property Used for Business.*

❑ Accounting or bookkeeping services
❑ Advertising expenses
❑ Books related to your business
❑ Briefcase or samples case
❑ Bulletin board
❑ Business gifts
❑ Business equipment
❑ Child care expenses *(see note 6)*
❑ Christmas cards for business associates
❑ Cleaning supplies/services *(business portion of home)*
❑ Commissions *(sales reps, agents, other sellers)*
❑ Computer, software, and related expenses *(see note 3)*
❑ Consulting fees
❑ Conventions and trade show expense
❑ Delivery charges
❑ Donations
❑ Dues to professional organizations
❑ Educational expenses, *(business seminars/workshops/classes)*

- ❑ Employee benefits
- ❑ Entertainment *(must be carefully documented)*
- ❑ Equipment lease costs
- ❑ Equipment purchases *(may be depreciated or expensed; see note 9)*
- ❑ Equipment repairs
- ❑ Exhibit/display expenses
- ❑ Freight and shipping charges
- ❑ Health insurance *(see note 7)*
- ❑ Indirect expenses on use of home for business *(see note 1)*
- ❑ Insurance premiums
- ❑ Interest on business loans or late tax payments
- ❑ Inventory purchases
- ❑ IRA or Keogh account deposits
- ❑ Labor costs *(independent contractors)*
- ❑ Legal and professional fees *(see note 2)*
- ❑ Licenses and permits
- ❑ Mail list development and maintenance
- ❑ Maintenance contracts on office equipment
- ❑ Membership fees in business-related organizations
- ❑ Moving expenses *(related to business portion)*
- ❑ Office decor *(drapes, blinds, carpeting, artwork, etc.)*
- ❑ Office furnishings *(depreciated or expensed; see note 9)*
- ❑ Office supplies
- ❑ Postage and postal fees
- ❑ Presentation packages *(sales)*
- ❑ Product displays, exhibiting expenses
- ❑ Professional services *(artists, designers, copywriters, etc.)*
- ❑ Refunds to customers
- ❑ Remodeling costs/expenses *(to business area of home)*
- ❑ Rental fees *(to malls, rent-a-space shops)*
- ❑ Repairs to area or room used exclusively for business
- ❑ Research and development expenses *(see note 2)*
- ❑ Safe deposit box *(for business-related documents or computer back-up disks)*
- ❑ Sales commissions
- ❑ Show fees
- ❑ Stationery and printing
- ❑ Subscriptions to craft or business periodicals

- ❑ Supplies and materials
- ❑ Tax preparer's fee *(portion related to Schedule C)*
- ❑ Telephone *(see note 4)*
- ❑ Tools of your trade
- ❑ Travel expenses *(meals and lodging; see note 8)*
- ❑ Uniforms or special costumes used only in trade or profession
- ❑ Vehicle *(see note 5)*
- ❑ Wages to employees *(including spouse or children)*

NOTES:

1. In addition to the *direct expenses* above—which may be itemized on your Schedule C tax form—you are entitled to deduct a portion of certain *indirect expenses* that benefit both the business and personal parts of your home. (See *Home Office Deduction.*)

2. Start up expenses, research and development costs, and legal and accounting fees incurred before your business has generated any revenue are not deductible, so try to defer such expenses until you actually have some money flowing into your business.

3. To deduct expenses for a computer that is also for personal use, you must calculate the percentage of time the computer is used for business to get the amount you can deduct as a business expense. Related supplies and materials are also deductible.

4. If your personal telephone is used for business, you may not deduct any part of the cost of the first line into your home, but you may deduct business-related long-distance calls and charges for extra lines, business extensions, call forwarding, etc.

5. When you use the family vehicle for business, you may deduct expenses either for business mileage or actual operating expenses related to business use (see also *Vehicle Used for Business*).

6. If you pay someone to care for your child or an invalid parent or spouse so you can work, a portion of the cost may be deductible.

7. For the year 1997, self-employed individuals may deduct forty percent of the cost of health insurance on page one of their annual tax return. This deduction will increase to forty-five percent for years 1998–2000, then gradually increase to eighty percent by 2006.

8. The deduction for business-related meal and travel expenses is currently limited to fifty percent. Spousal travel deductions are allowed only when the spouse is an employee of the company.

9. Some purchases must be depreciated while others (like inventory purchases bought for resale) are expensed only when actually sold. Expensing is a good strategy to use in years when your income takes a jump but your regular expenses remain the same. Currently, up to $18,000 worth of new equipment that would normally be depreciated can be written off ("expensed") each year. By the year 2003, this amount will have increased to $25,000.

Tip

The IRS considers payment has been made on the date of a credit card transaction, not when you actually pay the bill. Thus, business expenses charged to a third-party credit card (such as Visa or MasterCard) can be deducted even though the credit card bill hasn't been paid by year's end.

Business Name

See Business or Trade Name Registration/Protection; Checking Account; Employee Identification Number; Fax Machine; Hobby Business; and Supplies, Buying Wholesale.

Business or Trade Name Registration/Protection

Q: *I have a very small business. Do I really have to register my business name with local authorities?*

Registration of a business operated under any name other than your own is required by law because a fictitious name must be connected to the name of an individual who can be held responsible for the actions of a business. Moreover, if you like the name you've given your business, the only way to protect it is to register it locally. Otherwise, anyone can take it from you simply by registering your business name in connection with theirs.

Some states require registration even when one's real name is part of the business name, so you'll need to check this on your own. Simply call your city or county clerk (depending on whether you live within or outside city limits). Since registration of a business name is a simple and inexpensive matter, take care of it today. Don't worry about your failure to do this earlier if you've been in business for some time because the form you have to complete doesn't ask for the date your business was started. When you register, be sure to ask when you have to renew the registration of your name because you won't be notified.

You should also register your business name with the state to prevent its use by any corporate entity. To protect your name and business logo on a national level, consider filing a trademark.

See also Fictitious Name Statement; Printed Materials; *and* Trademark.

Tip

In selecting a business name, pick one that doesn't tie you down to just one activity since it's hard to tell where your business will lead you in the future. Avoid crafty-sounding names that might give suppliers and prospective customers the impression you're just a hobbyist. (Examples: *Kitty's Krafty Kreations, Homemade Treasures* or *Handmade by Sue.*) Since manufacturers and distributors will not sell to individual hobby sellers, you should do everything possible to remove the hobbyist image from their minds as well as from the minds of prospective customers if you want to make a real profit on the things you sell. Attaching your first name to your business may make you happy, but it can also be a signal that you're just a hobby seller.

Business Plan

Q: *I just want to make crafts and sell as much as possible. What do I need a business plan for?*

The primary reason for writing a formal business plan is to impress a banker if you're asking for a business loan. Since home business owners can't get a bank loan to launch a new business, you could logically conclude there is no reason to write a business plan for a small crafts business at home. As I see it, however, even a hobby business needs a plan of some kind. Otherwise, it's like going to the grocery store without a shopping list: you wander around trying to remember what you wanted to buy, you pick up impulse things you don't need, and end up at home without the lettuce.

Without a plan for your crafts business, you might dabble first in one craft and then another without ever developing a coordinated line of salable products. Or you might not make a point of doing market research to learn if one type of sales outlet might be better for you than another. A written business plan simply lays out a plan of action you can follow to be more efficient and productive in whatever you are doing. The more serious you are about making money from your activity, the more serious you will be about writing a plan. To begin, refer back to the Contents pages and note how business topics are listed under general categories such as *Accounting, Business and Office Management, Legal Issues,* and so on. Make a photocopy of this list so you'll have a worksheet. Then, with the list in hand, set up an outline for your business plan, including various listings under main category headings such as:

• **Business Statement**. Indicate how or why your business came into being. Briefly describe your business goals, products, or services (who you are and what you do).

• **Business Startup or Development Checklist**. Glean the entire list of Contents to find topics relative to your interests or present situation, paying particular attention to topics under *Banking, Insurance, Laws and Regulations,* and *Legal Issues*. Highlight information in the text for easy reference. Suggestion: Start a four-column list of (1) things that need immediate investigation or action; (2) things you want to check on or do in a few weeks; (3) things you want to investigate or do six months to a year from now and (4) long-term goals and plans related to or suggested by text topics.

• **Manufacturing/Production Plan**. Describe how you plan to produce goods for sale, listing any special equipment, tools, or facilities needed to make your products. Indicate where and how you will obtain necessary raw materials, what they will cost, and where you will store them. Explain how products will be made. Will you do all the work, hire family members, or outside workers? (See listings under *Employees/Labor Issues* and *Taxes*.)

• **Office Setup or Modification**. Describe how and where you're going to set up your office or improve current working conditions, acquire needed equipment, business services, stationery, office supplies, etc. (See listings under *Business and Office Management*.)

• **Financial Plan**. Indicate the amount of money needed for startup or expansion. Estimate your expected sales and expenses for a year and do a cash flow statement. (See listings under *Accounting, Banking,* and *Money Management*.)

• **Marketing Plan**. Describe your market, your customers, and your competition. List the individual products you plan to sell, including unique features or customer benefits related to each. Focus on these benefits when writing advertising copy or descriptive listings for your brochure or catalog. Indicate how and where you will advertise and what this will cost. List the market research steps you will take to learn more about new sales outlets that might be right for your products. (See all listings under *Advertising and Marketing* and *Pricing and Selling*. See also this book's companion volume, *Handmade for Profit,* for insider tips on how to successfully sell through sixteen different types of retail outlets.)

Tip

The greatest benefit of a written plan is that it forces you to think about your goals and the paths you must take to realize them. The biggest problem of a written plan is that it quickly goes out of date. For this reason, it's a good idea to put your plan on computer so you can regularly review and update it.

Business Pursuits Endorsement

See Homeowner's or Renter's Insurance.

Business Records, Protection of

Q: **What's the best way to protect my most important business records?**

I cringe every time I hear someone say they have lost everything in a fire, flooded basement, tornado, hurricane, or earthquake because there are many things people can do to protect themselves against such disasters. It's never too early to develop such a plan. Begin by asking yourself what would happen if you suddenly lost all your customer and prospect files? All the patterns and designs used to create products for sale? All your reference material for something you're writing? All your financial, tax, and insurance records? Printed materials, office forms, and correspondence? Once you decide which information and materials are vital to the success of your business, look at different ways you might protect them. Renting a safety deposit box is an excellent solution for protecting valuable materials off site, but if you need regular access to material, you might consider the purchase of a fireproof safe or file drawer.

• **Computer Files**. If you use a computer for your business, be sure to make regular backup disks or tapes of the software and files on your computer, including information on how to reinstall these files in case you lose the how-to manuals. In between trips to my safety deposit box to exchange my computer tapes, I regularly back up just the files (not the software) on one tape. I keep this tape in my purse, which goes with me any time I leave the house. I figure if the house burns down or is burgled while I'm gone, I'll have the bulk of my business in the palm of my hand. Back home, my purse hangs on my office door where it can be grabbed quickly day or night in case of fire.

• **Important Papers**. Make a list of all business documents, mailing lists, correspondence, artwork, designs, patterns, etc. that you consider absolutely vital to the continuation of your business. Copy as much of this material as possible for permanent storage in a safety deposit box or fireproof file. Since printed materials are an important part of any business, it's a good idea to get in the habit of setting aside a couple of master copies of everything you have printed. If the original art is lost and you don't have the printed piece on computer, at least you'll have an image to work from and all your valuable copywriting won't have been lost.

• **Other Files**. Material that can't be protected by copying should be centrally located in your home office, workshop, or studio so you can grab it at a moment's notice when you get a tornado warning or the smoke alarm goes off. For example, at my bill-paying desk, all the files and records I use every week are stored on one shelf so they can be grabbed quickly when the tornado siren warns of impending disaster. When I'm working on a new book, my reference files are vital so I keep them all together in a large filing tub I can grab in an emergency.

For a long time, I thought I was being prudent by keeping some of my valuable files on the lower level of our home. I figured if a tornado took off the roof, at least it wouldn't blow away all my files. I had never given flooding a thought because we don't live anywhere near a river. But when Naperville and surrounding cities flooded in 1996 after a "storm of the century" dropped twenty-two inches of rain in twenty-four hours, we found ourselves mopping water in the basement for fifteen hours straight. In our area alone, over two dozen homes were hit by lightning and eight thousand homes had serious flood damage. We escaped with only minor damage, but I suddenly saw the necessity of moving precious things and stored business records at least four feet off the floor. An old Arabic saying seems appropriate here: Trust in God but tie up your camel.

See also Financial and Tax Records; *and* Safety Deposit Box.

Business Reply Mail

This domestic mail service allows pieces bearing a specific address or label format to be mailed back to the addressee without prepayment of postage by the sender. Postage and fees are collected when the mail is delivered to the addressee who originally distributed the mail. Your postmaster will provide additional information on this topic.

Caller ID

It became law in mid-1995 that all telephone companies in the United States and Canada had to deliver Caller ID information on a national basis. What this technology has done is completely destroy our telephone privacy. Everyone you call who has opted for this service (and most businesses now use it) automatically knows your name and telephone number, even your unlisted number. With this information, people then have access to your address.

You cannot permanently refuse this service, but your telephone company is obligated by law to give you the option of their "*67 service." Although free, it's yet another aggravation in our daily lives. Has your telephone company explained this technology to you and told you that, to disable Caller ID, you now have to dial *67 every time you make a call? Although you may not mind doing this, what about your young children or elderly family members who use your phone? Do you want the people they call to have immediate access to their names and addresses?

Besides punching in extra numbers, the only way to permanently stop this flow of information every time you make a call is to install a technological gadget called a "Caller ID Blocker." This FCC-approved invention isn't promoted by telephone companies, but should be available through independent telephone accessory dealers.

Canadian Sales

Q: *What do I need to consider when soliciting orders from Canadian residents?*

Although you may be happy to send your catalog or brochure to any Canadian prospect who requests it as a result of your advertising or publicity, you may find, as I have, that sending unsolicited brochures and catalogs into Canada is prohibitively expensive. In addition to having to pay higher postage rates for Canadian mail, all of it (except for postcards) must be put in an envelope. This not only adds another dime or so to the cost of a mail piece, but the extra weight may throw the package over the one-ounce mark.

Canadian checks can also be a problem. Be sure to ask your bank about their policy for handling Canadian checks. Many banks in the United States are not equipped to handle foreign checks, so your deposit of Canadian checks might incur high handling charges. In addition, the service charge for handling a bad (returned) check through international channels can amount to $20 or more. For these reasons, and because the rate of exchange is constantly changing, you should ask Canadians (and buyers in other countries) to remit in U.S. Funds. Before you ask all your Canadian prospects to pay with a money order, however, consider the amount of business you might lose. I've been selling my publications to Canadians for nearly thirty years, and I've never received a bad Canadian check.

See also Money Orders; Shipping and Handling Charges; *and* United Parcel Service.

Tip

If you can accept payment by credit card, all your Canadian order problems will be resolved. You simply write the charge slip for the amount of purchase in U.S. Funds, and when your bank processes the charge slip, it credits your account with that amount and automatically calculates the rate of exchange for your Canadian customer.

Care Labels

In connection with its *Fabric Care Labeling Rule,* the Federal Trade Commission requires a permanently affixed care label on all textile wearing apparel and household furnishings. These labels must indicate if an item is to be dry cleaned or washed; if it is to be washed, indicate whether to use hot or cold water. Indicate whether bleach may or may not be used and specify at what heat the item may be ironed. You can design your own labels or order standard care labels from manufacturers such as Charm Woven Labels, GraphComm Services, and Widby Enterprises.

See also Labels or Tags Required by Law *and* Textile Fiber Products Identification Act.

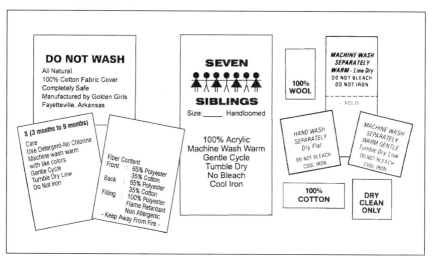

Samples from Widby Enterprises   *Samples from Charm Woven Labels*

Car Insurance

Q: *I use my car or van part-time for business, such as delivering prod-ucts to individual customers or shop outlets, driving to craft fairs, obtaining supplies, and so on. How will this occasional business use of a personal vehicle affect my car insurance?*

Your primary concern here is likely to be one of personal liability. The first thing you should do is sit down with your insurance agent and explain you plan to use your vehicle for business and what percentage of the time you would be using it this way. (If you use it mostly for business, it may be best to get it rated for business.) Find out if your present coverage would be sufficient in the event you had an accident while "doing business," such as delivering a load of finished crafts to a shop or traveling to/from a craft show. Also, if you have an employee who uses your vehicle for any reason, inquire about your need for "non-ownership contingent liability protection" that would protect you in the event your employee had an accident while working for you.

See also Labor Laws; Personal Liability Insurance; *and* Vehicle Used for Business.

Cash Discounts

A cash discount (generally two percent) is offered as an enticement to get early payment on an invoice.

See also Terms of Sale.

Cash Flow Projection

This is a picture that shows how cash comes in and goes out of your business. You can create cash flow projection worksheets for a period of one to six months as needed, but bankers may want to see a year's projection. Even if you never apply for a loan, you will find it helpful to occasionally make cash flow statements for your business, particularly when you find yourself coming into a period where you're worried about whether you will have sufficient income to meet anticipated expenses. By creating a cash flow projection in advance of an anticipated situation, you can identify if and when a financial problem is likely to occur and get a handle on what you might need to do to solve it. You might find you have to do something to generate extra income or apply for a short-term loan. Sometimes a cash flow projection proves that you aren't going to have a problem at all.

Realize, of course, that all you are doing here is estimating figures to the best of your ability and making wild guesses if you have no previous experience or financial records for reference. After you've been in business for a while, cash flow projections are easier to do because you can refer to earlier records of sales and expenses. (See sample worksheet nearby and article, "Solving Cash Flow Problems.")

Cash Method of Accounting

See Accounting Methods.

Catalog Houses, Selling to

In the United State alone, more than 55 billion catalogs are mailed annually. While this is a great market for manufacturers and publishers who can mass-produce items at low cost and high profit, it's not a good market for anyone who makes labor-intensive handcrafts. A four-time markup (sometimes more) is standard in this industry, which means a product that would normally retail for $29.95 would have to be wholesaled to a catalog house for around $7.50. This suggests that the only handcrafts that might conceivably be sold to a catalog house at a profit would have to be priced in the neighborhood of $75 or more.

If this is something you decide to pursue, contact catalog companies of interest and ask to speak to the Director of Merchandise or the Catalog Merchandise Buyer. If there is interest in your product, you may be asked to send an information package and photo. Do not send a sample unless specifically requested because it won't be returned.

See also article, "Selling to Catalog Houses."

How to Create a Cash Flow Statement

Begin with a blank columnar page and list the names of the months across the top. For each month, jot down the appropriate figures.

In the sample below, one-month totals are shown to illustrate how figures are added and subtracted in a cash flow statement. These figures, of course, are literally drawn out of the air and may seem high or low depending on whether you've just started selling or have been in business for a while. In this particular "financial picture," let's assume that a fellow who has been selling handmade furniture with great success for three months has an accident late in May that will prevent him from making or selling crafts in the months of June or July. (The income in June is from an invoice for goods delivered to a shop in May.) The question to be answered by this cash flow projection is whether money in the business checking account will be sufficient to cover fixed expenses that will continue in June and July whether there is income or not:

	May	June	July
Sales Receipts *(list all expected sources of income)*			
Total Sales	$ 1,800	350	0
Cost of Sales *(list expenses individually and subtract from Sales)*			
Total Cost of Sales	$ 540	0	0
Gross Profit	$ 1,260	350	0
Total Income this month	$ 1,800	350	0
Beginning Cash Balance	$ 175	1,375	1,125
Cumulative Cash	$ 1,975	1,725	1,125
Operating Expenses *(list individually and subtract from Gross Profit)*			
Total Cash Disbursements	$ 600	600	600
Ending Cash Balance	$ 1,375	1,125	525

(Carry forward to next month's column as "Beginning Cash Balance" figure)

As you can see, by the end of July, there will be sufficient cash to cover all operating expenses, but the amount lacking is small and these are merely estimates after all. For that reason, this business owner ought to make another cash flow projection at the end of June to see if the picture has become better or worse once exact sales and expense figures are known. The larger a business and the more important its profits are to a family's income, the more important cash flow projections like this will be.

Solving Cash Flow Problems

There is a knack to learning how to delay payment when money is tight or you're waiting for accounts to pay up. Here are some things you can do when your cash flow situation is desperate because of unanticipated or excessive expenses at a time when your income is not as high or as regular as expected.

Some bills can be delayed without hurting your credit rating while others must be paid on time to avoid late reports to the credit bureaus. Banks, finance companies, and major credit card companies generally report to credit agencies right away, so these bills always need to be paid on time. (Most credit card companies now add an extra ten dollars or so to your bill if you pay it late, and telephone and cable television companies also assess late charges.) You aren't likely to ruin your credit rating, however, by stalling a doctor or dentist bill, and gas companies may not report late payments until an account is several months overdue.

If you can't make your mortgage payment on time, call the financial institution that holds your mortgage and ask how many days of grace you have. (At least once a year, you have the legal right to pay only the interest due on your monthly mortgage payment.) Car and house insurance payments also have grace periods (usually thirty days) before the insurance would be cancelled, but double check with your agent to be sure.

If you have been doing business with a printer or other supplier for a long time and find you cannot pay a bill on time, call and explain your situation and ask if you can have a 30-day extension if you agree to pay a month's interest on the money. Few suppliers will say no because they won't want to lose you as a customer.

See also Cash Flow Projection.

CD ROM

A CD ROM looks the same as a musical compact disk (CD), only it is used with computer hardware and is capable of holding vast amounts of information. The term itself stands for "Compact Disk—Read Only Memory," which means you can retrieve information but you can't store data on it. Most new computers are now shipping with CD ROM drives so you ought to learn something about this technology if you are using, or plan to buy, a computer for your business.

Celebrity Rights Act

Q: *I'm thinking about creating a Charlie Chaplin "Little Tramp" doll. I figure this is okay because the movie star is now deceased. Right?*

Wrong. The rights of deceased personalities are protected either by special state laws known as the *Celebrity Rights Act*, or by attorneys or agencies who handle the estates of deceased movie stars. Without a license or special permission to use a particular personality's characterization in some way, no one may produce a product, advertise a product, or provide a service that in any way utilizes the name, voice, signature, photograph, or likeness of a deceased person during a period lasting fifty years after that person's death. Manufacturers who violate this law are not the only ones who must be careful here since distributors and retailers caught selling unlicensed products can also be sued. To find out who handles the estate of a particular individual, contact the Screen Actor's Guild or the Academy of Motion Picture Arts and Sciences in Los Angeles.

Cellular Phones

Over 36 million people use cellular phones today. They have proven invaluable to mobile retailers and vendors in outdoor markets and trade shows who use them for getting credit card authorizations. (If you plan to use a cellular phone to get approval for credit card sales, it's best to buy the phone at the same time you buy the electronic machine to transmit credit card transactions since some cellular phones may not be compatible with certain machines.)

Cellular phones are not inexpensive and there are countless choices in styles of phones and features such as expanded memory, call timers, ring modes, and so on. To save money when buying a cellular phone, check out the benefit of multiple phones that can share one number and bundled services that might be packaged at a discount, such as voice mail and paging. As is true with telephone service, different rate plans are available for cellular phone users, and some may be less expensive than others. Your carrier's customer service department can help you analyze recent bills to see if a different plan might be more economical for your special needs.

Tip

One downside of cellular phones is that sooner or later you may be a victim of cellular fraud. "Computer bandits" are literally stealing cellular numbers out of the air these days, so be sure to ask your carrier about installing a PIN code, which is to cellular phones what the Club is to cars.

Certified Mail

When you need legal proof that you have mailed something, send it by certified mail. (For international mail, it's called Recorded Delivery.) The post office records the actual delivery date. For an extra fee, you can get a postcard in the mail as proof of who signed for the package and the date it was delivered. Tax advisers recommend sending your annual tax return to the IRS by certified mail so you have evidence your return was filed on time.

Chamber of Commerce

Q: Is there any reason for a small homebased business to join the local chamber of commerce?

Throughout the United States, chambers of commerce support local businesses of all sizes, and home business owners are eligible for membership. In addition to the networking and marketing contacts you might make as a member (some chambers publish directories of licensed homebased businesses), you would also be eligible for United Chambers low-cost group health insurance program. Your local chamber will be happy to give you additional information.

See also Health Insurance.

Check Endorsements

When you endorse a check with only your signature, it's the same as cash to anyone who gets hold of it. When depositing checks by mail, then, always limit the endorsement by first writing "For Deposit Only." If you regularly take checks in your business, buy a rubber stamp to endorse them for deposit. Many sellers who take checks at fairs immediately rubber-stamp their checks for deposit before putting them in their cash drawer.

See also Checking Account.

Tip

To save money, don't order your check endorsement stamp through the bank because they will tack on a service charge that will make the cost of the stamp twice what you would pay if you ordered it from any other source.

Checking Account

: I don't have much business right now nor many bills to pay. Do I really need a separate checking account for my business in the beginning while it's so small?

Yes, use of a personal checking account for business is called "commingling of funds" by the IRS and it is strictly prohibited. The only way you can safely claim business deductions on your tax return is to conduct all business transactions through a separate business checking account. If an audit revealed commingling of funds, your deductions would most likely be disallowed, your taxes would be higher and you might incur interest and penalties on taxes due.

Although a separate checking account is the only way to keep accurate records for your business, you don't need an expensive "business checking account" to satisfy the IRS. A second small checking account whose checks have the name of the business imprinted on them will suffice. Simply deposit all business revenue into this account and pay all bills from it. (If the bank questions the fact that you have a business name on a personal checking account, you might tell them that your business is still in the hobby stage and you'll move up to a business account when you've had a chance to grow.)

To save money on service charges, compare the charges of several financial institutions in your area. Some will be much higher than others. In particular, ask:

- Is there a charge for deposits or each check deposited? (Some banks make a charge for each deposit while others charge for each out-of-state check deposited—very costly for mail order businesses.)
- Is there a charge for bounced checks? (Some banks charge up to twenty dollars per check.)
- Will the checking account balance draw interest?
- Is there a minimum balance requirement?
- Does the financial institution offer small business loans or a line of credit? Merchant credit card services? Savings and Loan Associations (what few are still in business these days) offer business checking accounts but do not make business loans or offer a line of credit or merchant card services.

I've always had my business checking account in a Savings and Loan Association because there are no service charges of any kind (except for bad checks), and interest is paid on my checking account balance. When I wanted a line of credit not offered by the Savings and Loan, I simply opened a second account with a local bank, where I later got merchant status as well.

See also Bad Checks; Check Endorsements; Checks Received in the Mail; Checks Taken at Shows; Credit History; DBA; Employee Identification Number; Partnership; *and* Stop Payment Order.

Tip

A big expense in maintaining a business checking account is the high cost of bank checks. You may already order personal checks by mail to save money, but did you know you can also order business checks and binders by mail? One check-printing company that has been in business for over seventy years is Checks In The Mail. Currently their cost for 300 three-on-a-page business checks and binder is about one-fourth what a bank would charge for the same order. For additional information, call 1-800-733-4443.

Checks

See Bad Checks; Checking Account; Checks Received in the Mail; Checks Taken at Shows; Mail, Undeliverable; Money Orders; Petty Cash; Refunds; Scams; *and* Stop Payment Order.

Checks Received in the Mail

Q: *Customers do not always write checks correctly. How do I handle "problem checks" I've received in the mail?*

Here are examples of typical problems and what to do about them:

• Check may indicate one figure on the amount line and a different one in the written description. (Example: the figure might be $10.95 but the written line reads "ten dollars and 00/100.") A bank will generally accept the amount that is written, rather than the amount shown as a figure. Knowing this will help you determine whether to return the check for correction and risk losing the order, or just let it go through as is.

• Check is unsigned. It may not be necessary to return the check. If the check is small, double-check with your bank to see if this alternative is acceptable: Write the word "over" on the signature line of the check. Then, on the back, type "lack of signature guaranteed." Include your business name, your name and title and signature. (If the customer doesn't honor the check, this tells the bank that you will take it back as a charge against your account.) If the check is for a large amount, and you feel uncomfortable about the customer honoring the check, returning it with an SASE might be preferable.

• Check is made out to an incorrect name (a common problem if you get publicity mentions for your products). I often receive checks made out to the titles of my books instead of my personal or business name, or sometimes my name is spelled incorrectly. In such cases I simply endorse the back of the check with the same name the check writer has used, write my personal name below that, and then stamp the check as usual with the rubber stamp that bears all my account information.

• Check doesn't have any name or address printed on it. Is there a sequence number on the check? It's possible you have received a temporary check, which new account holders use until their supply of printed checks is received. If you feel uncomfortable about the check, either call the customer to inquire about it or hold the shipment until the check clears.

See also Bad Checks.

Tip
Fill mail orders before depositing checks because people occasionally forget to include their name and address on a letter or order form.

Checks Taken at Shows

Q.: *I plan to take checks from my craft fair customers, getting a telephone number, driver's license number, and a credit card number. Is there anything else I can do to avoid accepting a bad check?*

When asking a buyer to give you his or her driver's license number, always take time to look carefully at the picture to make sure it's the same person you're dealing with. It does no good to ask for a credit card number, however, since you cannot legally cover a bad check with a customer's credit card. When taking a check, here are three other things you should do:

1. Be cautious about accepting checks that do not have a name and address imprinted on them.
2. Phony checks are generally smooth on all four sides, so look to see if the check is perforated on at least one side.
3. Check the routing number in the lower left-hand corner. The ink on a bad check will look shiny and slightly raised whereas the magnetic ink used on a good check will not reflect light. (Wet your finger and touch the ink if you're not sure. If it rubs off, refuse the check.)

See also Bad Checks *and* Scams.

COD Shipments

Q: *What are the advantages and disadvantages of shipping merchandise COD?*

Shipping COD (collect, or cash, on delivery) to first-time buyers has become standard policy in the crafts industry. While this can be a great solution for how to deal with customers you feel uncomfortable about invoicing, it is not without problems. While you can ship COD to an individual buyer or small shop, this is not an option when you're shipping to a hospital gift shop, department store, or catalog company. Some crafters have a policy that first orders from all new accounts must be shipped COD but others specify "No CODs" on their order form because they don't want the hassles involved with such orders.

"Sometimes you ship COD and get the package back, which means you're out the shipping charges," explains a professional crafter who often ships COD to questionable wholesale buyers. To avoid problems, she always calls the customer before shipping an order COD. "I tell them it's ready, give them the amount they need to have on hand, and ask them if it's okay to ship today."

This is a good idea for accounts you know, but this method leaves you at risk if you're dealing with a new customer whose check might bounce, or one of the con artists that are currently running COD scams at craft fairs. Here, the only way to protect yourself is to check the box on the COD form that says you will accept "Cash or Money

Order Only." (Both UPS and the Postal Service will accept cash, but the post office won't handle any COD package valued at more than $600.) Your customer, not you, should pay the extra amount involved in sending the order COD and some sellers add a note to this effect on their price list and order form. (Note: UPS will collect these charges for you, but if you ship by mail, the post office will collect only for the value of the goods in the box, not for postage or COD charges.)

Bernard Kamoroff, CPA, is the author and publisher of *Small Time Operator* (Bell Springs Publishing). Stung by COD con artists in the past, he offers this advice to others: "Be suspicious of large orders from unknown businesses, from businesses that don't have preprinted letterheads and purchase orders, and from businesses that don't list phone numbers. We always call Directory Assistance to see if a business is listed. And, like the old gambler's warning, we never ship more books than we can afford to lose. When you are dealing with hustlers, collection threats and demanding letters never work. Those people just laugh at you."

See also Bad Checks *and* Scams.

Tip

> If a customer asks you to send a shipment COD and it is packed in more than one carton or box, be sure to put a COD tag on each carton. A reader reported that a customer who ordered five cases of products returned the one case bearing her COD tag marked "delivery refused" but kept the other four cases and never paid for them.

Collateral

 What collateral can I use to back up my business loan request?

Collateral is security pledged for a loan, and banks are interested only in assets they may hold or assume to insure repayment of a loan. This generally includes property, stocks, bonds, savings accounts, life insurance, and current business assets. If an account owes you a considerable amount of money and you need to borrow money because their invoice hasn't been paid, the bank may consider the unpaid invoice as collateral for a loan.

Collection Agencies

Q: *How do collection agencies work, what does it cost to use one, and is this an effective way for a small business to collect accounts?*

When you decide you have done everything possible to collect unpaid invoices, you don't have much to lose by letting a collection agency try to collect for you. Be careful to select a reputable agency, however. A crafts manufacturer in my network told me about the problems she had with an agency. "When they solicited my business, I gave them $7,000 worth of unpaid invoices to try to collect," she said. "But I had a hard time trying to get reports of how they were doing and my phone calls often went unanswered. When they did talk to me, I was told accounts had been collected but it was weeks or months before I received any money from them. A year later, they had collected only half of the money I had hoped to receive, and by then some of the companies had gone out of business and other accounts were just too old to try to collect. I have since learned that not all collection agencies are reputable."

All the better agencies belong to the American Collector's Association, so before signing with an agency, ask if they are a member. Members of this association will collect accounts locally or nationally. (Out-of-state accounts are passed on to a member collection agency in the appropriate state.) All members of the American Collector's Association make regular ninety-day reports back to the originating agency. Agencies normally take forty percent of a local account or fifty percent if the collection is made by a member agency.

See also Invoices Not Paid *and* Small Claims Court.

Tip

Some of the home business/home office organizations listed in the resource chapter now offer low-cost collection and credit reporting services to their members. If so, this service would be described in the organization's membership brochure.

Collections of Art, Crafts, or Memorabilia

Q: *I have a large collection of art and crafts from around the world as well as memorabilia and collector's items. What's the best way to protect them against loss?*

You may have replacement cost coverage on your homeowner's policy, but if you check the fine print, you will find certain items are excluded from such coverage. This part of our policy specifically excludes ". . . paintings, etchings, antiques, pictures, tapestries, statuary, articles made of marble, bronze, or porcelain or any other articles which, because of their inherent nature, cannot be replaced with new articles." Further excluded are memorabilia, souvenirs, and collector's items. If you have any special collection of items valued at more than $1500, you may want to consider having the collection appraised so it can be insured on a separate all-risk endorsement.

See also Homeowner's or Renter's Insurance.

Tip

If you'd like to inventory your art or crafts collection on computer, or if you frequently buy and sell collectibles, check out the easy-to-use software offered by Bette Laswell of BDL Homeware (see resource chapter).

Collection Strategies

See Bad Checks; Collection Agencies; Invoices Not Paid; *and* Small Claims Court.

Commissioned Work

See Custom Orders.

Commissions

See Sales Commissions.

Computer Insurance

Personal computers used for business are not covered by a regular homeowner's or renter's policy, except possibly against loss by fire or theft. Damage or destruction caused by water or power surges would not be covered. The only way to insure your system against all loss is to cover it on a regular business policy or buy a separate all-risk policy such as the one offered by Safeware, The Insurance Agency, Inc. (1-800-848-3469).

See also Home Business Insurance Policies *and* Surge Suppressor.

Computer Software

See article; "Computer and Software Buying Tips."

Computer System, Purchase of

Q: *I'm ready to purchase a computer system for my business, but I feel so overwhelmed by all the choices available to me. How can I make the right buying decision?*

That's a tough question—one many authors have devoted whole books to—but here are four things you can do to get started:

1. Talk to others who use computers to do what you do and who speak the same language you do. Ask what hardware and software they are using and what they like best. (Basically, *hardware* is the machine and related peripherals; *software* is what makes it run.) Many artists and craftspeople now use computers in their business, so ask around when you go to fairs to see what various people are using and will recommend. Most towns and cities have computer-user groups who often meet in such places at the local library or school, so check to see if one exists in your community. Some are very help-

ful. As a computer novice, I attended several meetings of a local group in my area and got expert answers to dozens of questions and problems that had been plaguing me for months.

2. Know what you want a computer to do for you before you go shopping for one and investigate the various software programs available to do these jobs. Do research by browsing in computer stores and reading several issues of computer magazines available on newsstands. (One magazine especially helpful to beginners is *PC Novice—Personal Computers in Plain English.*)

In days past, you could buy a computer with nothing on it but DOS (disk operating system) software, and from that point you could simply install any programs you wanted, so long as they were designed to work with DOS. Life is not so simple today, however. Most, if not all new computers today are shipping with different disk-operating software and other programs that may not serve your particular needs. (Because Microsoft now dominates the computer market, all new PC-based computers ship with the latest version of its *Windows* software, which many experienced DOS users find difficult. For more information on this topic, see discussion under *Windows Software.*)

3. Shop around before making a purchase. Some brands of computers are sold exclusively by mail and computer stores carry only certain brands. When you buy a system "off the shelf," you have to take whatever comes with it. When I began to shop for my first 486 machine, I visited all the discount stores in the area and found that one system would have only a hard disk drive, while others might have both a floppy and hard disk drive. None had tape backup systems, and only some had modems or CD ROM drives. Some had sound systems, which I didn't need, and most came equipped with software that would have been useless to me. My problem was solved, however, when I connected with Gateway Computers, a company that sells exclusively by mail. From them, I was able to order exactly what I wanted, from size of hard drive to amount of RAM, to floppy/hard disk options, modem, tape backup system, and so on.

4. When you purchase hardware or software, ask what kind of support you will have when you have questions or run into technical problems. Most support is no longer free and sometimes the support offered is not very good. There are exceptions, however. One

reason I bought *WordPerfect* software for my word processing and desktop publishing work was because of the customer support offered by this company. Although customers must now pay for phone calls, *WordPerfect* users continue to get unlimited complimentary support for the most recent versions of *WordPerfect* software. And, one reason I will buy my next computer by mail from Gateway Computers is because they do not set a limit on giving customer service either. Knowing there is someone to call when you run into a "computer glitch" is very comforting.

See also CD ROM; Computer, Value to Business; Modem; Windows Software; *and article, "Computer and Software Buying Tips."*

Tip

Ideally, the dealer from whom you buy your machine will also be equipped to repair it in the event of problems. If you buy a computer from a discount store such as Best Buy, however, repairs could take up to two weeks due to the huge volume of repair work done on all the electronic equipment sold in these stores. I couldn't afford to be without my computer system that long if a problem should develop so this kind of repair guarantee is worthless to me and would be to others who also depend on their computer for a livelihood. My purchase of a Gateway computer, however, included a maintenance contract for a limited period of time that would give me on-site repairs if they were needed. (They never were.) When that contract expired, I found a nearby computer dealer that could repair Gateway computers on an overnight basis, should a problem develop in the future.

Computer, Value to Business

Q: *I've gotten along for years without a computer. Besides giving me access to the Internet, what else would a computer do for my small homebased business?*

In a few words, a computer will save you time, money, and aggravation, lower your stress level (once you're past the learning stage), and add excitement to your life. Professional artists, crafters, and other home business owners have learned to use computer technology to manage their business (correspondence, bookkeeping, inventory control, mail list development); design printed materials (stationery, flyers, brochures, catalogs, hang tags, and labels); market their work (online and by mail through regular promotional direct mailings or press releases); develop new designs (many software programs are now available—read computer magazines to learn about them); and explore desktop publishing opportunities (newsletters, directories, magazines, or books).

I've stated a computer will save you time. Let me qualify that statement by saying a computer will not save the kind of time that affords you more leisure; rather, it will enable you to do more for your business. Like capital plowed back into a growing business, time saved by computer technology is similarly used. For example, you might be able to produce twice as many products for sale if you could cut in half the amount of time you currently spend on paperwork, recordkeeping, accounting, and correspondence related to your business.

Even more important than increased profitability and greater efficiency in a business, perhaps, is the surprising impact a computer tends to make on one's personal life. Many of my readers have told me how using a computer has helped them to discover creative and organizational abilities they didn't realize they had. Others have explained how conquering their computer gave them new confidence in their abilities and automatically led them into exciting businesses. Individuals once hampered by the demands of a typewriter have suddenly found themselves able to write, design, and brainstorm on a computer. My research indicates that an individual's initial fear of computer technology is seldom justified. With time and patience—and the desire to do so—anyone can master a computer and learn to use it productively in both their homebased business and personal lives.

A lengthy discussion of why all small businesses should invest in a computer is beyond the scope of this book, but I've included a chapter on this topic in my *Homemade Money* book.

See also Business Records, Protection of; Computer System, Purchase of; Health Hazards; Internet and World Wide Web; *and* Surge Suppressor.

Computer and Software Buying Tips

from Bette Laswell, BDL Homeware

- From conversations with people like yourself, decide on the exact software you want. That will tell you how much computer you need and what capabilities the computer has to have. Don't buy a huge computer "to grow into." It will be at least two or three years—probably more—before you grow beyond your present needs. By then your needs may have changed and what's available surely will have changed.

- When you talk to salespeople about computers, insist they speak in a language you can understand, and realize you'll get better information about software from other users than you will from a hardware salesperson. Hardware people usually don't know software and often suggest what's well-known, not what will work for you. In my experience, many computer salespeople don't know—or don't care—what they're talking about.

- If you want to write letters and reports, you'll want a word-processing program. If you want to do bookkeeping, you'll need an accounting package. Beyond word processing and accounting, software breaks down into general purpose software and fixed purpose software. General purpose software, including databases and spreadsheets, are a one-size-fits-all proposition. It takes considerable time and knowledge to make them work for you, but you can get exactly what you want. Fixed purpose software, also known as structured software, comes already set up to do a specific job. You'll be able to use it easily and quickly, but it won't be a custom fit. You'll have to decide whether ease of use or a custom fit is more important to you. (Note: If you plan to keep your inventory on the computer, get an inventory program. Although general purpose packages are often recommended, they don't work well here.)

- If your computer needs are simple—and most are—consider buying a used computer. Used computer stores are popping up all over. They check out the computers before they sell them and often offer guarantees. Just make sure the software you want will run on them.

Consignment Laws

Consigned goods normally remain the property of the seller until they are sold to the retail customer. However, if an establishment goes bankrupt, merchandise left on consignment may be subject to the claims of creditors and be seized by them unless certain protective steps have been taken by consignors. (A standard consignment agreement is not enough to protect you in this instance.)

Several states have consignment laws designed to protect artists and craftspeople. Those known to me are California, Colorado, Connecticut, Illinois, Iowa, Kentucky, Massachusetts, New Hampshire, New Mexico, New York, Oregon, Texas, Washington, and Wisconsin. The pitfall in state consignment laws is that some states protect only "art" and may exclude protection to items that fall outside the area of painting, sculpture, drawing, graphic arts, pottery, weaving, batik, macrame, quilting, or "other commonly recognized art forms." Each state with a law on the books has a different interpretation of "art," and other states not listed above may or may not have a consignment law at all. For those reasons, everyone interested in selling on consignment should contact their state legislature for more information.

See also Consignment Selling.

Consignment Selling

 A shop in my area has invited me to place work on consignment. How can I make sure I get paid for everything in the shop that sells?

Never consign merchandise without a consignment agreement. If the shop doesn't provide one, create it yourself. In addition to a complete list of all items being left on consignment, a good agreement will include the following things, not necessarily in this order:

- the owner's name and telephone number
- the length of time items are to be displayed and any special display requirements you may have (i.e., "do not place in sunny window")

- what insurance, if any, is offered to seller
- the percentage of the retail selling price the shop will receive on each item it sells (may vary from thirty to fifty percent)
- a stipulation that items may not be sold for less than the retail price you have indicated; or, if they are, you will receive your share of the regular retail price
- when you will receive payments (usually monthly, with a report of which items have been sold)
- if products are being sent by mail or UPS, who pays for shipping expenses (Ideally, costs will be equally shared by shop and seller.)
- how merchandise will be returned to seller if shop no longer wants to carry it (Some shops have a clause in their contracts stating they can dispose of unsold merchandise if it is not claimed within thirty to sixty days after a notice has been sent to the consignor.)
- a detailed list of the individual items (and their prices) being consigned to the shop (Ideally, each of your products will bear a product code number the shop can use when it reports the sale of that item. As each item sells, cross it off the list and update the list as replacement merchandise is taken in.)

A discussion of the pros and cons of consignment selling is beyond the scope of this book but I've devoted a chapter to this topic in my *Handmade for Profit* book.

See also Consignment Laws; Insurance on Crafts Merchandise, Off-Premise; Inventory; Labels or Tags Required by Law; Sales Commissions; *and* Shop Failures.

Consumer Safety Laws

Q: *I plan to make toys for children, but I'm concerned about how to make them safe. What can I do to avoid legal problems here?*

The Consumer Product Safety Commission (CPSC), established by *The Consumer Product Safety Act of 1972,* enforces mandatory safety standards for consumer products sold in the United States. You should request free information from this agency if you (1) make toys or other products for children; (2) make garments (particularly children's wear); (3) use any kind of paint, varnish, lacquer, or shellac on your products.

One of the agency's most active regulatory programs is in the area of toys and consumer goods designed for children. Of most concern to craftspeople are these CPSC regulations:

- The small parts requirement, which prohibits small parts that could be a choking hazard in toys and articles for children under three years of age
- The sharp edge and sharp point requirements, which describe tests for identifying hazardously sharp edges and points in toys and articles for children under eight years of age
- Requirements for rattles that ensure that the ends or handles of rattles are large enough so they cannot enter a child's mouth and throat and cause choking
- Flammability requirements for toys that state a limit on the burning rate (Toys that pass this test may still ignite and burn, but they will not burn explosively.)

The *Federal Hazardous Substances Act* addresses products that are toxic, corrosive, an irritant, or a strong sensitizer, but these types of hazards are rare among toys and children's articles. If your toys (or other consumer products that might fall into the hands of children) are finished with paint, varnish, lacquer, or shellac, however, see the discussion under *Paints, Varnishes, and Other Finishes* for safety precautions you can take to avoid problems.

In summary, to be legally safe, *be careful*. All toys and other products for children should be (1) too large to be swallowed; (2) not apt to break easily or leave jagged edges; (3) free of sharp edges or points (including exposed pins, wires, or nails); (4) nontoxic, nonflammable, and nonpoisonous.

A wealth of consumer product information is available from the Consumer Product Safety Commission's toll-free Hotline, and several publications related to toys and children's products are offered. When you call 1-800-638-2772, you will get a menu of several extensions you can punch to order publications of interest or report your

When producing collectible dolls and other items that might look like toys but are not meant to be used by children, it's a good idea to protect yourself with a tag or label to this effect. The above examples were provided by Widby Enterprises.

dissatisfaction with any product or service you've purchased. One extension will connect you with CPSC's Small Business Ombudsman department, which offers information to help small business owners comply with CPSC statutes and regulations or solve problems related to them.

See also Flammability Standards; Lead Testing; Paints, Varnishes, and Other Finishes; and Product Liability Insurance.

Contracts

 Q: *Must a contract be in writing to be legal?*

Technically, unless a contract is for the sale of goods over a certain amount (which varies from state to state), a verbal contract is just as legal and binding as a written one. The problem with a verbal agreement, however, is that it is difficult if not impossible to prove in court. It makes much more sense to "get it in writing."

Whenever you make a simple verbal agreement with anyone, immediately confirm in writing what has been agreed upon. You don't have to use legal language to create a document that will stand up in court. Just state the facts clearly. Send two copies of your letter to the party involved and ask him or her to sign, date, and return one copy to you as confirmation of the facts stated. Voilà—a contract.

If you are entering into a more complicated legal arrangement with someone—such as a book publisher or a manufacturer who wants to mass produce one of your products—be sure to have the contract checked by an attorney familiar with the particular field involved. (An attorney friend who specializes in real estate deals may be inexpensive but unlikely to be familiar with the ins and outs of book publishing or selling designs.) Also remember that contracts aren't written in stone. If you are ever offered a "standard contract" that contains unacceptable clauses, don't blindly sign away your rights without first trying to negotiate those clauses.

See also Author/Publisher Contract; Consignment Selling; *and* Sales Representatives.

Tip

It's expensive to file a lawsuit out-of-state. When negotiating a contract with an out-of-state company, make sure it contains a clause that gives you the right to litigate or file a lawsuit in your own state's courts.

Copyright Categories of Protection

Q: *What can and cannot be protected by copyright, and what's the difference between a copyright, patent, and trademark?*

Here, from my *Homemade Money* book is an example to help you remember the difference: The *artwork* on a can of cola can be copyrighted. The *name—and the way it is expressed on that can*—can be trademarked. The *formula* for the cola itself can be patented. (See a discussion of patents and trademarks elsewhere in this book.)

Ideas themselves cannot be protected by a copyright, but you may protect your *expression of an idea* by copyright if it is in tangible form, such as a design, pattern, or other written or drawn material. Some creativity and originality must be incorporated into a work for it to be copyrightable, however. For example, you cannot copyright a common form, shape, or object such as a circle, triangle, heart, rose, or butterfly, but you *can* create original designs that incorporate such common forms, shapes, and objects. You cannot stop anyone else from using the same common forms, shapes, or objects in their own designs, however. For example, six artists could paint a picture of a butterfly sitting on a rose, and each artist could copyright his or her own original picture.

To further illustrate, you can copyright the design on a craft object when that design can be identified separately from the object itself, but you cannot copyright an ordinary object such as a ring, a plate, a coffee mug, or a box. You cannot copyright anything that has fallen into public domain, but you can make and copyright your own adaptation (see *Copyrights in Public Domain*). Names, titles, and short phrases may not be copyrighted, but may qualify for trademark protection. Although inventions are protected by patents, the written description or drawing of an invention can also be protected by copyright.

Different copyright forms must be used to protect different forms of intellectual property, which falls into five main categories:

1. SERIALS (use Form SE). This category includes periodicals, newspapers, magazines, bulletins, newsletters, annuals, journals, and proceedings of societies.
2. TEXT (use Form TX). Included in this category are books, directories, and any other kind of text or work written in words, such as how-to instructions for a craft project.
3. VISUAL ARTS (use Form VA). This category is used to register pictorial, graphic, or sculptural works, including fine, graphic, and applied, photographs, charts, technical drawings, diagrams, and models.
4. PERFORMING ARTS (use Form PA). Included in this category are musical works and accompanying words, dramatic works, pantomimes, choreographic works, motion pictures, and other audiovisual works.
5. SOUND RECORDINGS (use Form SR). This category includes musical, spoken, or other sounds.

See also Book Copyright; Copyright Registration; Patent; *and* Trademark.

Copyright "Fair Use" Doctrine

Q: *Who can copy my work under the "fair use" doctrine and how much of it can they use without permission?*

Anyone can make limited use of your work without permission as long as the material is being used for research, teaching, or in connection with news reporting, criticism, or comment—but only if such use does not affect the potential market for, or value of, the copyrighted work. For example, a writer may quote briefly from a book you have copyrighted if he or she gives you credit for it. A teacher may copy a small portion of your written work or one of your patterns or designs, *provided it is used just once, for one class.* However, this copy must bear your copyright notice, and the teacher does not have the right to use your material more than once without your permission.

See also Copyright Infringement *and* Copyrights of Others.

Copyright-Free Designs

Q: *I have no artistic ability and can't even draw a straight line, so how can I compete in today's crafts marketplace if I can't create my own designs?*

You *can* create your own designs! You may not think of yourself as an "artist," but don't ever say you are not creative or artistic. God gave all of us our own special streak of creativity or artistry—we simply need to discover it. Often, creativity is the discovery of something that's been there all along. Your special artistry may lie in such areas as your ability to arrange a bouquet of flowers, decorate a Christmas tree, or run a sewing machine.

I'm always amused by people who say they can't draw because every one of us drew pictures as children and thought they were wonderful. Some people have built businesses on child like (sometimes called "primitive") designs, so stop berating yourself for your inability to draw a picture or design that looks like other people's art and start creating your own kind of art. If you need help, ask one of your young children or grandchildren for advice, and always remember that "art" is in the eye of the beholder.

Tip

If you can wield a pair of scissors or move a pencil around, you can create original designs simply by adapting or mixing design motifs from the copyright-free design books published by Dover Publications. For more information on these books, see article, "Where to Find Copyright-Free Designs and Motifs."

Copyright Infringement

Q: *Someone has stolen something I have copyrighted. What can I do to stop them from profiting from my creativity, and where can I go for help in doing this?*

First, a definition of "copyright infringement." This occurs whenever anyone violates the exclusive rights covered by copyright. It requires only "substantial similarity" to establish infringement and the penalties can be high ($100,000 or more) if the infringement has affected the profits of the copyright owner. One copyright attorney says the test for infringement of copyright "is whether an ordinary observer, looking at your work and the work you claim is an infringement, would say that one work was copied from the other."

When you learn that someone has infringed one of your copyrights, the first consideration is whether you have filed a formal copyright registration of the work in question. Under present law, you cannot sue anyone who copies or infringes upon your copyright unless or until you have formerly registered your copyright with the Copyright Office. Although you can file the registration after you discover the infringer, late registration will limit the kind of damages you can sue for. (This could change, however. Congress has given consideration to abolishing the requirement that one must register a copyright in order to sue for infringement. If this becomes law, no one will be able to know whether anything is copyrighted or not, and to be safe, everyone will have to assume everything is protected.)

This is particularly true where cyberspace is concerned. If you are using the Internet, remember that the same laws, rules, and regulations that apply to all other areas of business also apply to the Internet and World Wide Web. To be legally safe, you must assume that *everything* on the Internet and World Wide Web is protected by copyright laws. This means you cannot pick up graphic designs, art illustrations, articles, and other material for posting to your web site, e-mailing to others or downloading to your printer for your own profitable use. The illegal distribution of copyrighted material over the Web or your illegal use of it off the Web could open you up to a lawsuit.

Where do you go for help when someone steals *your* creativity? Because the Copyright Office is prohibited from giving legal advice or opinions about your rights in connection with cases of alleged copyright infringement, your only options when trying to stop a copyright infringer are to (1) send a letter asking them to stop or (2) hire a copyright attorney to do this for you and pursue the matter beyond that point, if necessary.

If you are dealing with an individual who has innocently infringed your copyright, a friendly, yet strongly worded letter from you may be all it takes to resolve the matter. (It will carry more weight if it is typed on impressive stationery that at least gives the illusion you can afford to sue if necessary.) Explain that, as the legal copyright owner, you alone have the right to profit from the work in question and that you will take any legal steps necessary to protect your rights. Ask for a reply by return mail confirming that the infringement will cease at once. In many cases, this will do the trick. If you've been ripped off by a large corporation, however, skip the friendly letter and contact a copyright attorney at once. It won't cost much to have an attorney write a letter for you, but to proceed further than this will be costly.

In the end, you must ask yourself how valuable your work is to you and how much time and money you are willing to invest to protect it. I recall a very successful doll designer who quit the crafts business after years of doing battle in court with copyright infringers. They took all the joy out of her work and legal costs took all the profits she had accumulated from several years of selling.

See also Copyright "Fair Use" Doctrine; Copyrights of Others; *and article, "Coping With Copycats."*

Tip

> The best way to avoid copyright infringement problems is to follow the "Golden Rule" proposed by a United States Supreme Court Justice:
>
> "Take not from others to such an extent and in such a manner that you would be resentful if they so took from you."

Copyright Notice

Q: *Does it do any good to put a copyright notice on something if I have no intention of filing a formal copyright claim?*

Copyright protection exists from the moment a work is created. Although a copyright notice is no longer required by law, it doesn't cost anything to attach a copyright notice to every original thing you create, so you should always do this. (Lack of a copyright notice only makes it easier for others to steal your creativity and claim "innocent infringement.") Even when you place a copyright notice on your original work (thereby announcing to the world your ownership of the work), you are not required by law to file a formal registration. A proper copyright notice includes three elements:

1. the word "copyright" or its abbreviation, "copr." or the copyright symbol, ©
2. the year of first publication of the work (when it was first shown or sold to the public)
3. the name of the copyright owner. Sometimes the words, "All Rights Reserved" will be added, meaning that copyright protection has been extended to include all of the Western Hemisphere (*Example:* © 1998 by Barbara Brabec. All Rights Reserved.)

See also Copyright Categories of Protection, *and* Copyright Infringement.

Where to Find Copyright-Free Designs and Motifs

Thousands of copyright-free designs are available from Dover Publications, publisher of a series of inexpensive design books called the *Pictorial Archives.* Each of these paperback books contains hundreds of design motifs you can use in any manner or place you wish, without further payment, permission, or acknowledgement.

Anyone who claims they "can't draw a straight line" will appreciate these books and soon discover they *can* add their own creative ideas to a design or pattern created by someone else. Throughout history, artists have studied the work of others for inspiration and ideas, often lifting or adapting the best ideas of someone else for their own use. You can, too. The *Pictorial Archive* books offer a real treasure of usable patterns, ideas, and authentic motifs from many cultures, including American Indian, Japanese, Chinese, African, Mexican, Russian and East European, North African, Egyptian, and so on. The series also includes books on American folk art, flora and fauna, geometric design and ornament, and Art Deco.

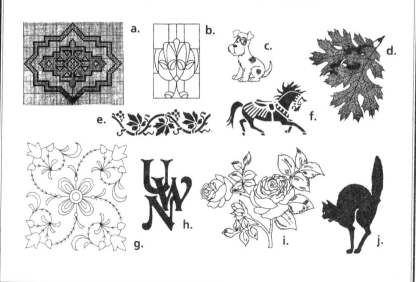

Coping With Copycats

Every craft seller hates them: the people who saunter up to a booth, pull out paper and pencil, and begin to copy the designs found on exhibited products, or worse, snap pictures. One crafter told me that at the last show she did, there were signs around the building stating "PLEASE: NO PHOTOS OR SKETCHES," but people ignored them, and she had two people in her booth sketching her work.

Another crafter reported in a magazine article that she has had some very rude and inconsiderate people stand in her booth and draw right in front of her. "I made them mad when I asked them to leave my booth," she said, "but at least they left." TIP: If you see someone with a camera taking pictures of you or your booth, ask for identification. Unless that person is with a newspaper or magazine, tell him or her to stop taking pictures at once. If your craft designs are copyrighted, emphasize that you have the legal right to sue anyone who copies your designs.

The minute you put a good idea out there, the public will copy it. So the secret is to come up with new ideas every year because then you'll be ahead of the copycats. By the time they get around to copying you, you have new merchandise. Phyllis Johnson sums it up nicely: "As soon as you have a new design or product, get it out there, saturate your market area, all the while dreaming up something new or a new twist on the old."

—An excerpt from Handmade for Profit—Hundreds of Secrets to Success in Selling Arts & Crafts *by Barbara Brabec (M. Evans).*

OPPOSITE: *These illustrations are but a tiny sampling of what you will find in Dover's* Pictorial Archive *books. More than 800 titles are available, giving artists and craftspeople access to more than 250,000 copyright-free images (many in full color) that may be used without permission. Illustrations shown here were clipped from the following books: a)* Folk Designs from the Caucusus for Weaving and Needlework; *b)* 390 Traditional Stained Glass Designs; *c)* 1001 Cartoon-Style Illustrations; *d)* Plants and Flowers; *e)* 2,286 Traditional Stencil Designs; *f)* Carousel Animals Cut & Use Stencils; *g)* Designs and Patterns for Embroiderers and Craftspeople; *h)* Modern Monograms: 1310 Graphic Designs; *i)* Traditional Floral Designs and Motifs for Artisits and Craftspeople; *j)* Old-Time Silhouettes.

Tip

Place the copyright notice where it can be seen. You can stamp copyright notices, cast them, engrave them, paint them, etch them, stitch them, print them, or write notices by hand. If you create fabric crafts, you can order custom, designed fabric labels that bear your copyright notice, logo, or any other information you wish to include.

Copyright Registration

Q: *How do I register a copyright claim and how much does this cost?*

Currently, it costs twenty dollars to file a copyright claim, and this is easy to do. Application forms include instructions on how to complete the form and they may be ordered by mail or by phone from the Copyright Office in Washington, D.C. (See sample copyright form nearby.) Telephone 1-202-707-3000 to get the Copyright Office's recorded information system. It offers a menu of recorded messages you can hear and enables you to order copyright publications or forms by mail or speak directly to an information specialist if you have a technical question. Note, however, that the Copyright Office cannot give you legal advice or opinions (see *Copyright Infringement*).

A copyright should be registered within three months of the "publication date," which is the date you first sell, display, give away, or otherwise distribute the copyrighted work to the public. Although it is not necessary to formally register a copyright claim, there is a "Mandatory Deposit Requirement" for all work bearing a copyright notice. There is no charge for this, and no forms to complete. You simply mail two copies of the work to the Library of Congress. For more information, request the Copyright Office's bulletin on this topic.

See also Copyright Categories of Protection *and articles, "Copyrights: Registering a Collection of Work" and "The Cabbage Patch Kids® Story."*

Copyrights:
Registering a Collection of Work

Instead of filing separate copyright forms for each design, pattern, or other written work you wish to protect, you can save money by registering them as a collection, with one application form and fee. To do this, all work must be from one author or creator, be assembled in an orderly fashion, and bear a single title that identifies the collection as a whole.

I once met Linda Fry Kenzle at a local print shop when she was in the process of preparing her designs for submission to the Copyright Office. She photocopied each design, one to a page, then turned the resulting pages into a book by adding a front and back cover of a stock heavier than the paper inside. The printer drilled three holes in it so she could bind the book. Linda's illustrations below first appeared in my newsletter, but her idea is as timely today as it was when first published.

See also Copyright Registration.

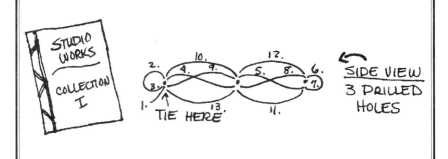

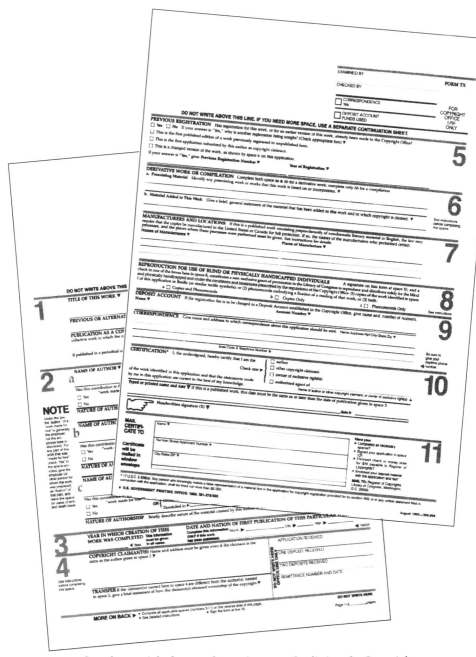

Sample copyright form used to register text. See listings for Copyright Categories of Protection *and* Copyright Protection.

Tip

With your copyright application form, you are required to send two copies of the best edition of any printed work. When registering three-dimensional objects, you need only send photographs (preferably 8x10 inches) or accurate drawings of the designs or patterns you wish to protect by copyright.

Copyrights in Public Domain

Q: *How long does a copyright last, and how can I tell if something is now in public domain?*

The copyright on all works created after January 1, 1978, lasts for the life of the author or creator plus fifty years after his or her death. For works created before 1978, there are different terms, which you can obtain from any book in your library on copyright law.

Material falls into public domain when the copyright has expired or has not been claimed by another, and once in public domain, material can never be copyrighted again. Examples of work in public domain include designs on ancient objects in museums or fairy-tale characters and other designs found in old books. One author of a book on copyright suggests that anything showing a copyright date more than seventy-five years old is probably in the public domain. If in doubt, however, a copyright search can be made. (Obtain the booklet "How to Investigate the Copyright Status of a Work" from the Copyright Office.)

In an article for *The Crafts Report,* attorney Leonard D. DuBoff once explained that no one could be stopped from copying a Tiffany lamp design in the public domain. "If you become creative when copying the Tiffany lamp and make substantial changes in the design," he said, "then your changes are copyrightable by you. Nobody can copy your adaptation, although they can work from the original and make their own variation."

Quilt designs offer an interesting example. You may have noticed the same quilt designs in several books. Because the old traditional quilt patterns were created before copyright laws were a reality, these works automatically fell into public domain. This means anyone can include traditional quilt patterns in yet another book and copyright the book. In effect, however, they are not copyrighting these old patterns themselves, *but merely the book and the way the patterns have been presented to readers.* Thus a contemporary quilt designer could take a log cabin design and make unique or dramatic design changes resulting in a new work that could be protected by copyright.

I have often been asked whether it's okay to use common expressions or sayings such as those being reproduced on scores of plaques, pictures, and sweatshirts today. Most are likely to be in public domain or could not qualify for copyright given their commonality. However, the *manner* in which such sayings are affixed to an object may be protected by copyright. For example, I believe several sellers might be able to get copyright protection for their own rendition of a common expression found on a plaque or sweatshirt simply by arranging letters or words in a unique way or adding special background art.

Note that I just said "I believe," meaning I don't know for sure. Copyright law is a complex topic. Although I am an "informed layperson," you must use all my remarks on this topic only as a guideline. Check your library for books on this topic by copyright attorneys and *always* get professional advice before entering the commercial marketplace with any product that is partly based on someone else's creativity.

See also Copyright-Free Designs.

Copyrights of Others

Q: *I am concerned about violating the copyrights of others, but I'm not sure what I need to do—or not do—to avoid legal confrontations with copyright owners. Would you offer some simple guidelines?*

As you work to protect your own intellectual property, you must also be concerned about violating the rights of others. To avoid problems, here are several things you should *not* do:

• Do not copy whole sections of any book for use as a handout in one of your classes. This is a serious violation of copyright law. (See also discussion under *Copyright "Fair Use" Doctrine.*)

• Do not use in a publication or on any product the poems or poetry of others without written permission. The use of an entire poem is a flagrant violation of copyright law because it represents the use of a whole work of an individual creator who is receiving no financial benefit from such usage.

• Do not reproduce for sale any part of any picture, photograph, painting, or piece of artwork you may have purchased. You may own the original object, but the creator still owns the copyright, and only he or she has the right to copy it as prints, postcards, greeting cards, calendars, etc., or grant the right to copy to someone else in the form of a license. (See *Licensing Arrangements.*)

• Do not make any item bearing a replica of any famous person or movie star. The fact that they are long dead does not mean others can capitalize on their fame. This topic is discussed under the listing for *Celebrity Rights Act.*

• Do not copy the designs on other handcrafted products and commercial gift items. All manufacturers and most professional craft sellers protect their work by copyrights or design patents and stand ready to take legal action against copyright violators. (Don't think you can get around this by changing some part of the design, using a different color or material or turning a two-dimensional design into a three-dimensional object. The Copyright Office says a work is a copy if it repeats a "substantial part" of someone else's design, and many people have gone to court to define "substantial part.")

• *Never, ever* make anything for sale that bears a famous copyrighted character such as Snoopy, the Sesame Street gang, or Walt Disney characters. The fact that you see others doing this does not mean it is legal to do so. Crafters who choose to ignore this advice "because everyone else is doing it" are inviting hefty fines or lawsuits. The Disney people are particularly aggressive in defending their copyrights.

• Do not *wholesale* items made from fabric that bears a copyright notice on the selvage. (See *Designer Fabrics, Commercial Use of* for a lengthy discussion about this.)

• Do not photocopy patterns for sale or trade because all patterns are protected by copyright, and your distribution of photocopies denies the creator the profit from copies that might have been sold. (For a lengthy discussion of the other copyright problems related to the use of patterns found in magazines or purchased in fabric stores or mail order catalogs, see *Patterns, Commercial Use of.*)

• Do not use rubber stamps to create a product or design you plan to sell until you have contacted the rubber stamp designer or manufacturer to get permission to do this. In a survey of many rubber stamp manufacturers, the editors of *Craft Supply Magazine* reported on their findings: "The overall feeling was that companies will allow a single artist or PC (professional crafter) to use the companies' copyrighted images for the single artist's or PC's work if the image is hand stamped." While this suggests it's okay for the individual crafter to sell products with rubber stamp designs on them if they personally stamp the products themselves (don't use employees to do it), it's important to remember that the policies of one stamp company may be entirely different from another, so to be safe, you should *always* get written permission to use rubber stamps for commercial purposes. (This includes the printed *images* of rubber stamps in a stamp company's catalog.) You must also be careful about using commercial rubber stamps on your printed materials. For an example of the kind of problems that can develop here, see the article, "Designer Paranoia."

• Do not clip illustrations, artwork, or designs from any publication (especially magazines and catalogs) and use them to illustrate your own publication or printed materials. The only illustrations that are safe to use for commercial or business purposes are those being sold as commercial clip art, or designs and motifs found in the *Pictorial Archive* books published by Dover Publications. (See *Copyright-Free Designs.*)

I realize this is a lot of "do nots," but my goal here is to keep you out of legal trouble and I know this is your goal, too.

See also Copyright Infringement.

Corporation

 I've been advised to incorporate to gain protection for my personal assets in the event of a lawsuit. What do I need to consider where incorporation is concerned?

The Cabbage Patch Kids® Story

In 1980, a Georgia dollmaker named Martha Nelson Thomas entered a million-dollar suit against Xavier Roberts and his licensed Hong Kong manufacturer and distributor, Coleco Industries, Inc., for "pirating" her soft sculpture *Doll Babies*. Four years later, Martha settled out of court for an undisclosed sum. By then, Roberts' dolls, named *Cabbage Patch Kids®* had become a $10.4 billion toy industry that gave Roberts even greater profits in the years that followed. Martha later enjoyed financial success as the designer of a plastic doll head that a manufacturer reproduced in several variations.

At the heart of this lawsuit was the fact that Xavier Roberts had filed a copyright on his doll and Martha hadn't, which brings me to the point I wish to emphasize here: *Only the person with the registered copyright has the right to profit from it, whether that person is the original creator or not.* By failing to protect her dolls with a copyright, Martha left the door open for someone else to take them, the judge pointed out.

The popularity of these dolls prompted many crafters to make "Cabbage Patch look-alikes," and at one point, Roberts was suing people right and left for selling such items. If you are selling a soft sculpture doll that has been "inspired" by a copyrighted doll on the marketplace, be forewarned: if anyone can see a resemblance between your doll and another's, there may be sufficient grounds for a lawsuit.

See also Copyright Infringement.

A corporation is the most complicated form a business can take, so it's important to get professional advice on this topic from a lawyer or accountant. Corporations are of two types: "C" (general corporation) and "S" (Subchapter S). While incorporation offers special legal advantages, it also involves extra paperwork and legal and accounting services. Unlike a partnership, a corporation is a legal entity unto itself that does not die with the retirement or death of its officers. Since it costs more to unincorporate a business than to incorporate it, you don't want to rush blindly in this direction until you have all the facts. Judith H. McQuown, author of *INC Yourself* (HarperBusiness) says it may not be worth it to incorporate if your net business earnings are less than $25,000 or $30,000 a year.

Many small business owners mistakenly believe that incorporation of their business will give them automatic protection for their personal assets in the event of a lawsuit. For businesses with employees, incorporation does serve as a kind of door that can be shut in the event an employee does something wrong and causes a business to be sued. In that case, the owner's personal assets would be protected by the "corporation door." However, if you are the business owner and you personally commit a wrongful act that prompts a lawsuit, the "corporation door" remains open and you will be held liable for that act.

If several individuals or families are involved in a business, a "C" corporation or Subchapter S Corporation (see below) may be the best route to take. As a sole proprietor, however, it may be easier and less expensive simply to purchase liability insurance for your business.

Subchapter S Corporation. Many new and low-income businesses establish an S Corporation, which operates like a regular corporation except it is taxed like a partnership (at the lower personal rate). Profits or losses are reported on a shareholder's Form 1040. The owners of a party-plan business reported to me that incorporation under Subchapter S was a good solution for them. Although it didn't offer any product liability insurance, it did work to protect their personal and family properties. Given the relative safety of their inventory, their insurance agent said this type of protection should be adequate for them.

See also Limited Liability Company; Partnership; Sole Proprietorship; *and* Taxes, Local, State, and Federal.

Tip

A professional writer incorporated his business after nearly twenty years as a sole proprietor because he wanted to keep working after he was eligible for social security. By incorporating, he said, he could avoid giving his social security checks back to the government at the end of the year.

Designer Paranoia

by Janet Burgess, Amazon Drygoods

I was using a rubber stamp company's images all over my envelopes (very funny and Victorian). When we outgrew having time to stamp, I had a large supply of envelopes printed with the designer's images. He gave his permission to do this in return for a free ad in our catalog that invited readers to send him a dollar to receive his catalog of rubber stamps. It was a nice trade-off until our envelopes were featured in a national trade journal for the direct marketing industry.

A business has no control over publicity like this, so when it happens I'm just delighted to receive it and glad if they get my name and address right. Well, the stamp company owner saw the article and just went crazy. The problem was that his name was not mentioned in this article, so his lawyer hit me with a demand for $10,000 in royalties to be paid annually, plus past royalties and damages. This problem cost me a great deal of time and money in legal fees. I was cleared on this because I had saved all correspondence on the matter and the stamp company's owner had saved nothing. I had not acted improperly other than inadvertently wounding his ego. In the end, I was forced to stop using the envelopes when my supply ran out, but they didn't get any money from me.

Cost of Advertising

To determine your advertising cost per lead, divide the dollars spent for advertising by the number of leads (buying prospects) generated. To determine cost per sale, divide the dollars you've spent to acquire leads and convert them to sales by the number of sales made. The formula looks like this:

$$ spent for advertising ÷ number of leads = cost per lead
$$ spent to acquire and convert leads ÷ number of sales = cost per sale

Cost of Goods

This figure is the total of purchase price of goods and any transportation or delivery costs involved.

See also Inventory.

Cottage Industry

Many people use this term loosely in connection with homebased businesses of all kinds, but a true cottage industry is a business that has a central marketing and management operation with production of craftwork done usually in the homes of people other than that of marketing and management.

See also Independent Contractors.

CPA

See Accountant.

Craft Cooperative

Q.: Several of my friends and I have discussed the idea of starting a handcraft cooperative, but we have no idea how to start such an organization. Should we pursue this idea?

Yes, and I can direct you to an authoritative source for detailed information on how to start a cooperative and manage it efficiently. In her booklet, *How to Start & Run a Successful Handcraft Co-Op in Your Own Community* (published by Front Room Publishers), Catherine Gilleland, founder of The Crafters, Ltd., points to the benefits of membership in a crafts cooperative: "A multifaceted guild is limited only by the energy and imagination of its members, and it is one of the few organizations that can actually offer something for everyone. What crafter wouldn't be thrilled at the thought of paying less for supplies? What artisan wouldn't be pleased to share the expense and energy required to promote her crafts? What novice handworker wouldn't welcome the chance to learn a variety of new techniques at low-cost workshops? These are just a few of the benefits awaiting each guild member, the most important of which may be the opportunity to share ideas and draw from the encouragement of other artists."

See also Art/Craft Organizations.

Tip

The success of a craft cooperative—or any organization, for that matter—depends on the willingness of members to contribute the time and energy necessary to get the group "up and running." Once things are rolling, new and existing members must understand the importance of sharing the work load. Many groups ultimately fold because a few individuals who don't know how to say no take on too much work. This leads not only to burnout for the individuals involved, but to feelings of anger toward those who aren't contributing their fair share.

Craft Fair Selling

See Brochure; Car Insurance; Cellular Phones; Checks; COD Shipments; Consumer Safety Laws; Custom Orders; Discounts; Home Office Deduction; Inventory; Juried Shows; Labels or Tags Required by Law; Merchant Bank Card Services; Patterns, Commercial Use of; Printed Materials; Sales Tax; *and* Show Listings.

Craft Mall Selling

Q: *I'm thinking about selling through craft malls. How do they operate and what kind of expenses are involved in this type of selling?*

Craft malls have been in existence since 1988 when Rufus Coomer opened his first mall in Azle, Texas. By the end of 1995, with a chain of malls in several states, Coomers was the nation's largest retailer of American handmade crafts, gifts, and decorations for homes and offices. Artisans were quick to see the advantages of selling in craft malls. Now they could:

- rent affordable shelf or booth space in a shop or store with steady traffic
- have control over how their wares were displayed without any responsibility for actually selling them
- have the benefit of a shop atmosphere without the problems of consignment selling
- enjoy year-round sales and regular monthly payments without the hassles involved in craft fair selling
- sell in many outlets across the country and deal with mall owners by mail through special "remote stocking programs" (Ask mall owners to explain how this works.)

The craft mall industry is huge and growing but, like the Internet, it has no rules or regulations so it has its own unique set of problems and pitfalls. Although others who have opened malls across the country have emulated the Coomers method of operation, each mall owner brings his or her own ideas into the business, which means each mall operates a bit differently. Monthly rental fees, service fees, and sales commissions may vary considerably, along with size of exhibit space and benefits offered to sellers, so you need to compare information from several malls to decide which ones are best for you.

For more information on this topic, see this book's companion volume, *Handmade for Profit.* Chapter nine explains how to select a good craft mall, avoid pitfalls, set up a good mall exhibit, deal with common craft mall problems and do the arithmetic that will help you determine a mall's profitability to you.

See also Insurance on Crafts Merchandise, Off-Premise; Inventory; Labels or Tags Required by Law; Product Liability Insurance; Rent-a-Space Shops; Sales Tax; *and* Shop Failures.

Craft Organizations

See Art/Craft Organizations; Craft Cooperative; Home Business Organizations; *and* Supplies, Buying Wholesale.

Credit

See Credit Bureaus; Credit History; Credit/Trade References; *and* Line of Credit.

Credit Bureaus

There are over 900 credit bureaus in the country but only three major credit rating firms: Equifax, Trans Union Credit Information, and TRW Information Services (see resource chapter for addresses). Credit bureaus used to serve local areas only, but thanks to computer technology, every credit bureau in the country now has access to everyone's credit information.

See also articles, "How to Check Someone's Credit" and "Solving Cash Flow Problems."

Tip

Depending on how information is processed by a credit bureau, errors can sometimes slip into your personal credit history. It's a good idea to periodically check your credit rating to make sure there are no problems. Prior to applying for a bank loan, for example, you could ask your bank which bureau it uses, then check your own credit first. Expect to pay a small fee for a credit report. (See also *Credit History.*)

Credit Cards

See Credit History; Personal Loans; Scams; *and article, "Personal Credit Card Tips."*

Credit Card Sales

Q: *How much difference is it likely to make in my sales if I give customers the option of paying with a credit card?*

Most sellers report a twenty-five to forty percent increase in sales once they begin to offer customers the privilege of charging purchases to a credit card. While this is great for retail sales, you should never let wholesale buyers charge purchases to a credit card. "It's amazing, the number of buyers who come to a trade show without a business card or any credit references," reports a frequent seller at trade shows. "They may be willing to give you a credit card for the sale, but you cannot legally charge them extra for what it will cost you to process that order (between five and seven percent), so this is a problem sellers should be prepared to deal with."

See also Electronic Marketing; Fax Machine; Merchant Bank Card Services; Price List; *and* Terms of Sale.

Credit History

If you do not have a personal credit history, this should be an immediate goal. If you're a married woman with a home business, be sure to open your business checking account in your name only. (If you add your husband's name, it becomes a joint account with credit history automatically going to his file.)

Some people are tearing up all their credit cards to avoid debt, but I believe it's a mistake not to have at least one credit card in your name you can use for business purposes. By charging business expenses to a credit card, you build not only a good paper trail of all transactions but a credit history in your name.

See also Credit Bureaus *and article, "Personal Credit Card Tips."*

How to Check Someone's Credit

How can you check the credit rating of a potential client, customer, or other business associate? It depends on who you are and whom you are checking on. While businesses can easily get credit information on individuals, individual business owners cannot get credit information on other businesses from credit bureaus.

• **Individual-to-Individual Business Transactions**. According to one of my credit bureau contacts, you can't get the credit rating of an individual client or customer unless you have a permissible purpose that includes a financial relationship with the individual or other party. Your best bet may be to call the Better Business Bureau to see if there have been any complaints against the party you're thinking about doing business with.

• **Business-to-Business Transactions**. If you are a small business interested in getting credit information on a specific company, check financial references such as *Dun & Bradstreet* (provided the company is large enough to be rated). If you just want to check the credit of a small shop across the country who wants you to ship and invoice, there's not much you can do to verify the shop's creditworthiness. If you know the name of the individual who owns the shop, however, you might be able to get a credit report on that individual by calling a credit bureau.

Credit Rating

See Credit Bureaus; Credit History; *and article,* "Solving Cash Flow Problems."

Personal Credit Card Tips

Credit cards are one of life's greatest conveniences, but if you happen to lose them or let even one of your credit cards fall into the wrong hands it can cause problems. Here are some things you should know:

- **Credit Card Insurance**. In spite of what you may be told by a smooth-talking salesperson who is selling credit card insurance, you don't need it, even when your card is lost, stolen, or illegally used by someone else. Under federal law, if you call the card issuer before unauthorized charges are made, you are automatically protected against loss. Even if you don't, you are liable for only $50 on each card. (In calling several credit card companies, I was told they generally waive the $50 fee if the cardholder reports the loss.)

Most of the credit card companies offer an inexpensive credit card and key tag/luggage registration service (about $15/year) that may be worthwhile if you have many cards that conceivably could all be lost or stolen at once. Such registration enables the service provider to immediately notify credit card companies of your loss, saving you the time it would take to do this yourself. If you haven't done this yet, do it now: Make a list of every credit card you use, with complete information on who to contact in the event of loss and keep it up to date at all times.

- **Credit Cards Used as Credit Reference**. When paying for a purchase with a check, some merchants may ask you to give them a credit card number for reference. This leaves you open to fraud, however, and by law you do not have to do this. Since merchants cannot legally cover bad checks with a credit card, there is no reason for them to have your credit card number. (It's okay to show a credit card as a credit reference; just don't let anyone copy the number.)

- **Telephone Solicitation**. Never give a credit card number to anyone on the phone who says they need to "verify a number for their records," or who has called you out of the blue to offer you some "special deal." In such cases, you may be dealing with a con artist.

Credit/Trade References

In the course of doing business, you will not only have to supply credit references to suppliers, but will need to get them from new accounts who ask for credit from you. What will you do the first time someone gives you a large order and asks you to ship and bill? Before agreeing to ship a large order to a new account you've never heard of before, ask that you be furnished with the following information and then check it out when you get it:

- owner or manager's name and phone number
- company's phone number, fax number, and e-mail address
- federal I.D. number
- three or more trade references with phone numbers and addresses
- a bank reference

Since you will be asking new customers for detailed credit information, it makes sense to create a standard form for the collection of all of the above. (Many buyers have already compiled this information on forms of their own which they give to suppliers at trade shows.)

A buyer's bank reference should include the bank's full address, buyer's account number, and written authorization for release of credit information. (Without such authorization, a bank won't even tell you whether a company has an account with them or not.) Be sure to check all the trade references to learn how long the buyer has had an account with each of them and whether they pay on time or not. If you have never heard of any of the trade references, call Information to verify that the telephone numbers you've been given are authentic. Be especially cautious if someone gives you an unusually large order and asks for shipment in a hurry. Con artists often set up phony references.

See also COD Shipments; Credit Bureaus; Credit Card Sales; Credit Rating; Order Policies; Pro Forma; *and* Scams.

Tip

If you are unable to get satisfactory credit information on a new customer or just feel uncomfortable about shipping that first order to them, you can either ship COD or pro forma.

Custom Orders

Q: *If someone asks me to do a custom order or commissions me to do a special art or craft project, do I ask for a deposit or bill them on completion of the job?*

Custom orders and craft commissions can be as simple as making a product in a particular size or color to decorating a nursery with creative artwork, stenciling walls, designing decorative tiles for a kitchen, or hand-carving a life-size figure. Because such work is often impossible to sell to anyone but the original buyer, you should always get a deposit to cover all material costs and insure against cancellation at the last moment.

The general rule is to ask for fifty percent down before you begin the work, but there may be times when you should make an exception. As artist Susan Young puts it, "Geography makes a difference. Down south, people's feelings are hurt if you ask for a deposit because they take this as a sign you don't trust them. Many of my customers would be offended if I asked them for a deposit for a custom-designed item, so I always trust my instincts here."

Some artists who accept commissions for pricey pieces may work a bit differently, taking an initial deposit until all details of the commission have been worked out, and then asking for an amount equal to one-third of the total price before supplies or materials have been ordered. To guarantee payment upon completion, finished pieces may be shipped either COD or Pro forma.

See also COD Shipments *and* Pro Forma.

DBA

This abbreviation—sometimes written as d/b/a—means "doing business as," and it is used by banks to connect a depositor to his or her fictitious (or assumed) name. (Example: Sondra Jones, dba Glass With Class). Some banks will not open a business account for you until you have filed a Fictitious Name Statement.

See also Fictitious Name Statement.

Dealer

See Distributor/Jobber.

Dealer Minimum

See Minimum/Maximum Order Policy.

Depreciation

See Business Expenses, Tax Deductible.

Design Business

See Business Records, Protection of; Contracts; *all listings on* Copyrights; Designer Fabrics,Commercial Use of; First Rights/All Rights Sales; Patterns, Commercial Use of; *and* Patent.

Designer Fabrics, Commercial Use of

Q: *I make a line of fabric crafts. Are there any restrictions on the use of designer fabrics in products that are to be wholesaled?*

Yes, there are limitations on the amount of fabric you can legally use without a licensing arrangement with the fabric manufacturer or a royalties payment to the fabric's designer. As you may know, all fab-

Using Designer Fabrics— One Manufacturer's Experience

Pat, a gift manufacturer who took her line of merchandise to a gift show, was thrilled when she learned that one of the designers whose fabrics she was using had stopped by her booth to chat. But a call from this designer's licensing agency a few days later stunned her. The designer, while friendly, wasn't just being friendly. What she was doing was *policing the use of her fabrics.*

If the designer hadn't liked what she saw in Pat's booth, legally she could have demanded that all products made of her fabrics be removed from Pat's line. As it turns out, she had no objection with the way Pat was using her fabric. What did concern her was the fact that Pat had mentioned her name in her brochure ("fabrics designed by xxx") which boiled down to Pat's illegally trading on the designer's reputation.

The designer asked her licensing agent to take care of this matter and also find out how much fabric Pat was using. Pat learned this particular designer had set a limit of 300 yards (in total) for use of her fabrics by unlicensed users. Usage beyond 300 yards would require a licensing arrangement and a five percent royalty on sales, she was told. Needing to use more than 300 yards, and not wanting to enter into a licensing arrangement, Pat decided to stop using this designer's fabric.

ric designs are copyrighted to protect other manufacturers from reproducing those designs. No one goes around checking to see how regular fabric is being used, but "designer fabric" is something else. Use of designer fabrics to make items for sale at craft fairs, holiday boutiques, or craft malls is not likely to be a problem, since few crafters would exceed the limitation that most designers find acceptable. (See licensing agent's comment on the next page.) A problem can arise, however, if you enter the wholesale marketplace with such products. Fabric designers often attend trade shows and gift marts looking for companies who are using their products and checking to see if they have a license to use their copyrighted fabrics.

The fact that you can buy designer fabrics from a fabric wholesaler or manufacturer does not mean you have unlimited commercial use of this fabric. The goal of a fabric manufacturer is to get fabrics into the marketplace. Distributors who wholesale these fabrics are supposed to notify buyers if there are any restrictions on the commercial use of them, but they are lax about doing this. The licensing agent for a well-known fabric designer explained that while most fabric manufacturers are happy to wholesale their designer fabrics, the goal of a designer's licensing agency is to make sure that *large users* pay for the privilege of making millions of dollars from the designer's fabrics. This means that someone has to keep tabs on who is using what, and how much, which explains why designers go to trade shows and marts looking for companies who are using their fabrics. (See related article, "Using Designer Fabrics—One Manufacturer's Experience.")

In my conversation with the licensing agent mentioned above, I learned there are no industry standards in the field of licensing. Everyone operates differently. The policy of one particular designer's licensing agency may be entirely different from the policy of another designer's agency. "The last thing we want to do is put small manufacturers out of business," the licensing agent told me. "On the other hand, we don't want to encourage the use of designer fabrics by individual crafters because we can't control the quality of the products they are putting on the market. We simply want to protect our licensees who have paid for the privilege of using our designer's fabrics for their exclusive product lines."

Tip

Before buying hundreds of yards of designer fabric for that new line of products you're planning to wholesale, ask the fabric distributor if there are any restrictions on its commercial use and whether you need to contact the manufacturer for additional information on this topic. If you're still buying fabric at the retail level, always observe the warning on the selvage. When you see a copyright notice with a designer's name, do not use this fabric to make items you plan to wholesale. If there is a notice to the effect that "this fabric is for individual consumption only," don't use it to make *anything* for sale. Avoid completely the commercial use of all fabrics with high profile designs such as copyrighted cartoon characters or NFL logos.

See also Copyrights of Others *and* Sports Logos, Commercial Use of.

You Can Publish Your Own Book

Thanks to computers, many creative people are producing their own books these days, and the secret to success as a small desktop publisher lies in publishing for a niche market. For example, if you are a woodworker, seamstress, or teddy bear designer who has learned secrets likely to benefit others in the same field, you're a book publisher just waiting to be born.

Although the fields of Art and Craft are big niche markets in their own right, each has many smaller niches of its own. Take woodworking, for example. Within this niche market are countless individuals interested in specific types of woodworking such as woodcarving, woodturning, woodburning, and marquetry to the kinds of products that can be made from wood, such as home accessories, furniture, toys, games, or jewelry.

"Niche publishing is the brightest and most profitable light in the publishing world as we go into 1997," says author and self-publisher Gordon Burgett in an article for *SPAN Connection* (newsletter of the Small Publishers Association of North America). He emphasizes how easy it is for anyone with a computer to publish books today and points to the market for books that are need-meeting or hope-fulfilling: "Today, anybody can produce a tightly-targeted book that is page-made at home, zip it off to the printer for a short turnaround, then sell it to several hundred or many thousands of eager souls at costs that make the pages a bargain."

As one who has published three books of her own and may publish others in the future, I can confirm the profitability of putting your words into book form and offering them to others. Book publishing is much too broad a topic to be covered in a book of this nature, but in the resource section of this book you will find a list of recommended business books that includes some of the best titles available on self-publishing. Reading any one of them will open a world of possibilities for you.

Design Patent

Design patents offer legal protection for ornamental designs. They are less expensive to obtain and maintain but give less protection than a regular patent. To qualify for protection, a design must have novel features. Examples: motifs on jewelry, furniture, or fabrics, or the unique shape and design of an object such as a belt buckle or a ceramic teapot in the form of a dragon. For more information on this topic, contact the Patent & Trademark Office in Washington, D.C. To hear a series of recorded messages, call 1-800-786-9199.

Desktop Publishing

See Book Publishing; Computer System, Purchase of; Copyright Categories of Protection; Copyright Infringement; Copyright Notice; Copyrights of Others; Directory Publishing; Newsletter Publishing; *and article,* *"You Can Publish Your Own Book."*

Directory Assistance

With deregulation of long-distance services and a mishmash of area codes that no longer reflect any geographic area, it has become difficult to get a correct number through Directory Assistance. Without trying to explain why this is so, let me just say that if you try to get someone's number and end up with a wrong number, try again.

Toll-free numbers are easy to obtain by dialing 1-800-555-1212, but only if a company has paid for a listing in toll-free directory assistance. While no charge is made to obtain toll-free numbers, you may have to pay as much as ninety cents for other telephone numbers obtained through Directory Assistance, so it really pays to let your fingers do the walking these days. (Don't you long for the old days when you could dial "Information" and always get the correct number?)

Directory Publishing

Q: *I would like to publish a directory of supply sources for artists and crafters, compiled from my own research plus information from current books and magazines. Is there any problem in doing this?*

Some writers and publishers, in a sincere effort to be helpful, list companies and their products in books or directories without ever checking to see if addresses are correct or whether advertised products or publications are still available. Never pick up information from other publications and put it in yours without going directly to the source to make sure the information is still up to date. Publishing inaccurate or out-of-date information is not only a disservice to readers but a poor reflection on both the author and publisher. It could also lead to legal problems if an incorrect listing were to cause financial loss to someone listed in your directory. (I'm still trying to locate the irresponsible publisher who put my name in a work-at-home directory saying I offer "homework opportunities." This is untrue and it has been costly to me to respond to such inquiries.)

Discounts

There are different types of discounts. For example, you may give customers a two percent discount off the invoice price if they pay within ten days, or offer a special ten percent discount to preferred craft fair customers who give you follow-up orders by mail. Professional discounts are often given to business owners who are bold enough to ask for them when they are doing business with other professionals in their industry, and local retailers and mail order suppliers may give trade or quantity discounts of ten to fifteen percent to those who buy larger-than-usual amounts of raw materials and supplies.

Tip

If you do not yet qualify to buy raw materials at wholesale prices, ask the retailers with whom you do business regularly if quantity or trade discounts are available to small business owners like yourself. Never do this in front of regular customers, however, and be prepared to prove you really are in business.

Distributor/Jobber

The chain of distribution for most products is manufacturer to distributor; distributor to dealer; dealer to individual buyer. As the maker of commercial art or handcrafted goods to be sold in quantity, you may not have enough room in your pricing formula to work with distributors (wholesalers), but are more likely to sell at wholesale prices to dealers (retailers), either directly or through sales representatives, trade shows, or gift marts.

See also Trade Shows.

Drop-Shipping

Drop-shipping is common in the book publishing industry and in many other product industries as well. This is a profitable way to work with others in your field who may be selling similar yet not competitive products or publications. The great advantage to sellers who work with you on a drop-ship basis is that they do not have to lay out cash for products until they have actually been sold, and there is no packaging or shipping involved. For example, several booksellers list my books in their catalogs, take orders for them, deposit the checks, and then write me a check for the total amount of orders less the agreed-upon sales commission. When I receive payment with a typed address label, I drop-ship orders directly to their customers.

EIN

See Employee Identification Number.

Electronic Marketing

Q: *How effective is this kind of marketing for artists and craft sellers?*

Although Internet hucksters say this is the hottest marketing medium in the world, it's not for everyone, and success stories about making sales directly on the Web have been hard to find. Since online advertising is so inexpensive, however, you don't have much to lose by trying it. Just don't believe all the hype about how easy it is to make direct sales on the Internet. A few craft sellers have reported an initial surge of inquiries for brochures or catalogs as soon as they went online, but orders have rarely resulted and after a while, response dropped off. As more and more artists and craft professionals set up Web sites on the Internet, response may only get worse. (Currently, it seems that the number of people offering things on the Internet is far greater than the number of people who might actually be interested in such offers. This may change in time, however.)

No one—including companies that have spent thousands of dollars on their Web sites— are reporting many direct sales. Many report, however, that the Internet is delivering a steady stream of prospects who may later become customers or clients. "By being on the Internet, our products and services have been noticed in ways we never before imagined," says publisher and web entrepreneur Bill Ronay. Through his *It's Happening! Events Link* web site, he provides listings of several thousand events per year. "Our unique compilation of nearly ten thousand festivals has attracted inquiries from around the world, opening up a completely new market for our publications," he says. Bill believes it takes extreme intelligence, insight, confidence, and patience to get successfully situated on the Web. "Design and maintenance are purely fundamental," he says. "Linking, registration, and locating the proper market on the Web is the difficult part."

The cost of online advertising is low. For as little as twenty to thirty dollars a month, you can have your own Home Page (online "store") that pictures several of your best items and tells people how to order them directly from you. Many people on the Internet offer home page design services, but if you have time to play around, you can buy software that will enable you to create your own. A good book for beginners who want to know how going online might help their business is *Marketing Online* by Marcia Yudkin (Plume). If going online has already been helpful to your business or simply exciting from a personal standpoint, I would enjoy hearing from you and possibly writing about you if you have a success story to share about marketing products or publications electronically. Meanwhile, for more information about my books and some article excerpts as well, visit these web sites:

- The Professional Crafter at http://www.procrafter.com
- National Craft Association at http://www.craftassoc.com
- Neighbors & Friends at http://www.crafter.com

See also Copyright Infringement; Copyrights of Others; Internet and World Wide Web; *and* Online Sales.

Tip

If you do try to market products online, you must be readily accessible by phone or fax, and your chance of capturing orders will increase if you have a toll-free number and can accept credit card payments. If you have a home page, promote it constantly. "Any idiot can get a home page," says Web entrepreneur Jeffrey Lant, "but what you need to succeed is constant promotion both inside and outside of the Net."

E-Mail

E-mail, or electronic mail, is one of the greatest communication tools ever to be developed and many people are going online today so they can communicate this way. Unless your online service charges for incoming messages, this is virtually cost-free communication and a great way for businesses or families to communicate with one another across the country or around the world. If not used properly, however, e-mail can be not only addictive but very time-consuming.

Some business owners say it can take a couple of hours a day to wade through all their e-mail messages, many of which may be advertising messages of no interest. (Millions of e-mail addresses are now available for rental to online advertisers.) For additional information on e-mail, check your library for any book about the Internet.

See also Electronic Marketing *and* Internet and World Wide Web.

Employee Identification Number (EIN)

This permanent federal taxpayer identification number is needed by all employers, partnerships, corporations, and nonprofit organizations. It can be used for more than one business, and you keep this number even when you change your business name or relocate to another part of the country. Sole proprietors without employees can obtain an EIN if they want one, but most simply use their Social Security Number. Some banks, however, may not let you open a commercial account without one. To apply for an EIN, use IRS Form SS-4, available wherever tax forms are found.

Tip

If you apply for an EIN but don't have employees, be sure to specify on the application form that you have no employees and are getting this number for banking purposes only. Otherwise you'll begin receiving employment tax forms you don't need and will have to explain why you're ignoring them.

Employees, Family

Q: *What are the tax advantages of hiring my spouse or children to work in my business?*

Spousal wages, deductible on your Schedule C tax form, will lower the amount of Self-Employment Taxes you must pay on Schedule C business profits. However, you must withhold state and federal income tax on spousal wages and file the necessary tax forms (your accountant can help you do this), and your spouse must pay Social

Security taxes on his or her earnings. The main tax advantage here is being able to place social security deposits where they are most advantageous to the family.

The tax benefits are considerably better when you can employ your children. A child under the age of eighteen doesn't have to pay FICA taxes on earnings, nor state and federal taxes up to a certain amount. (Check with an accountant on this.) As Julian Block, a former IRS agent explains: "Putting your youngster on your payroll can be a savvy way to take care of his or her allowance at the expense of the Internal Revenue Service. Significant tax savings can result merely by moving the money from one family pocket to another."

See also Employee Identification Number *and* Employees, Nonfamily.

Tip

The Tax Court has upheld deductions for children as young as seven, but if you hire young children, keep careful records of the hours they work and the kind of work they are doing for you.

Employees, Nonfamily

There are three types of nonfamily workers: regular employees, statutory employees, and independent contractors. Since each state has different laws about workers who perform duties in your place of business or in their own homes, you must contact your nearest Department of Labor for more information on this topic. An accountant or tax adviser can also explain the tax implications of hiring outside help.

As I was finishing this book, I received a fax warning that every business that has even one employee must post the new federally required labor law poster *or risk a fine of $7,500.* Outdated posters showing the old minimum wage of $4.25 must be replaced with the newest poster showing the $4.75 per hour figure and federal notices about such things as job safety, equal employment, and family and medical leave. Contact your local Department of Labor for more information.

See also Employee Identification Number; Independent Contractors; Labor Laws; Statutory Employees; *and* Workers' Compensation Insurance.

Endangered Species

If you use such "found objects" as feathers, bones, claws, or ivory, do not sell any products made of these items until you are absolutely sure none are protected by state or federal environmental protection laws.

You may know that eagles (every part of them, including feathers and claws) are protected under the *Bald and Golden Eagle Protection Act,* but you may be unaware that another law, *The Migratory Bird Treaty Act,* prohibits the sale of feathers of all North American migratory birds. Protected under other laws are certain waterfowl, marine mammals, and other endangered species. Just picking up a feather, tooth, claw, or bone of one of these endangered species and using it in a wall hanging could result in a fine of as much as $2,000. Sometimes you don't even have to sell the item to get into trouble; merely possessing it is a violation of the law.

Your state fish and game office can provide you with more information on this topic, and a complete list of protected birds, plants, and wildlife can be obtained from the U.S. Department of the Interior's Fish and Wildlife Service.

See also Found Objects *and* Nature Items.

Enrolled Agents

Q: *What's an enrolled agent and why should I consider hiring one to prepare my annual tax return?*

Enrolled Agents (EAs) are licensed by the Treasury Department to represent taxpayers before the Internal Revenue Service. Although they have more tax training than a CPA and are qualified to answer complex tax questions and prepare annual tax returns, their fee may be lower than that of an accountant or CPA. The National Association of Enrolled Agents (NAEA) is a 9,500-member national association of EAs with a nationwide network of affiliated state organizations. You can get a list of EAs in your area by calling 1-800-424-4339. Enrolled agents also provide their expertise free of charge on the NAEA Tax Channel area of America Online.

See also Accountant.

Environmental Protection

See Endangered Species; Licenses and Permits; *and* Nature Items.

Estimated Tax Payments

All self-employed individuals—and that includes even the smallest homebased crafts business—must file quarterly estimated tax payments if it is expected that taxes on regular and self-employment income will be $500 or more. These payments are due on the 15th of the month in April, June, September, and January. If you fail to accurately estimate your income and make the required quarterly payments, you could be socked with penalty and interest fees in April when you file your annual tax return. An accountant can help you do the estimate and give you the necessary tax forms for making quarterly payments.

Exporting

Q: *I think there might be a good foreign market for a unique product I can produce in volume. How do I get started in exporting?*

Before getting involved in exporting, you need to gain a basic knowledge of the field and an understanding of such things as payment terms, shipping terminology, and methods of shipping. To avoid the paperwork hassles involved in exporting, you may want to work with agent-buyers or bona fide distributors. A successful exporter in my network reported that it was time-consuming and often nonproductive to attempt to begin an export business by contacting foreign embassies or commercial trade offices. She recommended subscribing to a periodical that specializes in providing export leads (check a periodicals directory in your library). "This usually gives me a dozen or more prospects to explore each month," she says. "I contact them initially by fax and have been able to convert about fifteen percent of prospects to customers."

For more information, check your library for books about exporting and also contact the Department of Commerce for any free information booklets they may have on this topic.

Fax Installation Tips

When you get a fax machine, you have the option of hooking it up to your computer so you can fax directly by modem. When you do this, however, you automatically put your fax machine out of commission every time you use your modem to go online or shut off your computer at night. (I know many people leave their computers running all the time, but this is not something I want to do.) Many people also use the same number for both phone and fax—using a phone/fax switch that directs calls accordingly—but this means a fax cannot be sent or received when the phone is in use. And, since phone/fax switches won't recognize calls coming in to a voice mail system, your only option is to use an answering machine. (See also *Voice Mail vs. Answering Machine.*)

For these reasons, I elected to operate my fax independently on a separate line of its own. Since my use of the fax is minimal, I couldn't justify the expense of a second, expensive business line, but opted instead for "flex line" service. Initially, I paid a small installation fee but my only cost now is for the time I use the flexline to send or receive faxes (five cents a minute for both incoming and outgoing faxes). Although I send and receive dozens of faxes each month, my average monthly cost is rarely more than five dollars. Your telephone company undoubtedly offers a similar service, though they may call it a different name.

TIP: To protect your fax machine from damage caused by fluctuations in electric current, be sure to plug it into a surge suppressor. If you elect to fax by modem, make sure the surge suppressor for your computer system has a separate plug for the fax/modem.

See also Surge Suppressor.

Fabrics

See Designer Fabrics, Commercial Use of *and* Garment Manufacturing.

Fax Machine

Q: *I can't see any reason why a small homebased business should have a fax machine. Am I missing something here?*

Many business owners like myself finally caved in and bought a fax (facsimile) machine not because they felt they needed one, but because they wanted to accommodate customers or clients who preferred this method of communication. Within a month of installing my machine, however, I discovered all kinds of advantages to a fax that were never emphasized in the articles and advertising literature I'd read. Here are just some of the advantages of this inexpensive technology and how it can help a homebased business:

• **Saves time and money.** If you regularly deal with wholesale buyers, you can communicate more quickly and less expensively with them by fax to confirm receipt of new orders and shipping dates, announce a new products, or send an overdue invoice reminder. Doing the same things by phone will not only take longer, but cost more. (A study of my average fax costs reveals that each fax transmission costs me three cents less than a first-class stamp, and I save the cost of an envelope besides.)

• **Doubles as a copier.** The purchase of a plain paper fax also gives you a trouble-free photocopy machine. I always wanted a copier but couldn't justify the cost of one for the small number of copies I normally need in a week. Now I no longer have to make a special trip to the drug store every time I want a copy of something.

• **Serves as a marketing tool.** If you are selling anything by mail, you may find that some customers or clients prefer to fax orders to you with instructions to charge to a credit card.

• **Offers personal advantages.** It's handy to have a fax machine when you want your doctor to fax you a report on your latest blood test, get information to an insurance company about a claim you've filed, send an order for office supplies or other items you would normally order by mail, or just network with business pals.

See also Maintenance Agreements *and article, "Fax Installation Tips."*

Tip

By law, fax transmissions must have a special header that shows the date, time, business name, and telephone number. The fax instruction manual explains how to enter this information. If you unplug your machine for any reason, you will probably lose the time and date and have to reset it. Even if you never unplug your fax, you should periodically check the accuracy of information that appears on the header line of your transmissions.

Feathers

See Endangered Species *and* Trade Practice Rules.

Federal Laws and Regulations

See Care Labels; Consumer Safety Laws; *all listings for* Copyrights; Endangered Species; Estimated Tax Payments; Fax Machine; Federal Trade Commission Rules; Flammability Standards; Fur Products; Guarantees and Warranties; Health Hazards; Indian Arts and Crafts; Internal Revenue Service; Labels or Tags Required by Law; Labor Laws; Nature Items; Patent; Postal Regulations; Taxes; Trademark; Trade Practice Rules; *and* Trade Secret.

Federal Trade Commission Rules

Q: *Do FTC rules and regulations really apply to the average homebased business or are these regulations applicable only to "big" businesses?*

Every business—no matter how small—needs to be familiar with FTC rules. Among other things, this agency is concerned with truth in advertising, mail order marketing, trade practices, product labeling, unfair or deceptive acts and practices, and unfair methods of competition. Free booklets on all these topics are available from the FTC. Here are some rules of particular interest to the homebased business owner:

• **Truth in Advertising**. The FTC says it's not what you say in actual words, but what the "average" person (not the sophisticated or skeptical person) believes after reading your ad. You aren't likely to have any problems here so long as you make no false product claims (false representation) and are truthful about what buyers can expect to receive from you.

• **Use of the Word "New."** New products can be advertised as "new" for a period of six months only. Use of the word "new" to describe products older than this would be a violation of an FTC rule.

• **Thirty-Day Mail Order Rule**. This FTC rule is strictly enforced with penalties of up to $10,000 for each violation. Unless otherwise specified in your advertising or catalog, you must ship customer orders within thirty days of receiving payment for the order or you will be in violation of this Rule. (Now you know why so many advertisers include a note on their order form or other printed literature to "Allow six to eight weeks for delivery." It's not because they really think it's going to take that long for a customer's order to get shipped, but they are protecting themselves against unforeseen problems.) If you fail to indicate exactly how long it should take to receive an order, customers may legally expect to receive the product within thirty days after you get their order. (If you invoice orders after shipment, this rule does not apply to you.) If you find you cannot ship within the specified time, then you must notify the buyer of the delay, enclosing a postage-paid reply card or envelope. You must give the buyer the option either to cancel the order and get an immediate refund, or give you more time to ship the order. If the customer doesn't respond either way, the FTC rule says you may assume the customer is agreeable to the delay in shipping.

See also Guarantees and Warranties; Product Liability Insurance; Indian Arts and Crafts; Labels or Tags Required by Law; Organization, Formation of; Prepublication Offer; Scams; Testimonials; *and* Trade Practice Rules.

Fictitious Name Statement

This is a legal certificate that must be filed with your city or county clerk when you elect to operate a business under any name other than your own. Some states require that you publish notice of your assumed or fictitious name in a general-circulation newspaper in your county.

See also Business or Trade Name Registration/Protection.

Tip

If you're in violation of local zoning laws and don't want your neighbors to know you're running a business at home, the ad you run does not have to be placed in your home town paper but can be run in any newspaper in the county.

Financial and Tax Records

Q: *Which records are most important to my business, and how long do I need to keep them?*

Since a tax return can be audited for up to three years after it is due or filed, you need to keep all financial records related to your tax returns for at least this long. (There is no time limit on when the IRS can begin an audit on a return they consider to be fraudulent.) Specifically, keep all records pertaining to income and expenses, including accounts payable invoices, bank deposits and statements, employee records/payroll, petty cash records, sales commission reports, and manufacturing records.

Other records that should be retained permanently include business ledgers, financial statements, check registers, all legal papers (including contracts, patents, trademarks, copyrights, etc.), depreciation schedules, inventory records, and important correspondence.

See also Business Records, Protection of.

Financial Statements

Q: *I don't anticipate ever needing a bank loan, so why should I bother to prepare financial statements for my small homebased business?*

You may think your homebased business is too small for you to take the time to create financial statements, but if you're serious about what you're doing, you should have these reports for your own information. Even if you never plan to ask a banker for a business loan, your financial statements will provide a fascinating picture of how your business is doing and enable you to monitor cost-of-goods and inventory figures, overhead costs and net profits each year. Sometimes when you're not sure if you're just treading water or actually making gains, financial statements can offer surprising and comforting evidence that you're on the right track.

Financial statements include the Income Statement, Balance Sheet, and Profit and Loss Statement. (Look for samples of these forms in the appropriate alphabetical section of this book.) Depending on your particular needs, you may want to prepare statements on a monthly, quarterly, semi-annual, or annual basis. At the very least, you will need a set of financial statements at year's end to make preparation of your tax return easier. If you plan to apply for a loan, your banker will want to see a complete set of financial statements and may ask for your most recent annual statements as well as figures for the current month or quarter.

Bankers have always been impressed with my financial statements— particularly my income statements—so I've included a sample of that form as well as the balance sheet and profit and loss statement I have used in my publishing and mail order business for nearly thirty years. These were adapted from the financial statements used by a book publishing company I once worked for and have served me well. Of course you will find many other styles of financial reports in accounting books in your library or bookstore, and if you use a computer software program to do your bookkeeping, the forms will be different there, too. What's important where financial statements are concerned is not the style of form you use but whether you are giving bankers (and yourself) a true picture of your income and profit or loss from the business.

If you need help in bookkeeping, accounting, or the preparation of financial statements, one of the best books you will ever find is Bernard Kamoroff's *Small Time Operator—How to Start Your Own Small Business, Keep Your Books, Pay Your Taxes, and Stay Out of Trouble* (Bell Springs Publishing). This classic guide, regularly updated, includes all the ledgers and worksheets you will need for a year.

See also Balance Sheet; Cash Flow Projection; Income Statement; *and* Profit and Loss Statement.

Financing a Business

See Bank Loans; Home Equity Loans; Line of Credit; Personal Loans; *and* SBA Loans.

First Rights/All Rights Sales

Q: *I want to offer articles and how-to projects to magazines, but I'm confused about the difference between selling "first rights" and "all rights" to a publisher.*

In offering your work for publication—and this might be an article, a poem, a design, pattern, or how-to instructions for some project—you must consider whether you are going to sell only first rights or all rights to that publisher. If you elect the latter, which some beginners have to do just to get published, you will automatically lose ownership of the copyright to your material. Selling all rights means you have conveyed your copyright to the publisher, and you cannot use that material again without the publisher's written permission.

Selling first rights, on the other hand, means you have given the magazine permission to print your article once, for a specified sum of money, after which time you alone have the right to resell that article to someone else, reprint it in a publication of your own, include it in a book you are writing, incorporate it into kit instructions, and so on.

See also Book Copyright.

Flammability Standards

Q: *I plan to wholesale a line of garments for women and children. How can I be certain the fabric I'm buying from my wholesale supplier meets federal flammability standards?*

The Flammable Fabrics Act prohibits the introduction or movement in interstate commerce of articles of wearing apparel and fabrics that are so highly flammable as to be dangerous when worn by individuals or used for other purposes. It is difficult to tell by looking at a fabric if it is "so highly flammable as to be dangerous," explains a spokesperson for the Consumer Product Safety Commission.

"A quick test to help identify fabrics that comply with the children's sleepwear standard is to hold a match on the bottom edge of a small piece of fabric for approximately three seconds. If the fabric stops burning once the match is removed from the fabric, it is considered to be 'self-extinguishing' and will probably comply with the children's sleepwear standard (a very stringent flammability standard). If the fabric continues to burn, it will not comply with the children's sleepwear standard, but will probably comply with the flammability standard for all other fabrics intended for use in wearing apparel, doll clothing, and toys. Most fabrics comply with this latter standard, but it is difficult to make a determination of compliance by setting a match to a small piece of fabric held vertically because acceptance is based upon both the ease of ignition and the rate of burn. During the test, the fabric is held in a less stringent position (at a 45-degree angle, rather than vertical), and the flame touches the fabric in a less ignitable location (the top surface instead of the bottom edge)."

Most fabric manufacturers test their fabrics for compliance and issue a guaranty of compliance that is passed along the chain of distribution through a statement on the invoice that reads "Continuing guaranty under the Flammable Fabrics Act filed with the Consumer Product Safety Commission." If this information does not appear on the invoice you receive, ask the manufacturer, wholesaler, or distributor supplying the fabric to furnish you with a "statement of compliance" with the flammability standards. If you are purchasing fabrics at local retail outlets, you may contact the fabric manufacturer directly or call the Consumer Product Safety Commission to see if the fabric manufacturer has filed a continuing guarantee under *The Flammable Fabrics Act.*

NOTE: If you spin your own wool yarn for sale or use it to make products for sale, contact The Consumer Product Safety Commission for information on what you must do to have your wool meet the standards of *The Flammable Fabrics Act.*

See also Consumer Safety Laws.

FOB

This means "freight, or free, on board" and is generally used in printed sales literature or on invoices to indicate the point to which a seller will pay freight. Since title of the goods legally changes hands at the FOB point, this notation could be important in the event a large shipment is lost or damaged in transit.

EXAMPLES: If you live in San Francisco and are buying a heavy piece of equipment from a company in Chicago, a notation of "FOB Chicago" means you have to pay the freight charges. If it reads "FOB San Francisco," it means the equipment seller is paying the freight. Thus, if you are shipping an order from San Francisco to Chicago and the customer is paying the freight, the FOB notation would read "FOB San Francisco."

Foreign Sales

See Canadian Sales *and* Money Orders.

Found Objects

Q: *I believe in recycling, so many of the craft items I make are made from discarded objects, nature items, and other "found objects." Are there any restrictions on selling such items?*

It's great to recycle, so long as you don't violate environmental and safety laws when you collect and use materials whose manufacturers or origins are unknown. The list of endangered species grows longer every day, and elsewhere I have discussed this topic at length, along with problems related to use of certain nature items. Many found objects are perfectly safe and there are no restrictions on using them to create art products for sale. Given their "handicraft nature," however, they will undoubtedly have a limited market.

One thing you should never do, however, is use egg cartons or plastic meat trays to make handicraft items because there is no way to wash off the salmonella, *E. coli,* and other harmful microbes that may be lingering on them. You could become ill from using such items for craft projects, and if you sold them to someone who got sick, you could find yourself facing a lawsuit.

See Endangered Species *and* Nature Items.

Fourth-Class Mail

See Mail, Classes of.

Freebies

Q: *Do you think it's a good idea to offer customers something free from time to time?*

Yes, everyone loves a freebie. Common freebies used by craft sellers include bookmarks and calendars. Artist Ruby Tobey uses a small yearly calendar as her business card, printing them in October so she can include one with each purchase during the Christmas sales season. I also recall a home sewer who created an interesting freebie by printing on the back of her regular business card a handy fabric conversion chart. She then laminated the card to make it a practical purse or wallet reference when shopping.

Some sellers who make toys, dolls, and other products for children often create little giveaway items from scrap materials, reasoning that if they give something to a child, they will automatically attract the parent's attention. Stewart Madsen, who makes custom-designed Halloween costumes, prints his name and address on vinyl black half-masks, including a couple with each completed costume and telling the kids to give them to their friends.

If you have an inexpensive freebie to offer consumers, check out *Freebies Magazine,* which is always interested in running freebie offers at no charge to advertisers. This magazine has such a large circulation that free offers in it often generate two or three thousand requests, so be careful what you advertise here and *never* offer anything entirely free, but tack on a shipping charge of two or three dollars so your offer gets into the mail free along with your catalog or other sales material.

Freight Charges

See Shipping and Handling Charges.

FTC

See Federal Trade Commission Rules.

Fur Products

If you make wearing apparel that contains any kind of fur, the *Fur Products Labeling Act* requires a very specifically worded and sized label on all such products. Request additional information on this Act from the FTC.

Games

See Toy and Game Brokers.

Garment Manufacturing

See Consumer Safety Laws; Designer Fabrics, Commercial Use of; Flammability Standards; Fur Products; Homework Laws; Labels or Tags Required by Law; Patterns, Commercial Use of; Textile Fiber Products Identification Act; *and* Wool and Other Textiles.

Gross Price

Gross price is the total (list) price of a product before deductions or allowances have been made. For example, your gross annual income would be the total of all income received in a year, while net income is what's left after all expenses have been deducted.

See also Net Price.

Guarantees and Warranties

To comply with FTC rules, a guarantee must clearly disclose the terms, conditions, and extent of the guarantee, plus the manner in which the company will perform the guarantee. It is not enough merely to say "Satisfaction guaranteed or money back." (For examples of some guarantees used by craft sellers, see *Guaranty of Satisfaction.*)

Warranties are of two kinds: *implied* and *express.* An implied warranty means a product will perform as similar products of its kind under normal conditions (i.e., buyers can expect that the ceramic mug they have purchased will not crack when hot coffee is poured into it). An express warranty states a specific fact about how the product will perform (i.e., "the handpainting on this ceramic coffee mug is dishwasher safe"). It is best not to make express warranties since doing so opens you to the possibility of legal obligations should the product turn out to be defective.

See also Guaranty of Satisfaction.

Guaranty of Satisfaction

Q: *Do you think it makes a difference in the number of orders a mail order seller will get if customers are guaranteed satisfaction? Are there any rules about guarantees that would relate to a crafts business?*

Yes to both questions. All of the large mail order catalog houses allow buyers to return merchandise that is in any way unsatisfactory, so I believe most consumers would expect small businesses to offer the same kind of guarantee of satisfaction. Certainly this would give them more confidence in ordering from you. Such guarantees are particularly important to booksellers like myself, but I don't see many crafter's catalogs offering them and there are no rules that say you must. However, if you do offer a customer guarantee, the Federal Trade Commission requires more than just a "Satisfaction Guaranteed" statement. You must also disclose the specific terms, conditions, and extent of the guarantee, plus the manner in which you will perform the guaranty. As a mail order bookseller, I have used a guarantee like the one below for twenty-five years, and I can't remember the last time someone returned a book:

> SATISFACTION GUARANTEED! Book orders carry a money-back guarantee. If for any reason you are not satisfied with your purchase, simply return the undamaged book in its original mailer within ten days of receipt to receive a refund of the book's cover price.

Here are a couple other examples of guarantees I have found in the literature of craft sellers:

> SATISFACTION GUARANTEED! If you are not completely satisfied with the quality of our products, return your purchase in undamaged condition within ten days to receive a refund of the retail price.

> OUR GUARANTEE: We take pride in our products. If for any reason an item does not meet your expectations, you may return it within ten days for exchange, credit or refund (except custom-made or personalized items).

See also Guarantees and Warranties; Order Form; Price List; *and* Refunds.

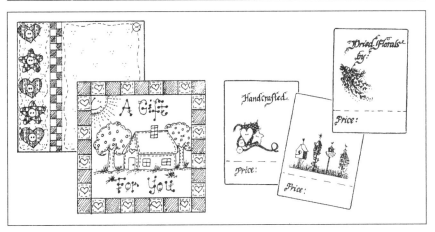

Preprinted Hang Tages from Wood Cellar Graphics (left), and E & S Creations (right).

Hang Tags and Labels

Q: *My crafts sell very well without fancy hang tags or labels, but a fellow crafter has urged me to start using them. Would this really make a difference in sales?*

Many sellers have reported that their sales increased after they began to use hang tags and labels. One reason may be that the average consumer has grown accustomed to seeing hang tags and labels on commercial items and thus expects to see them on handcrafted merchandise as well. They may even expect to pay more for a product that bears a striking hang tag or designer label.

Tags and labels speak volumes about your professionalism and often add personality and sales appeal to products. They can be any size, shape, or color and may be laser-printed on lightweight card stock or printed inexpensively at any quick-copy print shop or office center that offers photocopy services. Also check out the tags and labels offered by mail order suppliers listed in the resource directory. For example, GraphComm Services and Grayarc offer custom hang tags and sew-on fabric labels, jewelry tags and labels, foil-stamped address labels, and special-message information labels such as "Thank you," "Made in the USA," etc. Designer labels are avail-

What to Say on a Hang Tag

The size of a hang tag and the message you put on it are up to you; options are unlimited. For starters, anything that makes you or your products unique is information that can be put on a tag, such as:

• Type and source of materials used to make the product (Georgia clay, seashells from around the world, hand-dyed yarns)
• A statement about the quality of the product ("Our treenware is designed to give you fitness for purpose, beauty of form, and a love of old-time craftsmanship.")
• Colorful information about a business ("It was our grandmother's idea to start this business. . .")
• How products are made (interesting technical information about the manufacturing process)
• Care and cleaning instructions
• Consumer safety warnings ("This is not a toy—keep out of children's hands!")
• History of an old or little-known art or craft
• A whimsical note designed to tug at a buyer's heartstrings (often the most effective way to get higher prices)

The designer who shears her sheep to make handmade felt that is turned into toys . . . the ornament maker whose wax creations are replicas of museum pieces . . . the rosemaler whose designs are completely authentic—all should use such information to their advantage on a hang tag because such stories give a product personality, and personality *sells.*

I'm reminded of a little handpainted picture on wood my husband and I once bought. It was just a sailor standing by a rowboat, and we never would have bought it except for the fact that beneath the picture was a "personality message" that made it the perfect gift for Harry's old school chum, a sailboat enthusiast: "Old sailors never die; they just get a little dinghy."

—an excerpt from the revised fifth edition of Homemade Money *by Barbara Brabec (1997, Betterway Books)*

able from Charm Woven Labels and Widby Enterprises. A delightful collection of preprinted hang tags that can do double duty as price tags are available from Wood Cellar Graphics and E & S Creations. (See addresses in resource chapter.)

See also Care Labels; Labels or Tags Required by Law; *and article, "What to Say on a Hang Tag."*

Health Hazards

Do you suffer from chronic fatigue, headaches, nausea, or dizziness that cannot be explained? These and other symptoms could be caused by the raw materials and substances you are using to make products for sale. If any of the following information "rings a bell" with you, be sure to discuss it with your doctor. (It may be necessary to consult with an internist, neurologist, or occupational health consultant since the average doctor may not take your complaints seriously.)

• **Harmful Materials and Substances**. Artists and crafters routinely handle materials that can be harmful if not used properly, such as paints, paint thinners, dyes, lead, plastics, photo chemicals, and dozens of other materials or substances. "One hundred million Americans may be using dangerous materials without knowing it," says a national clearinghouse for information on this topic. Because many materials give off dangerous hydrocarbons for months, they urge individuals to be especially cautious if they work with varnishes, lacquers, artificial leather, rubber, or plastic cement.

Toxic substances can enter the body by skin contact, through the mouth and digestive system, and through breathing. Never eat, drink, or smoke in your workshop area, and do not inhale fumes, sprays, or dusts. Improper ventilation is the major health problem in all the crafts, so take special precautions to always have adequate ventilation in your work area. (If you can smell the substance you're working with, your ventilation is inadequate and dangerous to your health.) Many materials can harm the skin directly, causing rashes, burns, and other skin problems. A good rule of thumb is to wear protective gloves when using any liquid other than water. Acute lung diseases result when strongly irritating substances burn the tissues of the air sacs in the lung and certain fumes are injurious to the kidneys and liver with effects being cumulative. Symptoms such as weakness, fatigue, palpitations, or pale complexion may be caused by chemical substances that affect the red and white blood cells, and the entire nervous system can be affected by certain substances. Since children are more susceptible to toxic substances than adults, keep them away from your workshop. (See special tip below.)

• **Dust and Other Airborne Materials.** All dust is irritating to the mucous membranes in the nose, throat, eyes, and respiratory tract. Some people also have allergic skin reactions from the dust of certain woods. (Included in the list of allergenic woods are certain members of the birch, pine, dogwood, beech, mahogany, mulberry, and myrtle families.) Wear a dust mask when sawing, sculpting, grinding, or carving any materials to keep minute particles of dust from penetrating your lungs. Also wear a face shield or eye goggles. In cleaning up dust, never sweep but vacuum, wet-mop, or both.

• **Computer Hazards.** If your face gets red and itchy for no apparent reason, your doctor may tell you it's nerves, but your computer may be the culprit. According to the author of *Don't Get Zapped by Your Computer* (Peachpit Press), your face may simply be reacting to the dust and particles that are being propelled toward it by the electrostatic field of the video screen. Author Don Sellers says there has been an increased incidence of facial dermatitis (reddening, itching, prickling of the face) among people who sit in front of computers all the time. His book addresses the "epidemic of modern times" that is affecting the health of millions of Americans who use computers, and covers everything from eyestrain to pregnancy issues to carpal tunnel syndrome to back problems.

The Art & Creative Materials Institute (see resource chapter) offers a free booklet, "What You Need to Know about the Safety of Art & Craft Materials." It contains a wealth of tips for crafters, teachers, retailers, and manufacturers in this industry.

See also Found Objects; Labor Laws; Lead Testing; *and* Paints, Varnishes, and Other Finishes.

Tip

Always read the label on the materials you or your children use to make handcrafts—particularly paints, varnishes, lacquers, sprays, and glues—and take any preventive action necessary to protect your health. By law, all art materials manufactured in the United States must be evaluated by a qualified toxicologist and labeled, if necessary, for chronic toxicity according to the chronic hazard labeling standard of the *Federal Hazardous Substances Act*. The label on such products must contain any necessary cautionary information or safe use instructions. (For example, if a material improperly used can cause lung cancer or harm to a developing fetus, this must be noted on the label. Instructions must be provided on how to use the product properly and safely and a warning given if the product is inappropriate for use by children.)

Health Insurance

Q: *My husband and I would like to quit our jobs to work full-time on our home business, but that would mean giving up the hospitalization/major medical insurance coverage our family now enjoys. Is there an affordable solution to this problem?*

Unless you have preexisting conditions that make it difficult to get coverage, you can probably get individual insurance through Blue Cross/Blue Shield. This is very expensive, however, and periodic premium increases are common. One solution is to join your local Chamber of Commerce so you can get into its United Chambers group health insurance program. One couple told me they were able to cut their insurance premiums in half this way. Another option is to join one of the many home business organizations that now offer group insurance programs to their members. Most of these programs are HMO or PPO programs, but rates are more affordable than what you would pay for an individual policy. (I've listed a few of these organizations in the resource chapter. Each will send you more information on request.)

See also Chamber of Commerce *and* Home Business Organizations.

Hobby Business

Q: *At this time I do not foresee having enough income to allow me to deduct any business expenses. Are there advantages to being a registered business that I'm missing out on by maintaining hobbyist status?*

There is nothing wrong with selling to support a craft hobby, but you should deduct all expenses related to your hobby income to keep your state and federal taxes on this income as low as possible. (See *Hobby Income* for information on how to do this.)

The two main disadvantages of treating your activity as a hobby instead of a business are that (1) your profit margin on finished crafts will be less because you cannot buy supplies and materials at wholesale prices; and (2) you cannot give your hobby business a business name unless you register it with local authorities.

See also Hobby Income; Purchase Order; *and* Sales Tax.

Hobby Income

Q: *How does the Internal Revenue Service treat hobby income, and at what point does a "hobby business" become a "real business" in the eyes of the IRS?*

Hobby income must be reported on Schedule C of Form 1040. You may deduct all expenses incurred to earn this income up to, but not exceeding, the amount of your hobby income. When your hobby business shows a profit, taxes will be due on this income. If you show a loss, however, it will not be deductible against other income.

A "hobby business" becomes a "real business" in the eyes of the IRS at the point where you can state that you (1) are trying to make a profit, (2) are making regular business transactions, and (3) have made a profit at least three years out of five.

See also Home Office Deduction.

Tip

If you call your activity a business for tax purposes but fail to keep proper records or meet other IRS criteria, it will be ruled a "hobby" and any losses you may have deducted in the past will be disallowed.

Holiday Boutiques

See Checks; Personal Liability Insurance; Sales Commissions; Sales Tax; *and* Zoning Laws.

Home Business Insurance Policies

A growing number of insurance companies now offer special home office/home business policies that offer much greater coverage than a rider or business pursuits endorsement on your homeowner's or renter's policy. For example, the In-Home Business Policy offered by RLI Insurance Co. provides up to a million dollars in general liability (product and professional), up to $50,000 in all-risk protection for business personal property, theft coverage away from premises, coverage for loss of business income, and up to $5,000 per person medical payments. Premiums are as low as $150/year with a standard $100 deductible. For an independent agent near you who sells this particular policy, call the Independent Insurance Agents of America at 1-800-221-7917. Check your Yellow Pages for the names of other insurance companies that offer homeowner's insurance, since many of these same companies have added in-home business packages to their line. Some that have come to my attention are Aetna, Liberty Mutual, and Firemen Insurance Co.

See also Home Business Organizations *and* Insurance on Crafts Merchandise, Off-Premise.

Home Business Organizations

Q: *What will I get from membership in a home business or small business organization?*

There are hundreds of small business organizations in the United States, but only a few national organizations serve the special interests and needs of homebased business owners and other self-employed individuals. Some are primarily educational or advocacy groups but several offer attractive membership packages that include some or all of the following benefits: discounts on business products, publications, services, online networking opportunities and forums, travel discounts and long-distance telephone savings, group insurance programs (major medical, hospital, life, disability, dental), general home business insurance packages (including personal and product liability coverage), low-fee merchant card programs, collection services, and business loan programs. Some organizations have also arranged for their members to get special discounts from such service providers as UPS, Airborne Express, and Kinko's Copy Centers.

The resource chapter includes a list of organizations you may wish to investigate. Most have a presence on the Internet; all will send you additional information by mail on request. To find the names and addresses of other organizations, check such library directories as *National Trade and Professional Associations of the United States & Canada* (Columbia Books) or *Encyclopedia of Associations* (Gale Research Co.).

> *See also* Art/Craft Organizations; Collection Agencies; Long Distance Carriers; Merchant Bank Card Services; Organization, Formation of; Prepaid Legal Services; *and* Trade Associations/Publications.

Home Equity Loans

Q: *I need access to cash, but I can't get a traditional line of credit from my bank because my business is just getting started. Do you think it's a good idea to tap the equity in our home?*

It can be dangerous to borrow against the equity in your home unless you are a good money manager. On the other hand, if you have thousands of dollars of equity in a home and need cash right now, a home equity loan could be the perfect solution to your problem. Although it is common knowledge that homeowners can get home equity loans based on the amount of equity they have in their home, what is not as well known is that home equity *lines of credit* are now available from many lenders. The interest on this kind of loan is tax-deductible, and the money can be used to finance or expand a business.

With a regular home equity loan, you would borrow a specific amount and make monthly principle/interest payments until the loan is satisfied. However, if you just want to know you have a source of money to tap in case you need it in the future, you can set up a line of credit. You would then be able to write checks to yourself or business suppliers up to the maximum amount of your credit line. Each month you would be required to pay only the interest on the amount borrowed and, depending on your bank's policy, you might have up to ten years to pay back the loan.

See also Personal Loans.

Home Office Deduction

Q: *I've heard that if I take the Home Office Deduction, it's a red flag for the IRS that might trigger an audit. Is this true?*

The latest industry research statistics show that perhaps 31 million individuals have homebased businesses, yet in 1994 (the latest year for which tax figures were available), only 1.5 million tax-payers claimed the Home Office Deduction. Don't let a nervous accountant rob you of this legal deduction. The IRS says they do not audit returns merely because this deduction is taken, and I've yet to meet anyone who has been audited even after years of taking the deduction (myself included).

If you are an artist or crafts professional, you may not have an "office," per se, but any space in your home (studio, workshop, or back bedroom) regularly used for business is an "office" to the IRS. You qualify if you spend most of your income-producing hours in your homebased office, studio, or workshop. (Not everyone who works at home can qualify for the Home Office Deduction, but artists and craftspeople generally have no problem. An accountant can give you more information on this topic.)

If you qualify for the Home Office Deduction, you may deduct expenses for the business use of your home on your Schedule C tax form, thereby lowering the amount of self-employment tax you must pay. First you must be able to show the part of your home that you use for business (take photos and file them with your tax returns). Then you must calculate an appropriate percentage of expenses that can be deducted. (Generally this is done by dividing the square footage of your office by the total square footage of your home.) Expenses that fall into the home office deduction area are:

- mortgage interest or rental fees
- real estate taxes paid on your home
- home owner's insurance premiums
- utility bills (gas, electric, oil, water)
- trash collection service
- general home repairs and maintenance
- depreciation of your home (see *TIP*)

To take a tax deduction for using a part of your home in business, that part must be used *exclusively and regularly for business*—meaning the space can't do double duty as a bedroom or den. If, however, you regularly use *part* of a room strictly for business, then you can deduct expenses for the percentage of space that is used exclusively and regularly for business. You may also take the Home Office Deduction for expenses related to the operation of any structure that is not attached to your house or residence, such as a garage, studio, garden shed, or barn.

NOTE: If your business shows a loss, some or all of your home office expenses may not be deductible in that year, but may be carried to a future year. For more information on this topic, obtain IRS publication #587, "Business Use of Your Home."

See also Business Expenses, Tax Deductible.

Tip

If you depreciate your house, there may be tax complications when you sell it. Be sure to discuss this with an accountant or tax professional, and pay particular attention to this statement from IRS publication #587, *"Business Use of Your Home"*:

"Basis Adjustment. You must decrease the basis of your property by the amount of depreciation you could have deducted on your tax returns under the method of depreciation you selected. If you took less depreciation than you could have under the method you selected, you must decrease the basis by the amount you could have taken under that method."

Homeowner's or Renter's Insurance

Q: *We have quite a bit of money invested in tools, equipment, raw materials, and finished handcrafts. Since everything is in our home, we assume our homeowner's insurance covers everything, right?*

Wrong! Homeowner's (or renter's) insurance is strictly limited to personal possessions. Anything in the home used to generate income is considered to be business-related—including "goods for sale"—and thus exempt from coverage on a personal policy. It's important to tell your insurance agent that you run a business at home because your regular homeowner's or renter's policy will not cover business equipment, supplies, or inventory nor, in all probability, any losses due to fires that may be caused by such things. You must protect them either with a special rider or Business Pursuits Endorsement to your homeowner's or renter's policy, or with an individual business insurance policy. (If you are storing over $3,000 of inventory, you should probably obtain a separate fire, vandalism, and theft policy.)

Although a business rider on your home insurance carries no personal liability coverage for your business, a special Business Pursuits Endorsement may cover materials and products you are storing as

Is Your Insurance an All-Risk Policy?

When the sump pump failed one year causing our basement to flood about six inches, I faced the clean-up job secure in the knowledge that the home business rider I had placed on our homeowner's insurance policy would cover my business loss. When I called our insurance agent to report on all the books and printed materials I had lost, however, I learned yet another small lesson about insurance.

"I lost some of my book inventory and catalogs," I said, "but that should be covered on the business rider I took out—right?"

"Wait a minute," he said. "Let me see if you have an all-risk policy."

"What do you mean—all-risk?" I asked nervously. "When I bought the business rider, I asked you to sell me a policy that would protect my book inventory from damage or destruction. You didn't say anything about all-risk coverage at that time."

The agent then explained that since our regular home insurance policy was an all-risk policy, the attached business rider was automatically all-risk coverage as well. "But if you had purchased a separate policy for your business," the agent said, "you might not have collected in this instance unless the policy specifically said you had all-risk coverage."

Let this serve as a reminder to check your insurance policy to make sure your coverage is all-risk. Your insurance agent may not advise you about the fine print until the damage is done.

well as provide some liability coverage for people who may come to your home for business purposes. If you have turned your garage or some outbuilding into a studio or workshop, be sure to check with your insurance agent about the need for a rider that would cover all the tools, supplies, materials, and merchandise normally stored there. Ask specific questions, such as "What would the policy pay if everything was destroyed by a fire, flood, or tornado?" or "If a thief breaks in and steals my tools, craft merchandise, or electronic machines, am I fully covered against loss?"

In times of tragedy, the homebased business owner has twice as much to lose as the ordinary homeowner—both home and business. For this reason, you might want to have a chat with your insurance agent about some "special disasters" that could befall your home. Find out if you are covered, and if not, how much it would cost to add a rider or two.

Remember that regular homeowner policies do not cover such things as cracks in the foundation due to earth movement, sink holes, damage from earthquakes, sewer problems, or water damage from hurricanes and other storms. As thousands of homeowners in my community learned in 1996, you don't have to live in a flood plain to sustain serious water damage to your home. When a twenty-four-hour "storm of the century" flooded nearby streams, they overflowed into streets throughout our area, ultimately pouring tons of water into the lower levels of nearly eight thousand homes in our city alone. In talking to my insurance agent about our own problem (a crack in the foundation that was ultimately repaired), I learned that the typical homeowner policy will cover water damage to one's furnace, water heater, washer and drier, but not furniture, artwork, and other home furnishings in lower-level (basement) family rooms. I was surprised to learn that if we had sustained water damage because of our foundation leak, our policy would not have covered the loss; however, if our basement had flooded because the power failed and the sump pump couldn't work, then we would have been covered because we have a sump pump insurance rider. Insurance is tricky and you must ask a lot of questions to find out exactly how much coverage you've got.

See also Computer Insurance; Home Business Insurance Policies; and Insurance, Replacement-Value.

Tip

If you have a special collection of art or craft objects valued at more than $1500, consider having the collection appraised so it can be insured on a separate all-risk endorsement. (See also *Collections of Art, Crafts, or Memorabilia.*)

Home Page

See Electronic Marketing.

Home Shows and Sales

See Checks; Personal Liability Insurance; Sales Commissions; Sales Tax; *and* Zoning Laws.

Home, Used for Business

See Business Expenses, Tax Deductible; *and* Home Office Deduction.

Homework Laws

Homework laws have been in existence in many states since 1937 when the legislature became aware of homework abuses and passed a federal *Industrial Homework Law*. Generally, homework laws still in effect today prohibit the manufacturing at home of such products as food and drink, wearing apparel, toys and dolls, cosmetics, and jewelry. In some cases manufacturing may be allowed if a special homeworker certificate or permit is obtained.

Readers may recall the massive media coverage given to the case of the Vermont Knitters back in the 1980s. When these knitters united to protest government restrictions on their industry, they eventually won exemption against extreme opposition from labor unions. In 1984, thanks to their efforts, the forty-year-old nationwide ban on home knitters was lifted along with bans against five other home industries that had been restricted since the 1940s under the *Fair*

Labor Standards Act: the manufacture of jewelry, gloves and mittens, buttons and buckles, handkerchiefs, and embroidery.

Because the problem of "sweatshops" still exists in large cities where women's and children's apparel is made, a ban still exists on hiring homeworkers to produce such goods. Knitting garments at home is also illegal in some states that have special homework laws. This means that if you are a crafter who designs and makes garments of any kind for women or children, you will not be able to expand your business by using homeworkers (independent contractors) without violating U.S. Labor Department laws. For more information on this topic, contact your state's Department of Labor.

See also Independent Contractors *and* Statutory Employees.

Income Statement

See Financial Statements *and sample Income Statement.*

Incorporation

See Corporation.

Independent Contractors

Q: *Can I hire homebased workers (independent contractors) to produce my products, give them the materials they need, and pay a per-piece price for each finished item?*

For years, small business owners have acted on the advice of accountants and attorneys to hire such labor on an independent contractor basis instead of an employee basis. They have been told that this will avoid the usual tax and paperwork problems associated with the hiring of employees. This is now a very dangerous thing for any business owner to do.

In recent years the IRS has been on a campaign to reclassify millions of independent contractors as employees, and if they have their way, someday there will be no independent contractors at all. Thousands of businesses that have had their workers reclassified by the

INCOME STATEMENT WORKSHEET

INCOME STATEMENT
(business name)

For Period Ending _____

REVENUE: $_____
   Gross Sales $_____
   Less Returns $_____
                                                               $_____
   Other Income $_____
   Total Income

COST OF GOODS SOLD:
   Inventory (type of) 1/1/____ $_____
   Inventory Purchases $_____
   Other Costs (specific to your business) $_____
   Subtotal $_____
   Less Inventory as of (12/31/   ) $_____ $_____
   Total Cost of Goods Sold
                                                                        $_____

TRADING PROFIT:

SELLING EXPENSES:
   Advertising $_____
   Postage $_____
   Shipping Expense $_____
   Exhibitor fees $_____
   Sales Commissions $_____ $_____
                                                                        $_____

SELLING PROFIT:

ADMINISTRATIVE EXPENSES:
   Bank Charges $_____
   Postal Fees $_____
   Office Supplies $_____
   Dues/Subscriptions $_____
   Insurance $_____
   Telephone $_____
   Repairs/Maintenance $_____
   Legal/Professional Expenses $_____
   Auto Expense $_____
   Sales Tax $_____
   New Equipment (write off or depreciate) $_____
   Interest $_____
   Travel Expenses (meals & lodging) $_____
   Wages
                                                                        $_____
   Total Administrative Expenses
                                                                        $_____
NET OPERATING PROFIT BEFORE TAXES:

IRS and the Department of Labor have been fined massive amounts in back taxes and related penalties.

Small craft businesses and cottage industries are not exempt. The problem arises when you hire an individual to work for you and that individual, in truth, is not a self-employed business person. You may have an agreement stating that an employer/independent contractor relationship exists between you, but it won't hold water if you are questioned by the IRS or Department of Labor. If you can't prove the legitimacy of the relationship, you could be liable for back taxes and penalties on all wages paid to such workers. To quote the IRS: "If an employer-employee relationship exists, it does not matter what it is called." In other words, an employee is an employee if the IRS or the Department of Labor says so. A note from the IRS's *Tax Guide for Small Businesses* reads: *"Penalty for treating an employee as an independent contractor. If you classify an employee as an independent contractor and you had no reasonable basis for doing so, you can be held liable to pay employment taxes for that worker. Further, if you do not withhold income, social security, and Medicare taxes from his or her wages, you may be held personally liable for a penalty equal to such taxes if you are the person responsible for the collection and payment of withholding taxes."*

See also Homework Laws; Sales Representatives; and Statutory Employees.

Tip

If you are presently using independent contractors to produce craft products for your business and feel you may be on unsafe legal ground, it would be wise to immediately consult with an attorney who specializes in labor law. (See article, "How One Manufacturer Solved Her Independent Contractor Problem.") Meanwhile, to avoid undue attention from legal authorities, avoid publicity or advertising of any kind that suggests you may be using outside help. Some businesses fall under scrutiny when an independent contractor is let go and then files for unemployment insurance or employee benefits under workman's compensation.

How One Manufacturer Solved Her Independent Contractor Problem

After reading my comments about the dangers of using home sewers to produce a line of goods, Jane, a homebased manufacturer in my network, began to worry about her situation. In consulting a labor attorney as I had advised, she learned that all the "good advice" she had been receiving from CPAs, accountants, and tax attorneys was dangerously incorrect.

While they said it was okay for Jane to continue using independent contractors, the labor attorney told Jane she was in a situation where her sewers had to be employees. To "go legal" when she had been operating illegally to that point was a frightening step. By filing with the U.S. Department of Labor, Jane would actually be raising her own red flag. But she followed her attorney's advice and was told by the Labor Department that, because she had voluntarily declared herself and had always paid minimum wages or above to her workers, there would be no penalties or back taxes imposed. Thus, if you are in a similar situation—wanting to switch over to employee status but afraid to do so—start looking for an attorney *who specializes in labor law*. (Jane found hers simply by asking around.)

Indian Arts and Crafts

A little-known FTC regulation relates to the production of Indian arts and crafts, which must meet specific requirements in order to be advertised as made by American Indians. If you are producing American Indian handcrafts, request additional information on this topic from the Federal Trade Commission.

Indicia

An indicia is an imprint on mail that indicates postage has been prepaid. It includes a special permit number that has been assigned to your company. An annual fee paid to your post office will cover all first- and third-class mailings you wish to make each year.

Insurance

See Car Insurance; Computer Insurance; Health Insurance; Homeowner's or Renter's Insurance; Insurance on Crafts Merchandise, Off-Premise; Personal Liability Insurance; Product Liability Insurance; *and* Workers' Compensation Insurance.

Insurance on Crafts Merchandise, Off-Premise

Q: *If I consign my crafts or place them in a craft mall or rent-a-space shop, will the shop or mall owner's insurance policy cover loss or damage to my products?*

Except for shops and stores in shopping malls—which are mandated by law to buy liability and fire insurance whether they own the merchandise in a store or not—you are unlikely to have any insurance coverage unless you buy it yourself.

Generally, craft shop and mall owners buy fire and theft insurance on their building and equipment only. If the shop burns down or your goods are otherwise damaged or stolen, you will lose all. If you ever find yourself placing a great deal of merchandise in a single location, it would be prudent to purchase a business insurance policy that includes coverage for merchandise off-premise.

Professional craft sellers who sell regularly at fairs may wish to investigate the benefits of membership in the American Craft Association (1-800-724-0859). In addition to offering health insurance, this organization offers a property and casualty insurance policy that lets individuals choose the types and amounts of coverage needed for such things as protection of buildings, machinery, equipment, inventory, raw materials, goods on consignment, goods at fairs and shows, and losses due to theft, burglary, or robbery. Liability insurance is also offered as part of this particular policy.

American Family Mutual Insurance has an affordable "Arts, Crafts, and Hobby Stores" business policy that offers protection against fire on merchandise consigned to stores. A policy covering goods for $20,000, with $300,000 liability and a $250 deductible for property damage, would cost about $346/year. (This particular policy would not cover items stolen or damaged in a shop, or loss of merchandise at a craft fair, such as an exhibit that blows over in the wind and destroys goods.)

Insurance, Replacement-Value

With regular insurance, what you get in the event of loss is figured on the current value of items after depreciation is taken into consideration. When you buy replacement-value insurance, however (which costs about fifteen percent more a year), the amount you receive is the amount it would take to replace items at today's prices.

If you have added a business rider to your homeowner's policy to cover equipment and materials in your workshop or studio, note that the replacement-value insurance coverage stops at your business door. That is, any loss to business materials and equipment will be figured on a depreciable basis and limited to the amounts shown on your special business rider. Since your computer system may be one of the most expensive items in your business area, it's a good idea to insure it separately with a company that specializes in this type of insurance.

See also Collections of Art; Crafts or Memorabilia; *and* Computer Insurance.

Internal Revenue Service

See Accountant; Accounting Methods; Bookkeeping; Business Expenses, Tax-Deductible; Checking Account; Employees, Family; Employees, Nonfamily; Hobby Income; Home Office Deduction; Independent Contractors; Inventory; Organization, Formation of; Statutory Employees; *and* Tax Audits.

Scams on the Internet

In spite of all the glowing articles about how great the Internet is, cyberspace is an industry running amok with no rules or regulations or anyone in control. Shady opportunists and con artists are just one of the Internet's big problems. Scheming individuals who previously used the mail and telephone to prey on unsuspecting consumers were among the first to get on the Internet and World Wide Web. The U.S. Postal Inspection Service is now working with other federal law enforcement agencies to monitor computer online services for fraud and direct marketing scams, but investment scams, gambling, and pornography are running rampant and only just beginning to be investigated by legal authorities. Be especially cautious when dealing with individuals or companies you've never heard of before. Don't automatically equate an impressive home page with credibility or business integrity.

The business benefits of the Internet are obvious, but this technology also has a dark and seedy side that could be dangerous to one's soul if not one's very life (as evidenced by the mass suicide of Heaven's Gate Believers that made headlines in 1997). Clearly, adults must be discerning when they go online and children should be closely monitored at all times.

See also *Scams.*

Internet and World Wide Web

Dozens of books on this topic are available to anyone who wants additional information, so my discussion here will be limited. As you surely know, the Internet is a computer network that connects millions of computers worldwide through telephone lines, fiber optics, and modems. The World Wide Web is simply a way of publishing and accessing information on the Internet. Business owners see the Internet as one of the greatest marketing and communication tools ever to come down the pike, but not everyone in business has an interest in, or need for, this technology. More information than anyone could use in ten lifetimes is already available online and more is being added every day. (I read somewhere that in a few years there will be 50 billion sites on the Web. If we all just stopped everything else we were doing with our lives and began to browse the Web all day every day for the rest of our lives, we could never cover it all.)

Experts predict that by the turn of the century 300 million people may be surfing the Internet and I'm sure I'll be one of them. For now, however, I am resisting this time-consuming technology because I have not yet seen a need for it in my professional or personal life. I am still very uncomfortable with the idea that anyone with a modem and a computer hacker's skill could tap into my computer's hard disk while I'm online and gain access to all the information on it, including all my business and accounting records, work-in-progress, private journals, and personal financial information. (The minute you go online with that kind of information on your computer's hard disk, you are literally offering it to the whole world.) Computer hackers are only part of the privacy problem, however. Internet service providers now rent the names and addresses of their subscribers and they are capable of collecting an enormous amount of other personal information about online users. Until such time as Congress enacts preventive legislation, Internet service providers are free to divulge "personally identifiable information" to third parties without the written consent of their subscribers.

I do understand that the Internet is exciting technology that can be used to enrich one's life but it's the worst invasion of our privacy we've ever had, and it's certainly the greatest time-waster ever devised. Many people have become addicted to spending their lives in front of a computer. Whole families are losing their ability to communicate with one another as each family member goes to his or her own personal computer terminal to work, play games alone, or chat with strangers online. Some call this progress but I find it frightening. As we all bend to accommodate the new technology that is literally being forced upon us day by day, we must be careful not to get so carried away with the wonder of it all that we forget it's people, not machines, that are important.

See also Electronic Marketing *and article, "Scams on the Internet."*

Inventor's Clubs and Associations

If you think you have invented something worth protecting with a patent, don't do anything about it until you've had a chance to communicate with other inventors. You do this by joining an organization such as Inventors Workshop International or subscribing to a magazine such as *The Dream Merchant* (see resource chapter). "Find someone who has been through the entire routine of patents, applied R&D, and stages of financing," advises the U.S. Small Business Administration. "It doesn't matter if the end result was a financial success or failure. Getting the nitty-gritty of the process is what's important."

See also Patent *and* Scams: Invention Hucksters.

Inventory

As crafters begin to sell what they make, they are not likely to concern themselves with keeping inventory records for tax purposes, but the longer one is in business and the more one sells, the more important this becomes.

First, the IRS requires everyone who sells products to keep inventory records, so if you're not doing this now, it means the information on your annual Schedule C tax report is incorrect. Keeping track of what you spend each year versus what you owe is only part of the recordkeeping you must do as a professional craft seller. What the IRS wants to know is how much inventory you are sitting with at the end of any given year. Only the amount of raw materials and supplies that ended up in the products you sold that year is deductible. The value of the inventory that's left must be carried forward to your next year's tax return (line 33 on your Schedule C report). For tax purposes, the inventory of a craft seller includes:

- what has been spent on raw materials and supplies used to make products
- the value of the raw materials and supplies (not the retail price) in partly finished craft items

- the value of the raw materials and supplies in finished crafts still unsold at the end of the year, including orders awaiting shipment and all goods on consignment or in craft malls and rent-a-space shops.

This sounds complicated, but it really isn't. You need to keep these records anyway if you want to know whether you're making a true profit on your crafts. Following is the information the IRS will expect you to provide on your Schedule C tax return. (See also article, "How to Keep Inventory Records.")

Schedule C (Form 1040) 1995   Page **2**

Part III   Cost of Goods Sold (see page C-5)

33   Method(s) used to value closing inventory: **a** ☐ Cost   **b** ☐ Lower of cost or market   **c** ☐ Other (attach explanation)

34   Was there any change in determining quantities, costs, or valuations between opening and closing inventory? If "Yes," attach explanation   . . . . ☐ Yes   ☐ No

35   Inventory at beginning of year. If different from last year's closing inventory, attach explanation   . . | 35 |

36   Purchases less cost of items withdrawn for personal use   . . . . | 36 |

37   Cost of labor. Do not include salary paid to yourself   . . . . | 37 |

38   Materials and supplies . . . . | 38 |

39   Other costs . . . . | 39 |

40   Add lines 35 through 39   . . . . | 40 |

41   Inventory at end of year   . . . . | 41 |

IRS Worksheet (page 2 of Schedule C, Form 1040) for cost of goods sold.

Invoice

The standard three-, four-, or five-part invoice sets available in office supply outlets will probably be sufficient for most small businesses, but you may prefer to create your own computer-generated invoices. As your business grows and you wish to make a stronger impression on your customer accounts, your local "quick printer" can custom-print multiple-part invoices for you at a reasonable cost.

An invoice should include seller's name and address; buyer's name and address; ship-to address (if different from sold-to address); customer's purchase order number and date of invoice; shipping

How to Keep Inventory Records

Inventory records can be kept on computer (special programs are available) or by hand with the use of ledger sheets or a notebook. To simplify record-keeping, break down purchases of raw materials and supplies into logical categories, using a separate page for each (wood, clay, wire, screws, component parts, paint, fur, fabric, etc.). Log purchases specifically, such as "ten yards red velvet ribbon" or "500 lamp bases."

Barbara Massie, who publishes how-to business guides for creative people, suggests that craft manufacturers create a chart with headings of Date, Materials Purchased, Number Purchased, Cost Per Item, Number Used, Number Left, and Cost of Items on Hand. "This will give you a worksheet to monitor all the supplies purchased and the cost of the supplies used in an item," she says. (Barbara's column, "Barb's Bench," appears regularly in *Neighbors & Friends* magazine.)

At year's end when you do your physical inventory, remember that the figure the IRS wants to see on your tax return is the total of unused supplies and materials on hand *plus* the amount of materials and supplies in products-in-progress, finished items on the premises not yet sold or shipped, plus unsold merchandise in consignment shops, craft malls, and rent-a-space shops. To come up with these figures, you will need to refer to records you have kept (or should be keeping) of how much materials cost you have in each of the products you sell. Whether you make one-of-a-kind creations or sell hundreds or thousands of items each year, this is information you need to record not only for yourself, but to satisfy IRS requirements.

Don't stay up nights worrying about your inventory records, but do the best estimate you can. (Many crafters simply "eyeball" their inventory of raw materials and unsold craft merchandise to arrive at a good estimate for their tax return. If you were ever audited, the IRS would have a hard time proving your estimate was incorrect.)

See also Tax Audits.

date and method of shipment (parcel post, truck line, UPS, etc.); invoice number (optional); customer's purchase order number; terms of payment (Net 30 days, etc.); quantity and description of items shipped with unit price and total amount indicated; along with shipping charges. To protect yourself against unauthorized returns, you may also wish to include your Returns Policy on the invoice. Larger stores may request a "blind invoice copy" which is the same thing as a packing slip (a copy of the invoice that describes the merchandise but does not indicate any prices).

If you make a single shipment to an account, invoice them and find thirty days later that payment has not been received, send a copy of the invoice with "SECOND NOTICE" written across the top and a note saying "This invoice is now overdue. Please remit promptly to retain your good credit rating with us." If you have made several shipments to this account and some of the invoices have been paid while others have not (some of which are not yet overdue), a statement should be sent that lists the dates and amounts of outstanding invoices.

See also Invoices Not Paid; Returns Policy; Minimum/Maximum Order Policy; Packing List; *and* Statement.

Invoices Not Paid

Q: *What steps should I take to collect overdue invoices for merchandise shipped to shops and other buyers?*

Begin with a series of reminder letters. After one crafts wholesaler in my network let her unpaid accounts build up to $10,000 (because she was so busy producing goods she didn't take time to monitor this situation closely), she got serious about collecting the money due her.

After her statements were ignored, she sent a friendly reminder ("Has this slipped your mind?"). Thirty days later, she sent a stronger notice ("Your account is now sixty days overdue.") To this she added a personal note that brought a twenty percent response. It read: "This invoice represents (number of hours) of handwork. Please consider the time and effort we have put into manufacturing this product and sending it to you on time."

Along with the statements and reminder notices, this seller also made telephone calls. "Phone calls work better than letters when you're trying to collect," she says. "Always try to work out a payment arrangement because few people want to be hounded by a bill collector and will finally pay just to avoid this hassle."

The final notice read "Your account is seriously past due. If payment is not made immediately, it will be turned over for collection." In the end, this particular business was able to collect only about a third of her accounts. She turned the rest over to a collection agency that took more than a year to collect half of them. The balance had to be written off. "It was an expensive lesson," she adds.

See also Collection Agencies *and* Small Claims Court.

Tip

Many problems can be avoided if your customers have your payment terms in writing and you communicate with them as soon as an invoice becomes overdue. When it's time to put on your bill-collecting hat, try not to think of yourself as the person who created the products that haven't been paid for, but the practical manager of your business whose goal is to increase cash flow. If the first call doesn't bring results, be persistent and call again.

Invoicing Policies

See Credit/Trade References; COD Shipments; Order Policies; Invoices Not Paid; *and article, "Selling to Catalog Houses."*

IRA

Self-employed individuals who wish to shelter some of their income from taxes while also building a retirement nest egg should consider opening an IRA (Individual Retirement Account). Currently, individuals who do not participate in the pension plan of an employer may put up to $2,000 of earnings into an IRA and take a deduction for the amount of the deposit on their annual income tax return.

A great advantage of an IRA is that you can contribute varying amounts each year or make no contribution at all. Withdrawals from an IRA may begin at age 59½ or be delayed up to age 70½. Taxes on this income will be due at the time of withdrawal.

See also Keogh Plan.

ISBN Number

This is a unique product identification code, helpful to publishers as an inventory code, to buyers as an order number, and for a variety of bibliographic purposes such as library catalog cards and online ordering systems.

If you plan to publish a book, you need to write to the ISBN Agency (see resource chapter) and request a block of numbers based on the number of books you intend to publish. (Even one-book publishers should do this, as books without an ISBN number won't be acceptable to bookstores and libraries.)

Jewelry Making

See Homework Laws *and* Trade Practice Rules.

Juried Shows

Q: *I tried to get into a juried show but was rejected. What's wrong with my work?*

All the better art and craft shows today are juried events. That is, hopeful exhibitors must submit slides or photos of their work to show promoters or organizers to demonstrate both the quality of their work and its appropriateness for sale at a particular show. Some sellers will be juried out of a show because they are producing handcrafts not in keeping with a show's theme or type of art or craft wanted for sale. For example, a traditional craftsperson might not gain entry to a contemporary crafts show, while a hobby crafter might be excluded from a show because his or her work does not qualify as true art or craft in the opinion of the show promoter. Try not to take such rejections personally. Being juried out of a show doesn't mean your work is not good, only that it is not appropriate for sale at that particular show. Sometimes sellers are rejected because too many other sellers are offering the same type of product and a limit has been placed on the number of sellers in a particular product field that will be allowed in the show. Entering events earlier could solve this problem. Subscribe to show listing periodicals to learn about such events months in advance.

See also Show Listings.

Tip

Failure to gain entry to a juried show could lie in the way you are presenting your art or craft to a show promoter. They are as likely to be interested in the way you plan to display your work as they are in the quality of work you do. You will need good photos that show your work and sales exhibit in the best possible light.

Keogh Plan

Self-employed individuals who wish to shelter a larger amount of earnings than is possible with an IRA should consider setting up a Keogh plan. (If you have employees, you may have to include them in your plan.) Ask a financial adviser whether an IRA or Keogh Plan is best for your particular needs.

See also IRA.

Kitchen Laws

Q: *I'd like to sell some homemade jams, jellies, and dried foods along with my craft items. Are there any problems in offering food products for sale?*

Anyone who sells food items of any kind should investigate their state's "commercial kitchen" law and find out if any local permits or licenses are required. In many states, it is very costly, if not impossible, for anyone to set up a food-related business in their home.

There are exceptions, however, and some states draw the line between commercial food businesses and small operations such as bake sales and farmer's markets. Iowa, for example has a "home bakery provision" that allows home bakers to operate without a license if they earn less than $2,000 per year and agree not to advertise their products.

Tip

Many clever food sellers have gotten around commercial kitchen laws in their state by renting a kitchen in a commercial building such as a local pizza parlor or church. One woman met her state's requirement by buying a storage building and putting in the required sinks and two Coleman stoves to make her jams and jellies in her backyard.

Labels, Address

When you want to make a great impression, use printed address labels to add pizzazz to your professional image. Check office supply catalogs for two-color mailing and shipping labels that can be ordered either with your business name and address preprinted on them, or blank if you prefer to add this information with your laser printer.

See also Office Supply Catalogs.

Labels or Tags Required by Law

Q: *If I'm only selling at craft fairs or in a consignment shop or craft mall, do federal labeling laws apply to my small business?*

Yes, you become a manufacturer in the eye of the law as soon as you begin to put products on the consumer market, even if all your products are one-of-a-kind creations. Certain labels and hang tags are required by law by the Bureau of Consumer Protection and the Federal Trade Commission, so you must comply with federal labeling rules if you make any of the following products for sale:

- Textile, suede, or leather products in the form of wearing apparel or household furnishings, piece goods, yarn, rugs, or anything else made of fiber (see *Textile Fiber Products Identification Act)*
- Stuffed toys, dolls, quilts, pillows, soft sculpture, and all other items with concealed stuffing (see *Bedding and Upholstered Furniture Law)*
- Any product made of wool, or any wool or textile product that uses imported fibers (see *Wool and Other Textiles)*
- Any product made of fur (see *Fur Products)*
- Any kind of garment (see *Care Labels)*

These federal labeling requirements may seem imposing, but it is not difficult to comply with them. You can make your own hang tags and labels or order commercial tags and labels from a number of suppliers listed in the resource chapter. (See E & S Creations, GraphComm Services, Widby Enterprises, and Wood Cellar Graphics.)

See also Hang Tags and Labels *and* Toymaking.

Labor Laws

Q: *What labor laws are applicable to a homebased business?*

If you hire only family members to work for your business, the U.S. Department of Labor's only concern is that you are paying your family employees at least the minimum wage. If you later hire non–family members to work for your business, you should familiarize yourself with these labor laws:

• *The Fair Labor Standards Act of 1938, as Amended.* This law establishes minimum wages, overtime pay, record-keeping, and child labor standards for employees individually engaged in or producing goods for interstate commerce, and for all employees employed in certain enterprises described in the act, unless a specific exemption applies. Direct specific questions on this topic to the Wage & Hour Division of the Department of Labor. (See "U.S. Government" in your telephone book.)

- *OSHA (Occupational Safety and Health) Act of 1970.* This statute is concerned with safe and healthful conditions in the workplace, and it covers all employers engaged in business affecting interstate commerce. Employers must comply with standards and with applicable record-keeping and reporting requirements specified in regulations issued by OSHA. If your crafts business uses paints, varnishes, and other materials that might conceivably be hazardous to your employees, check with state regulators to find out what safety requirements you must meet. If you are investigated after someone has reported you to officials, it could be very costly. I recall the story of one craft business that was put out of business by OSHA after being reported by a former employee who had been fired. When this person was denied unemployment benefits he decided to get even by claiming he had been working in an unhealthy environment due to paints and other chemicals. The crafts business owner spent thousands of dollars making modifications in his production line to meet OSHA requirements, but in the process he lost so much time and so many orders that he finally had to close up shop completely.

OSHA regulations also extend to employees' use of your vehicle. If one of them were to be hurt in an automobile accident, you could be held responsible, particularly if they were injured because they weren't wearing a seat belt. Details about OSHA regulations are available from area offices of the U.S. Department of Labor.

See also Employees, Nonfamily; Homework Laws; Independent Contractors; *and* Statutory Employees.

Laws and Regulations

See Local Laws; State Laws; *and* Federal Laws and Regulations.

Lawyer

Q: *Do I need a lawyer to start a homebased craft business?*

No. Hiring a lawyer to hold your hand while you start a small business at home would be comparable to hiring a limousine to drive you across the street. For what you would pay a lawyer to answer your business start-up questions, you could buy an entire library of small business reference books that will serve you for years. There may come a time in your business, however, when legal help is prudent, if not actually necessary, because the alternative could cost far more than your legal fees.

• **When You Need a Lawyer.** Unless you have a good understanding of "legalese," you would be wise to consult a lawyer any time you are asked to sign a contract, exclusive dealer or distributor agreement, licensing or franchise arrangement, or royalty contract. Legal counsel is also recommended if you decide to form a partnership, corporation, or cooperative. And never purchase property or buy a business without the guidance of a lawyer who will make sure you're not placing yourself in an uncomfortable legal or tax situation. At some point in your business, you may need the help of an attorney who specializes in patents, copyrights, or trademarks, but note that you do not need an attorney to get a simple copyright. A lawyer might charge you one hundred dollars to file the same form you can file for just twenty dollars. (See *Copyright Registration*.)

• **How to Find a Good Lawyer.** Like doctors, lawyers specialize in certain areas. Make a prospect list by first asking for recommendations from friends, business acquaintances, or your accountant. Also check the local Yellow Pages or call your city, county, or state bar association to get the names of lawyers in your area who handle cases of your type of concern. To check a lawyer's credentials, visit your library and ask for *The Martindale-Hubbell Law Directory,* a nationwide directory that details each lawyer's education, professional background, association memberships, and areas of expertise. (The international version of this directory lists Canadian lawyers.)

• **Initial Consultation**. Many lawyers offer free, initial consultations or may apply the fee for same toward your bill if you decide to hire them. Because lawyer's fees can vary dramatically, always ask about a lawyer's fee before you go in for a visit. Once you decide to hire a lawyer, make sure he or she puts in writing exactly what you will be paying and what you're going to get for your money.

• **Free Legal Assistance**. Strapped for funds and can't afford a lawyer? Artists and craftspeople who need advice, but cannot afford it, should contact the Volunteer Lawyers for the Arts. Headquartered in New York, this organization has branches in many states and is dedicated to providing free legal assistance to artists and arts organizations in all creative fields.

See also Prepaid Legal Services *and* Small Claims Court.

LC Number

If you plan to publish a book that will be sold to libraries, you must obtain an LC (Library of Congress) number and add it to the copyright page of your book. Through its CIP program (Cataloging in Publication), the Library of Congress makes printed catalog cards available to libraries throughout the world. The purpose of the number is to reduce cataloging costs and speed the delivery of books to readers. To acquire this number, submit a "Request for Preassignment of LCCN" to the Publications Section of the Copyright Office in Washington, D.C.

Lead Testing

Q: *We are careful about firing our ceramics to the temperature recommendation of the glaze manufacturer to make sure our products are free of lead and safe for food use. Do we need to take any other precautions to ensure the safety of our products?*

If you are selling ceramic items that come in contact with food or drink, you should test them for lead content before sale, *even though glazes are said to be food-safe or lead-free by the manufacturer.* I first wrote about this problem in 1972 and, unfortunately, it still exists today. For a long time, consumers were led to believe that it was only imported products that were hazardous because of improper glazing and firing. That is not the case, however. Any piece that is under-fired or incorrectly fired by an amateur potter may contain a dangerous level of lead. This is a potentially serious problem in schools where kilns are not as carefully regulated as those of professional ceramists. In other words, drinking out of that mug Junior just brought home is likely to be hazardous to your health.

The Food and Drug Administration (FDA) regularly makes random tests of pottery being shipped in interstate commerce, and they are empowered to confiscate products that fail to meet their lead release guideline of less than 0.5 parts per million. As ceramist Judith Leigh Pearson has learned, being careful about regulating the temperature of her kiln and following manufacturer's firing instructions to the letter is not enough. In an article for *The Crafts Report* she brought this problem to light while sharing her unusual experience with the Food and Drug Administration and her state's Department of Health. When the FDA was doing random lead testing in her area, they called Judith's studio to schedule a test of her products. So she would know what they were going to find, she immediately purchased a lead test kit (available in the paint department of most hardware stores). She was stunned to learn that many of her pieces tested positive, but not nearly as stunned, she said, as the manufacturer of the glaze she was using. According to their tests, this particular glaze was food-safe when fired to the temperature indicated on the label—the one Judith had used.

This article left several questions unanswered, but it emphasizes the importance of testing the ceramics you're putting into the commercial marketplace *if there is any chance they might be used as food containers.* No craftsperson can afford a lead poisoning lawsuit. "We as craft producers have to go the extra mile," Judith cautions, "and read beyond the labels to make sure that products are safe."

Here are some additional tips to help you avoid problems:

1. No glaze should ever be used by the hobbyist for food surfaces unless the manufacturer's label states the glaze is approved for such use when fired according to instructions—and these instructions must be followed *to the letter*.
2. Never fire by time alone—always use pyrometric cones.
3. Ceramic makers who are concerned about the safety of their products or uncertain about their ability to control their end use should design and fire decorative pieces only or make items undesirable for holding food and beverages by drilling holes in the sides or bottom, thus rendering them useless as containers.
4. If supervision is required in a teaching situation (such as elementary schools, hospitals, nursing homes, or other institutions), only non-toxic, lead-free hobby glazes should be used.

5. Depending on the size of the kiln and the quantity of ware being fired, the atmosphere around a kiln can constitute a very real health hazard. The kiln should be fit with a hood exhausting to the outdoors, and should be located in an area where adults, children, or pets will not unwittingly be exposed to lead fumes.

See also Consumer Safety Laws; Health Hazards; *and* Product Liability Insurance.

Legal Forms of Business

See Corporation; Partnership; Sole Proprietor; *and* Limited Liability Company.

Liabilities

The small homebased business will be concerned with only two kinds of business liabilities: Current and Fixed. Current liabilities are all the unpaid bills you have at the time you prepare a balance sheet (your Accounts Payable), any short-term loans that will be paid off within a year, plus any taxes due but not yet paid. Fixed liabilities would include any long-term business loan you may have taken.

Liability Insurance

See Corporation; Insurance on Crafts Merchandise, Off-Premise; Personal Liability Insurance; *and* Product Liability Insurance.

Libel/Defamation of Character

Be careful what you say about others, since you can be held legally accountable for defamation of character if you disparage another's business reputation or character with untrue statements. In an article for *The Crafts Report,* attorney Leonard D. DuBoff emphasized there is a big difference between promoting your work and reputa-

When using lead-free glazes, be sure to tell your prospective buyers you have done this. The sample tag above is a good example of how to convey this information. Note the inclusion of two additional buyer benefits as well; products are both *dishwasher-safe* and *microwave-proof*.

tion and undermining another's, so be careful about intentionally undermining a competitor's product or integrity when talking to strangers. "You can say your products are first-rate, but it would be risky to say that your work is better than another's unless that fact can be established," he says.

Licenses and Permits

Q: What's the difference between a license and a permit, and do I need either of them to sell my crafts at local fairs and shops or by mail?

A *license* is a certificate granted by a government agency that gives one permission to legally engage in a business, occupation, or activity. Depending on the type of business you plan to operate, you may need a license from certain municipal or county agencies. Food-related businesses, for example, are subject to special restrictions and inspections by both local and state health departments. If you work with flammable materials, you may need some kind of permit or official okay from the Fire Department. If your business causes the release of any materials into the air or water (even a ceramic kiln), you may need approval from the local environmental protection agency.

A *permit* is similar to a license, except it is granted by local authorities. Some communities require a permit for almost everything while others require it only for businesses that involve food, direct selling, and home shops. In years past, permits were rarely required for small craft businesses. Now, however, many communities see homebased entrepreneurs as a great source of extra revenue. So, depending on where you live, you might have to pay between fifteen and two hundred dollars for a "home occupation permit" that contributes to community coffers but does absolutely nothing for you.

If a license or permit is required and you operate without it, you run the risk of discovery, which could lead to a fine or an order to cease your business. No one goes around checking to see who has a license and who doesn't, but authorities sometimes discover unlicensed businesses by checking state sales tax returns and resale licenses, or they might read about a crafter's homebased business in the local newspaper and check their records to see if the business is registered. Call your city or county clerk for more information on this topic.

See also Bedding and Upholstered Furniture Law; Business or Trade Name Registration/Protection; Kitchen Laws; *and* Zoning Laws.

Licensing Arrangements

Q: *I have been contacted by a company interested in mass producing a doll I have designed. What kind of royalties are common in such an arrangement and what are the pitfalls in this area?*

A license grants specific rights to someone to do something that could not legally be done without the license. Creators of ideas or products may grant licenses for such things as the use of a name, a graphic image or design, a cartoon character, or an invention or unique product. In return for granting a license to a manufacturer to produce a product, a licensor is compensated with a royalty on the wholesale price that can vary from five to twelve percent but will more likely fall somewhere in between. An advance on royalties is common. The amount of royalties and size of advance has much to do with the industry and how marketable the product appears to be.

A licensing arrangement can be made for a period of one to five years, but most contracts are set up for two years with renewal options. If you use an agent to sell your idea or product to a manufacturer, expect to pay that person either a flat fee or a commission of between ten and fifteen percent of your total royalties. Don't sign a licensing contract until a patent or copyright attorney has checked it.

Licensing works in reverse, too. That is, you may someday want to use someone else's designs on your products. A licensing arrangement with another creative person like yourself could be mutually profitable. For more information on this aspect of licensing, see article, "Licensing Tips for Small Manufacturers."

See also Copyrights of Others; Designer Fabrics, Commercial Use of; Lawyer; Patent; Patterns, Commercial Use of; Sports Logos, Commercial Use of; *and article,* "The Cabbage Patch Kids® Story."

Limited Editions

Q: *I would like to create a limited-edition doll for collectors and offer perhaps no more than 250 for sale. Besides giving customers a certificate that states the item is a limited edition, is there anything else I should do?*

Licensing Tips for Small Manufacturers

When working with major companies or institutions, licensing arrangements are likely to be expensive and usually involve royalties that may range from six and a half to seven and a half percent of gross sales. But small business owners may be able to work with other individuals on a mutually profitable basis. For example, I recall two needlework designers who made a profitable arrangement with an artist whose work they admired. They sold him on the deal simply by stitching one of his paintings and explaining how they would market an entire line of his designs in cross stitch and needlepoint. Working with an attorney, they came to an agreement on royalties and term of contract (which included renewal options and a termination clause). Here are three tips they shared with me:

1. You or the licensor may want to branch out into other related fields, so you need a "Right of First Refusal" clause that will give you first chance at the opportunity to expand into a different area of business. If you decline, the opportunity may then be offered to others.

2. Be sure to work out what will happen in the event of death of either licensor or licensee.

3. Specify the territory in which you plan to sell . . . and don't limit yourself to a small area.

Although you may never have any intention of obtaining such a license, you may someday find yourself in a position to license others to reproduce a design you've created. Before entering into a licensing arrangement, be sure to register appropriate patents, copyrights, or trademarks and establish quality-control standards for the manufacturer of your designs. A licensing agent or attorney can represent your interests.

—A tip from the revised fifth edition of Homemade Money *by Barbara Brabec (1997, Betterway Books)*

In an article for *The Crafts Report,* attorney Peter H. Karlen of La Jolla, California, explained that many states now have laws that impose strict disclosure and warranty requirements on sellers who offer limited editions of art or craftwork. These laws require the inclusion of specific information on printed materials that advertise such items by mail, and the certificate of authenticity must contain a whole list of disclosures that become warranties. "If any of the disclosures are untrue," he states, "you have a breach-of-warranty problem on your hands."

Given the complex legal nature of this topic, anyone thinking about offering a limited edition item should work with an attorney who can draft the proper certificate forms.

Tip

There is a big difference between producing a limited number of items of a particular design (called multiples) and a "limited edition" run of that item as discussed above. If you're not into mass production of handcrafts, don't apologize for the fact that you make only multiples of your work. Instead, emphasize the uniqueness, rarity, or exclusivity of your products. Even large department stores are buying one-of-a-kind originals and craft multiples today.

Limited Liability Company

Limited Liability Companies (LLCs), which first appeared in the late 1980s, are now available in most, if not all states. An LLC reportedly combines the best attributes of other business forms while offering a better tax advantage than a limited partnership and personal liability protection similar to that of a corporation. Owners do not assume liability for a business's debt.

Although this legal form of business has been hailed as *the* business formation of the future—especially suitable for entrepreneurs, professional partnerships, and other small business owners—some business advisers are suggesting caution in selecting this type of business structure because it is still too new and hasn't yet been tested in the tax courts.

For more information, check with an accountant or see the book, *How to Profit by Forming Your Own Limited Liability Company* by Scott Friedman (Upstart).

See also Corporation.

Line of Credit

Q: *Is there any way a small business owner can get a line of credit?*

If you have a growing crafts business, you're likely to have cash flow problems. If you have been doing business with a local bank for some time and have a good credit rating, you may find it easy to get a $10,000 line of credit against which you can borrow funds as needed. Since banks love to give money to people who don't need it, the best time to apply for a line of credit is when all your bills are paid and you have some money in the bank. If you wait until you're financially strapped and can't show how you're going to repay any loan you make, you are likely to be refused credit.

By obtaining a line of credit before you actually need the money, you'll have added peace of mind that you'll be able to handle unexpected business expenses in low cash flow months, take advantage of special sales on supplies or equipment, or make major business purchases earlier than you might otherwise have been able to do.

The rules for borrowing on a line of credit are simple. During a period of a year, you can borrow and repay money as often as necessary, but the bank will want to see inactivity in your account for a period of at least thirty days during the year. If you can meet this requirement, your credit line is likely to be renewed every year. Although line-of-credit loans are payable on demand, few banks call them in unless they are unduly concerned about a lender's ability to repay.

See also Home Equity Loans.

Loans

See Bank Loans; Home Equity Loans; Line of Credit; Personal Loans; *and* SBA Loans.

Local Laws

See Business or Trade Name Registration/Protection; Fictitious Name Statement; Kitchen Laws; Licenses and Permits; Taxes; Telephone; *and* Zoning Laws.

Long Distance Carriers

Q: *I'm always getting calls from companies who want me to switch my long distance service, but I don't understand why one company may be better or worse than another. Help!*

The three major carriers are AT&T, Sprint and MCI. Because the FCC charges AT&T a higher tariff due to their enormous size and power, their rates are a few pennies higher than Sprint and MCI. AT&T and MCI continue to dangle enticing carrots to get people to switch their long-distance service. After receiving an offer of a $50 check and a free clock, I switched our home phone from MCI to AT&T. MCI immediately called and offered us three months of free long-distance service if we'd just switch back. I said I didn't think this was a nice thing to do after I'd just accepted $50 from AT&T, but I was told people do this all the time. I couldn't believe it when the sales rep added, "Some people change their long-distance service providers every 24 hours."

If you have a business phone, you can get lower rates by buying your long distance service from a reseller. Many companies now buy time from AT&T and resell it to small business owners at rates lower than those offered through regular long-distance companies. These companies are known as "AT&T SDN Resellers" (Software Defined Network), and by signing up with one of them, you may be able to save up to twenty percent on long-distance calls, getting the same low rates enjoyed by major corporations. Such companies advertise in business periodicals, and all the craft and home business organizations work with such resellers, offering their members special savings on long-distance services.

In selecting a long-distance provider, ask how charges are determined. The two biggest money-makers for companies are charging for ring time (customer pays for a call even when no one answers) and charging by the minute instead of in six-second increments. (Even when you're on the phone for only half a minute, you pay for a full minute. This really adds up when you consider that every call you make is likely to have an extra minute's charge attached to it.) Also ask what the rate is for calls made out-of-state.

All long-distance companies offer a variety of plans so before you switch your service, consult with a representative on which plan is best for your particular needs. What you spend per month on average, where you call, and when you make most of your calls has much to do with the rates you can get. Competition is so fierce in this industry that merely by complaining about your phone bill and suggesting you might switch carriers could get you lower rates.

As I was putting the final touches on this book, I switched my long-distance carrier once again, this time to Connect America, a national service provider who offers the lowest interstate rates in the nation—just 10.9 cents per minute for interstate calls and 8.9 cents for calls within my state with 6-second billing. For more information call 1-800-745-9650.

See also Telephone *and* Home Business Organizations.

Mail, Classes of

In mid-1996, the U.S. Postal Service announced it was improving mail standards with its "Classification Reform" program. In addition to offering special discounts for mailers who can prepare mail for automated processing, it introduced a new and very tedious system for sorting and bundling bulk mail. Now there are only four classes of mail:

1. Expedited (Express) Mail offers guaranteed next-day delivery for packages up to seventy pounds.
2. First-Class Mail includes pieces weighing eleven ounces or less (after which point it is called Priority Mail). Postal cards and postcards make up one subclass; letters and sealed parcels make up the other. The minimum volume per bulk mailing is 500 addressed pieces for each mailing. Barcoded and presorted first class mail is entitled to special discounts.

3. Periodicals (formerly called second-class) must meet certain requirements to qualify for the special periodicals rate. Check with your postmaster about this.

4. Standard Mail (formerly third- and fourth-class) is all mail not sent as First-Class Mail or entered as Periodicals. Submitted in bulk (200 pieces minimum), Standard Mail can include samples, ordinary papers, and circulars.

See also Bulk Mailings; Business Reply Mail; Certified Mail; Indicia; Mail, Size Regulations; Mail, Undeliverable; P.O. Box Address; Postage Meter; Postal Regulations; Priority Mail; Registered Mail; Return Receipt Mail; Self-Mailers; *and article, "State and City Abbreviations."*

Mail Lists, Rental of

Q: *I've developed a sizable mailing list of customers who have purchased my products by mail and I would like to rent this list to other mail order sellers. Is there any problem with this?*

Some people do not want their names sold to others, and they have the right to privacy. In the Privacy Protection Study Commission named by former President Ford, it was recommended that list sellers give their customers (or members, subscribers, etc.) the option of having their names removed from any rental list. The following "disclosure notice" in your catalog or other mailers should suffice:

> "We occasionally make our customers' names available to other reputable companies who offer quality products that might be of interest to you. If you prefer not to receive such offers, copy your name and address as it appears on the mailing label and send it to us."

Before you advertise any mailing list for rent, make sure it's up to date. Because today's society is very mobile, a list can go out of date in a few months, After a year, thirty percent of the addresses on any mailing list could be bad. It is unethical to rent an out-of-date list, so you will need to "clean" your list by mailing to it again. When you place an "Address Correction Requested" notice on your mail piece, the post office will send you new addresses or indicate which ones are bad. (Check your postmaster for the current cost of this service.)

See also Bulk Mailings.

Tip

Don't think you can keep a list clean simply by always mailing it First Class. True, the Post Office will forward your mail piece to people who have moved, but unless you ask for address correction information, you won't be notified of their new address. Future mailings to the old addresses will result in your mail being returned with a notice that the forwarding order has expired, and you will have lost these prospect and customer names for good.

Mail Order Business

See Better Business Bureau; Break-Even Point; Canadian Sales; Checking Account; Checks; COD Shipments; Federal Trade Commission Rules; Guaranty of Satisfaction; Mail, Classes of; Mail Lists, Rental of; Money Orders; P.O. Box Address; Postal Regulations; Prepublication Offer; Refunds; Shipping and Handling Charges; Sole Proprietorship; Trade Practice Rules; *and* ZIP Code.

Mail Order Rule

See Federal Trade Commission Rules; Prepublication Offer; *and* Price List.

Mail, Size Regulations

Your postmaster will be happy to give you a booklet detailing all the size regulations of mail, so I'll just mention here a couple of problem areas that need emphasis.

• **Catalogs and Self Mailers.** Before printing your new catalog or self-mailer or figuring what it will cost to mail a newsletter, ask your postmaster for a booklet that explains the various types of mail and all the rules and regulations related to each. You must be concerned not only with the size and design of mail pieces but how they are

State and City Abbreviations

Thousands of people write to me every year requesting information about my books and reports, and every week I toss mail without answering it for three reasons: (1) I can't read a person's handwriting or decipher a number in their address; (2) they have abbreviated the name of their city and I can't figure out what it is; or (3) they have failed to include their ZIP code.

City abbreviations are particularly annoying. Do you know what R. S. M., CA is, or Bnvl, IN, or W. W., OK? I wasn't sure until I checked my z.c. dir. to decipher these abbreviations, which turned out to be Rancho Santa Marguerita, Boonville, and Woodward. (A rubber stamp of your address or mini-address labels will not only save you time when ordering information or products but will speed delivery of your mail and fulfillment of your orders.)

Even when the people you write to have a ZIP code directory, not everyone will take the time to look up address information you should have provided in the first place. Therefore, to speed delivery of your mail and always get a reply to your mail, write legibly, don't abbreviate the name of your city, use the proper two-digit abbreviation for your state and always include your ZIP code. (If you don't know the two-letter abbreviations for each state, your postmaster will be happy to provide you with a list of them.)

addressed. "We changed the format of our newsletter to resemble a book layout, putting the address area on the upper third of the back side," a reader reports. "When I delivered the mailing to the post office, I was told that because the address area was more than 6¼ inches from the bottom, I had to pay a penalty fee of about four cents per piece. Prior to printing our new catalog, I took a mock-up to the post office to confirm that its size and design met their regulations and qualified for the lower rates."

- **Postal Cards**. I frequently receive 3 x 5 index cards as a substitute for postal cards, and it's a wonder they are delivered, because they do not meet U.S. Postal regulations. To be acceptable by the post office, a postal card may be no smaller than 3½ x 5 inches. The largest size that can use the regular post card stamp is 4½ x 6 inches. While smaller cards may simply be rejected, the use of larger cards will result in extra postage charges.

See Postal Regulations *and article, "Money-Saving Postal Tips."*

Mail, Undeliverable

Do you know that undeliverable mail without a return address will be opened by postal employees and searched for an address or items of value? Letters that do not contain anything of value will be destroyed because of the Privacy Act, but any checks, money orders, stocks, or bonds found in such mail will be returned free of charge. Undeliverable parcels are held for 90 days, then put up for auction.

Maintenance Agreements

Q: *Are maintenance agreements on office machines worth the money they cost?*

In my experience, it depends on which machine you are talking about. Because my dot matrix and laser printers have worked beautifully for years without a hint of trouble, I wouldn't encourage anyone to buy a maintenance agreement for a printer. I haven't found any reason to buy a maintenance agreement on computers, either, since they come with a guarantee that is long enough to get you past the point at which trouble is likely to occur. (If a machine is defective, problems tend to develop very early, while the guarantee is still in effect.) This is not to say that you won't need repairs on your system from time to time; only that I have found it more practical to pay for them at the time they are needed. Note there is a difference between a maintenance agreement on your computer system, and *computer insurance,* a topic discussed elsewhere.

Although electronic typewriters may soon be a thing of the past, getting a maintenance agreement on my Adler typewriter was the smartest thing I ever did. Electronic typewriters do need regular cleaning, and parts wear out. The last part I had replaced would have cost me $500, and the older this machine gets, the more I am going to need a maintenance contract.

Perhaps the most important equipment to cover with a maintenance contract is a fax machine. Since the cost of an annual maintenance agreement is about the same as the minimum charge for service, it seems prudent to buy one. My failure to do this when I bought my fax almost cost me $250 in repairs, or half what I had paid for it in the first place. One day after only a few months of use, my fax suddenly stopped in the middle of a multi-page transmission and began to chirp like a bird. A call to the manufacturer revealed I might have a problem with the power pack. After some discussion, a technician said to unplug the fax for a while, then try plugging it in again since my machine had an automatic reset button. This did the trick, but I suddenly saw the need for a maintenance agreement on this particular machine. If the power pack goes bad in the future, at least now it won't cost me a small fortune to get it replaced.

See also article, "Commercial Use of Home Sewing Machines."

Manufacturer's Rep

See Sales Representatives.

Markups

This is the percentage a retail outlet adds to the wholesale price it pays for any item. In the gift and crafts industry the wholesale price is generally doubled (marked up 100 percent) to arrive at the retail price, but there are exceptions to this rule. Sometimes a crafts producer cannot wholesale an item at half the normal retail price, but buyers may want the product anyway because they know they can triple the purchase price and still sell it in their particular area. Even when you do wholesale products at half your standard retail price, buyers always have the option of using a higher markup, depending on what their traffic will bear.

Money-Saving Postal Tips

Here is a collection of tips I've compiled over more than twenty-five years of doing business by mail:

- If you're not using an accurate postal scale, you could be wasting postage on pieces that fall on the line between one ounce and another. Either double-check the weight of those pieces at the post office or get a more accurate electronic scale.
- Keep your postage costs low by designing your brochures and catalogs so they weigh an ounce or less. A change of paper weight or cover stock can make a big difference.
- If you use a business name and move, make sure you file a forwarding order for both your personal and business names. Otherwise you may miss some of your mail.
- Although you may guarantee forwarding postage on periodicals when you move, remember that third class bulk mail is not forwardable even when forwarding postage is guaranteed.
- If you are developing a mailing list for your business, delete any address that says "General Delivery" because such mail is forwardable for only thirty days.
- When addressing mail, always use the standard two-letter abbreviations for states with a ZIP code to enable automatic scanning and sorting. Abbreviate where you can and avoid punctuation. (AVE and ST are preferable to Avenue or Street.)
- It's a myth that you must use all caps and no punctuation for fast processing and delivery of your mail. That was true years ago when computers and optical scanners were less sophisticated at reading addresses but no more. If you prefer to use upper and lower case letters in your computer database files, that's fine so long as you avoid the use of hard-to-read exotic typefaces.
- Always include your address on both sides of a postal card because the postmark on the front often obliterates part of an address making it impossible to read.

Higher markups of 150 to 400 percent or more are common in other industries, so the product you make and the wholesale price you set may or may not permit selling to them.

See also Catalog Houses, Selling to *and* Pricing Guidelines.

Merchant Bank Card Services

Q: *My local bank won't grant me merchant status because my business is too small and too new. I need to be able to offer my customers credit card privileges, but don't know how to do it.*

Until recently, it has been difficult for home business owners to get merchant status from their local bank. If you live in a small community or are well known by your bank, you may not have a problem getting merchant status, but if you do, one option is to join a home business or small business organization that offers this service to its members. Many organizations have made special arrangements with banks that are favorably inclined toward homebased businesses. Membership in one of these organizations will cost around fifty dollars a year, and as soon as you're a member, you can apply for merchant status. (See resource chapter for some home business and art/craft organizations that offer bank card services.)

Offering a charge card service to your customers is no longer as simple as writing up tickets by hand and running them through an imprinting machine. Now everything is done electronically with special equipment that must be purchased or leased. You will need a certain level of income to justify the cost of doing business this way, or at least feel confident that sales will increase substantially once you begin to offer your customers charge card privileges. Your discount rate (the percentage you will pay on each sale) may vary from two to five percent depending on the size of your average order and your annual sales volume. In addition, there will be also be charges for each telephone authorization you make, each ticket deposited (transaction fee) and each chargeback made.

In earlier years, professional craft fair sellers could accept credit card sales but had no way of verifying if a credit card was good or not. Now, thanks to technology and cellular phones, craft sellers can

Commercial Use of Home Sewing Machines

Here's an interesting story about sewing machines and Sears' maintenance contracts. When the owner of a sewing business took her machine to Sears for servicing, she made the mistake of mentioning to the clerk at the service desk that she had her own home business. Later, when her service contract came up for renewal, Sears wouldn't renew it. "I was told by Sears that their sewing machine is to be used only for home (family) sewing—never for something to be sold," she reported. "I'm sure a lot of other people don't know this."

On the warranties of many Sears' appliances, there is an exclusionary clause that states, in effect, that commercial use invalidates the terms of the warranty. It's not surprising that Sears would want to protect themselves in this way. Obviously, a machine put together for light duty will not have the stamina for nearly-industrial use. Thus, the exclusion.

check a customer's card before making a sale. Back home, they simply deposit funds in their bank account electronically by keying in sales to a terminal attached to their phone. One organization that offers several bank card "service packages" to artists and crafters is Arts and Crafts Business Solutions (call 1-800-873-1192). Their least expensive package (without a cellular phone) is around $500.

An even more affordable solution is offered by Novus Services, Inc., the umbrella company for the Discover, Bravo, and Private Issue credit cards. Currently, crafters with a good personal credit rating can now get merchant status for their business for around $300, which covers an electronic terminal, a connector to your phone, and a charge slip imprinting machine. The only information Novus requires is your social security number or federal tax I.D. number (Employee Identification Number) so they can run a credit check on you. When you apply to Novus for merchant status, they can also get you set up to take Visa and MasterCard as well. However, while Novus automatically accepts brand new businesses with a good credit rating, some Visa and MasterCard processors won't grant acceptance unless one has been in business for at least two years. Novus has twenty district offices around the country. To talk to a local representative about getting the Discover card, call this toll-free number: 1-800-347-2000.

Finally, merchant status can be obtained through an Independent Sales Organization (ISO), but this is the most expensive route you can go and some companies in this field have questionable business ethics. In one publication or another, crafters have reported on their experience with ISOs and some of them have been badly burned after paying $2,000 or more for equipment worth only $300 and getting stuck for fifty-dollar-a-month lease fees on a noncancelable four-year lease. The problem with ISOs is that they charge much higher equipment lease fees than banks and they also have higher application, installation, programming, and site inspection fees. Before applying to my local bank, I checked out a couple of ISOs and found their fees and lease costs totally impractical for my needs. The ISO I was considering would have charged me thirty-five dollars a month to lease the terminal ($1680 over a period of four years), or I could buy it for $1,000. Imagine my surprise when my local bank told me I could get the same equipment from them, including the software needed to make direct deposits to my bank account, for just $350. That gives you an idea of the high markups ISOs are taking on equipment.

Before signing with any ISO, be sure to compare all service charges, discount rates, and equipment lease fees against what you would pay if you got merchant status through another source.

See also Cellular Phones *and* Credit Card Sales.

Minimum/Maximum Order Policy

Q: *I'm trying to establish minimum/maximum order and reorder policies. What things do I need to consider here?*

Craft producers may have a minimum order policy of $50 to $200. More important than your minimum order policy, however, is the amount of additional merchandise you will ship to new accounts that have no credit history with you.

A crafts manufacturer explains the big ego trap many new crafters and even some old pros fall into: "Be especially cautious about invoicing large orders from new accounts. The people who are out to trick you or who have bad credit tend to order in large quantities. New crafters are so excited by large orders and rave comments that they may ship and invoice an order without question. Then, especially if it's around the holidays when shops often sell out their first shipment immediately, they may get a second order before the first order is past due. Everything looks great but before you know it, you can have three or four invoices totaling a thousand dollars or more that aren't past due yet."

The ceiling amount you set for new customers and reorders is up to you, but a good guideline would be to ask yourself how much money you could afford to lose if an account doesn't pay, and set that amount as your maximum amount. While a large crafts business might feel comfortable with a minimum of $250 to $500, the beginning crafter may not want to risk more than $100.

See also article, "Selling to Catalog Houses."

Tip

If you do not establish a high enough minimum order for dealers, you may find (especially around Christmas) that shop owners are buying your work at wholesale prices for themselves or for personal gifts. This may not bother you, but remember that very small orders can be a nuisance if you are primarily wholesaling your work.

Modem

A modem enables your computer to communicate with other computers through your telephone line. It works in conjunction with communications software (many different programs are available). Modems come in different speeds. The faster the modem, the faster you can access information online.

See also article, "Fax Installation Tips."

Money Orders

Q: *When is it advisable to ask for payment by money order instead of a check?*

If someone is replacing a bad check, you should ask for repayment by money order since if one check was bad, the replacement check might be bad, too. Always give your mail order customers the option of paying by money order, but don't insist on this type of payment for customers in the United States. (If you ask the average individual to pay by money order when they are used to paying by check, they will probably not order at all because it takes too much time to go out and get a money order.)

If you solicit orders from buyers in countries other than Canada (particularly when selling on the Internet), insist on payment by credit card or International Money Order. If you are selling by mail to Canadian buyers, see *Canadian Sales* for perspective on asking for payment by money order versus check.

Nature Items

Q: *Are there any laws against collecting and using natural materials in products I make for sale?*

Many crafters make products of dried nature materials such as tree bark, flowers, grapevines, pine cones, pods, dried grasses, weeds, and so on. Some also sell these dried materials to others. Legally speaking, the place from which you collect such items and the way you use them is important.

First, it's against the law to remove anything from a state park or forest preserve, including dead, dried materials. The idea here is not to disturb the balance of nature. Endangered species and their parts, from plants and wildflowers to animal bones, claws, and feathers are also protected by state or federal environmental protection laws. In some cases merely possessing one of these protected items is a violation of the law.

If you plan to sell or are already selling nature crafts or raw materials, here are four suggestions on how to avoid problems or fines:

1. Never pick up *anything* from a state park or forest preserve.
2. Make sure you sell nothing that is protected by law.
3. Either gather all your nature items on your own property, or get written permission to collect them from other public or private areas.
4. Look in your Yellow Pages under the state government listings for the Department of Natural Resources and inquire about commercial permits that might be offered to collectors of nature materials. (Some states apparently authorize the removal of certain items at certain times, such as when greenery needs cutting back, trees need topping, or an area has to be mowed for some construction purpose.)

Finally, a note about bugs. As I was writing this, I wondered if there were any restrictions on shipping nature crafts or dried materials by mail because of tiny insects that might be clinging to such products. In checking with the post office I was amused to learn that the U.S. Postal Service Manual specifically says that "thoroughly dried dead insects" are mailable, so you will have no problems if your products are properly dried. (Tiny insects too small to see could be killed by freezing them overnight or zapping them in the microwave.)

See also Endangered Species *and* Found Objects.

Net Price

"Net" means free and clear. A net price is one from which deductions have been taken; net profit is what's left after all business expenses have been deducted. The opposite of net is gross.

See also Gross Price.

Selling to Catalog Houses

Could your business survive if you shipped $11,000 worth of merchandise and didn't get paid for it? That's what happened to Susan, a crafts designer in my network who prefers anonymity. She shared her story with me so others wouldn't get caught in a similar trap.

Susan was thrilled when a prestigious catalog company ordered 150 of her hand-decorated gourds for an invoice total of $11,000—the biggest order of her life. Uncomfortable about filling such a large order, Susan was reassured by the buyer who said not to worry—she was an investor in this reputable company.

So Susan put in hundreds of hours of around-the-clock production to meet the catalog's shipping date of August 1. Unable to do all the work herself, she hired a woman to help her, agreeing to pay her $1,000 for this work as soon as she got paid by the catalog house. Total expenses for this order—not counting Susan's time—were $4,000.

The last of the items were received by the catalog house on August 2. On August 3, the company filed for Chapter Eleven bankruptcy and Susan got caught in a terrible trap. Because her merchandise arrived before the court date, the company was not obligated to return it and could actually count it as part of their inventory, even though it was unpaid.

"While a company in Chapter Eleven can continue to operate and is protected against creditors, I have learned that creditors have no rights at all," writes Susan. "The papers I received stated that, as a creditor, I (1) could *not* call to demand payment; (2) could *not* put a lien on anything owned by the company; and (3) could *not* take repossession of my property. (Only the company's top twenty creditors had the legal right to file a

(continued on next page)

(continued from previous page)

priority claim or reclamation papers.) All I was allowed to do was fill out a proof of claim form documenting that I was, in fact, owed $11,000 plus shipping charges. And I was given the right to seek legal counsel, which I could not afford."

How can a company accept merchandise from a supplier one day knowing full well they are going into court the next day to declare bankruptcy? Susan never got the answer to this question. "If individuals operated like this, they'd end up in jail," she says. "This may not qualify as fraud, but it is surely immoral." Susan advises other crafters who are considering this kind of marketing to *never* ship such a large first-time order to a mail order catalog house. "Such companies demand thirty-day terms but rarely pay within sixty days," she says. "The prudent thing for a small supplier to do is sign a contract stating they will supply whatever quantity of merchandise the buyer anticipates needing for whatever period they plan to sell the item. (I had to agree to supply them for a one-year period.) Insist, however, that shipments go out in small batches, and that new shipments will not be made until outstanding invoices have been paid."

You may find this hard to believe, but a week after Susan got the bankruptcy papers, she received a new order for $3500 worth of merchandise to be sent COD. Because she needed cash so badly, she agreed to ship this order, but insisted on a check up front and didn't ship until it cleared the bank. Although Susan tried every legal strategy she could afford, she never got her merchandise back and she never got paid for the initial shipment. This experience not only put her out of business but left her totally discouraged and in deeply in debt.

Newsletter Publishing

Q: *I would like to share my enthusiasm for crafts by publishing a newsletter. This sounds easy to do, but I wonder if I'm overlooking something. Are small newsletters profitable?*

Few small newsletter publishers expect to make a lot of money when they begin and fewer still realize the enormous effort it takes to get and keep subscribers. Yet all seem to enjoy the creative challenge of producing a periodical for a select and appreciative audience of readers, no matter how small it may be. Fortunately, the very act of publishing a newsletter tends to lead one into more profitable areas, including teaching, consulting, writing a book, etc. At the very least, a newsletter enables one to "go forth and meet the world."

Because there are so many newsletters in print today, new publishers entering this field must offer something new and different to entice readers. It's fine to publish a newsletter "for the love of it," but if your goal is to realize a financial profit as well, there are many things to be considered, not the least of which is the impact the Internet is having on the sale of information. Now that we are all drowning in information and millions of people have access to free newsletters online, it's going to be harder than ever to sell subscriptions. I predict many small newsletter publishers will soon cease publication because of this.

Newsletters are supposed to be free of advertising—which is one of the things that makes them valuable to readers—but novice publishers often attempt to sell advertising when they begin. Classified advertising that benefits your subscribers may work, but display advertisers are not likely to advertise in a small newsletter that has less than 5,000 readers. Novice publishers also tend to look at the profitability of a newsletter by figuring what it will cost to print and mail four or six issues, subtract this amount from the amount they plan to charge for a subscription and figure the rest is profit. For example, it might cost $4.50 to deliver six issues of a newsletter to a subscriber who may pay $18 for a subscription. That leaves a gross profit of $13.50 for the publisher. From this, you must deduct a host of other expenses such as clip art and design costs, the costs of building and maintaining a mailing list (all those additions, deletions, and corrections on a continuous basis), printed materials to sell the newsletter, renewal notices, subscription forms, office forms, invoices, and so on. Last, and most expensive, you have the continuing cost of advertising and promoting the publication. Before long, that $18 you're getting from each subscriber has dwindled to mere pennies of profit, and I'll bet you still haven't taken into consideration the time it's going to take to write, design, and produce each issue, design all the special printed materials that go along with newsletter publishing, get out mailings, answer subscriber correspondence, dig up new material for each issue, keep subscription and renewal records and so on.

During my fifteen-year stint as the publisher of a home-business newsletter, I saw many new publications come and quickly go because people just didn't understand the realities of marketing a newsletter, and few could understand at the beginning how hard it was going to be to get and keep subscribers. What finally wore me down, however, were the relentless deadlines. The longer I published, the closer those deadlines seemed to be, and I began to feel strangled by all the time this work was taking. Because I wanted time to write more books before I die, I decided to cease publication in 1996.

I'm glad I'm no longer publishing a newsletter (to every thing there is a season), but I don't want to discourage others from trying this because even when financial profits are low, there are other reasons for publishing. First, having your own newsletter positions you in your industry as an authority and this may bring you invitations to speak or teach that will yield far greater profits than the newsletter itself. The most successful newsletter publishers always have something else to sell, and high on the list will be books and related products, business services, consulting, or one's availability as a speaker. Because newsletters are such good marketing tools, many small businesses publish free newsletters that are mailed regularly to customers and others who have responded to advertising and promotional efforts.

See also Desktop Publishing *and* Mail, Size Regulations.

Tip

If you include book reviews in your periodical, you can build a great library of books in your field because publishers will usually send free review copies of new books to any periodical publisher who expresses an interest in giving it print publicity. Some manufacturers may also send you sample products in return for reviews.

Office Supply Catalogs

Q: *I am miles away from an office supply store. Can you recommend companies I can order from by mail?*

Even when you live near office supply stores, it's a good idea to collect several catalogs of mail order suppliers so you can compare prices of basic supplies such as ribbons, ink cartridges, laser or copier paper, envelopes, shipping supplies, labels, and so on. Here are some of my favorite suppliers who offer immediate shipment by UPS. Call to request a free catalog from:

Office Depot 1-800-685-8800 (free delivery)
OfficeMax 1-800-788-8080 (free delivery on orders of $50 or more)
Quill 1-800-789-1331 (free delivery on orders of $50 or more)
Viking 1-800-421-1222 (free delivery on orders of $25 or more)

See also Preprinted Papers; Presentation Folders and Table Signs; *and* Scams: Office Supply Scams.

Online Sales

Q: *I plan to offer my products to buyers online, through my own home page as well as through other web sites or malls. How should I handle sales?*

All sales made online should be handled the same way you treat sales by mail. The same laws and regulations apply to both.

See also Electronic Marketing *and* Mail Order Business.

Order Forms

Every business needs one kind of order form or another. Some craft sellers create separate order forms and price lists while others combine the two into one form. (See sample of the latter near the text on *Price List.*)

An order form should include your full business name, address, telephone, and fax number, with space for the same information about your customer. It should show the date the order was placed and the delivery date you've promised. Depending on what you sell, you may want to create an order form that allows you to write in the items that are being ordered, or one that lists all the products with their code or identity numbers listed along with the price of each. Your order form should also include your terms of payment, freight or delivery information, any special ordering instructions, and your guarantee, if one is offered.

See also Purchase Order.

Tip

Keep a pad of order forms by your phone. I create forms using my word processing software, setting them up four-to-a-page, then cutting and stapling batches together.

Order Policies

See Credit/Trade References; Invoicing Policies; Minimum/Maximum Order Policy; Payment Methods; Price Lists; Returns Policy; Shipping and Handling Charges; *and* Terms of Sale.

Organization, Formation of

Q: *I would like to form an organization or association for creative people. What do I have to do to operate legally?*

Many people erroneously assume that all organizations and associations are run by a group of people. Actually, an organization or association of any kind may be started by one or more individuals and operated either on a profit or nonprofit basis. The thing that makes any organization "a group" is its members, not its management.

Carolyn D. Duronio, an attorney with Reed Smith Shaw & McClay in Pittsburgh, confirms anyone can start an association, and there are no legal rules about the formation or registration of associations except that a nonprofit association must have some sort of organizational form. Incorporation is a matter of choice, not a legal requirement for any nonprofit or for-profit association. To obtain tax-exempt status, however, a nonprofit association must file a tax-exemption application with the IRS. If approved, the IRS then issues a "Determination Letter."

While FTC laws dictate that we cannot represent ourselves to be something other than we are, there is no law that says the owner of an association has to broadcast the fact that he or she is a one-person organization. Leading people to believe you are a nonprofit organization when you are really a for-profit business, however, would be in violation of both FTC truth-in-advertising regulations and mail order laws.

Organizations

See Art/Craft Organizations; Home-Business Organizations; and Trade Associations/Publications.

OSHA Regulations

See Labor Laws.

Overhead

Overhead expenses are all costs not directly related to the production of your products (raw materials and labor). Overhead includes selling costs (show fees, sales commissions, display expenses, photography, packaging, samples, advertising, promotional mailings, and the cost of accepting credit card charges); general office expenses (telephone, fax, and computer supplies, office supplies and stationery, postage and postal fees, bank charges, legal and professional expenses, subscriptions, memberships, and conference fees); other expenses (travel and auto expenses, equipment purchases, maintenance and depreciation, employee or independent contractor expense) and "home office expenses" (a percentage of your rent or mortgage expense, taxes, insurance, and utilities).

If you are serious about business, you will take overhead costs into consideration when figuring prices for your products. After totaling your annual overhead costs, divide this figure by the number of hours you worked during the year to come up with an hourly overhead rate that can be incorporated into your pricing. For example, if your hourly overhead costs are three dollars and you can produce a dozen miniature products per hour, you would add twenty-five cents overhead costs to each product. On the other hand, if you're making an item that takes three hours to complete, you would add nine dollars to the price just to cover overhead costs.

See also article, "Pricing Formulas for Handcraft Sellers."

Packing Charge

See Packing Materials *and* Shipping and Handling Charges.

Packing List

Each shipment to a wholesale account should include a packing list that describes the contents of each box or carton in the shipment. The information on the packing list must agree in description and number with the information shown on the invoice except that it need not include prices. Make two copies of the list, one for your files and one to be included either inside one of the cartons being shipped or, preferably, on the outside of one of the cartons. (Any office supply store or catalog sells handy stick-on packing-slip envelopes for this purpose.) When shipping more than one box or carton, be sure to mark the cartons themselves by writing "Box 1 of 3 boxes," "Box 2 of 3 boxes" and so on.

See also Invoice.

Packing Materials

Q: *What's the best way to pack art or craft objects for shipment?*

Crumpled newspaper is cheap, but it can be a problem when newspaper ink rubs off onto objects. A shop owner says shredded paper is a pain because it gets all over everything. Styrofoam peanuts and bubble-wrap are the most popular packing materials and they can be ordered by mail from most office supply catalogs.

Shipping cartons can be a problem because box manufacturers often require minimum orders of 500–1000 cartons. If you can't afford to buy cartons directly, contact box manufacturers for the names of distributors who can sell to you in smaller quantities. You can get started, of course, by purchasing these items at retail from one of the many office supply catalogs available today. Several have been listed in the resource chapter.

See also Office Supply Catalogs *and* Packing List.

Paints, Varnishes, and Other Finishes

Q: *I'd like to offer handpainted toys and other products for children. How can I find out if paints and other finishes are lead-free, and what other things should I do to avoid problems here?*

Under the *Consumer Product Safety Act* there is a ban of paint and other surface coatings (varnish, lacquer, and shellac) that contain more than 0.06 percent lead by weight. A spokesperson for the Consumer Product Safety Commission tells me the agency has no objection to the use of paint or other surface coatings on children's products so long as they comply with the lead-in-paint ban. All paints sold for household use in the United States must comply with this ban. Only paints intended for specialized uses are exempt, and such paints must bear a label that warns the paint contains lead, may be harmful if eaten or chewed, and should not be applied to toys, children's articles, or furniture.

There is one important exception: Artist's paints are exempt from the lead-in-paint ban, yet they are not required to bear a warning label regarding lead. Therefore, these paints should never be used on children's articles.

See also Consumer Safety Laws; Health Hazards; *and* Lead Testing.

Partnership

Q: *A friend and I are thinking about forming a business partnership. What are the most important things we need to consider here?*

Partnerships between or among friends often end the friendship when disagreements over business policies occur, so serious consideration should be given to the advantages and disadvantages of such a business arrangement. There are two kinds of partnerships: General and Limited. Each type may have two or more partners.

• **General Partnership**. This is easy to start and no federal requirements are involved. Owners report their profit or loss on their personal tax returns and the business ends with withdrawal of any one of the partners. Each partner shares the work load, contributing work, time, or money in amounts agreed to by all. The disadvantages of a General Partnership are that there can be conflict of authority, liability is unlimited, profits are divided, and the debts incurred by one partner must be assumed by all other partners. If the business fails, creditors can attach each partner's personal income and assets, as in an individual proprietorship.

• **Limited Partnership**. Here, general partners run the business while limited (silent) partners have no liability beyond invested money. Profits are divided per partnership agreement, and earnings are taxed as personal income. The minuses of a Limited Partnership are that it is more complicated to establish, there are special tax withholding regulations, and a legal contract must be filed with the state. Limited partners have no say in the business and general partners have unlimited liability.

See also articles, "A Solution to the Partnership Checkbook Problem" and "Three Partnership Tips."

Patent

Q: *I've been told I should patent the unique product I've designed, but is this worth the time and money it would take?*

Patents are a complicated and expensive way of protecting "intellectual property" and, in my opinion, few if any craftspeople should consider them. The process of getting a patent can take up to ten years and cost as much as $20,000 or more in patent attorney fees. Once you've got your patent, you must pay periodic maintenance fees to keep it from lapsing. These could run as much as $2,000.

Obviously, before laying out this kind of time and money, you need to determine whether there is actually a market for your product and, if so, whether you would make and sell the product yourself or have it made under license. "Patentability has nothing to do with marketability," emphasizes one marketing consultant. "Of the more than seven million products that have been patented in the United States, less than one percent has ever been marketed." Inventor Jeremy Gorman, who has over thrity-five years of experience in getting new products and ideas into the marketplace, says that ninety-seven percent of the U.S. patents issued never earn enough money to pay the patenting fee. "They just go on a plaque on the wall or in a desk drawer to impress the grandchildren fifty years later," he says. "Except for your ego, nothing is helped by having a patent on an unsalable idea, no matter how creative it is."

All a patent really does is give the inventor the right to exclude anyone else from making, using, or selling his invention. This means that if you had a great idea and were successful in getting it patented, any large company with plenty of money for lawyers could easily prevent you from selling your patented product simply by proving that your patent resembled some item they had already patented. This would automatically void your patent.

Patent attorney Mary Helen Sears believes that some inventors might be better off selling their ideas to manufacturers for a flat fee up front, or on a royalty basis. Before submitting a patentable item to a manufacturer, however, you must get the manufacturer to commit in writing that you are the owner of the idea. "Don't do this without competent legal help or you will lose all," she emphasizes.

It would be foolhardy to file for a patent without an attorney's help because there are many requirements of disclosure and conduct in the patent statute that the average person is not going to know about. When you try to do your own patent, you create more opportunity for someone to defeat your patent based on some legal rule or pitfall you've overlooked. An attorney will be more knowledgeable about these pitfalls and help you avoid them. (Based on the number of patents that are granted each year to applicants who act without the help of a patent attorney or agent, your chances for success are only about two out of a hundred.)

To hear a series of recorded messages on this topic, call the Patent and Trademark Office's toll-free number: 1-800-786-9199. For more information, subscribe to *The Dream Merchant* or join Inventors Workshop International (see resource chapter).

See also Copyright Categories of Protection; Design Patent; Inventor's Clubs and Associations; Patent and Trademark Searches; *and* Trademark.

Patent and Trademark Searches

Q: *I can't afford to hire an attorney or a trademark search firm to do a patent or trademark search for me. How can I do this myself?*

The Patent and Trademark Office (PTO) has a public search room in Arlington, Virginia, as well as a nationwide network of depository libraries (usually large city libraries) where you can conduct a search. (You can get a list of these libraries from the Patent and Trademark Office in Washington, D.C.) The depository libraries have CD-ROMs that contain the complete database of registered and pending marks. Check with your local library to see if it subscribes to an online computer service such as *Trademark Scan*. If so, they can do an economical trademark search for you. Also check to see if they have the annual directory, *Trademark Register of the U.S.*

Lists of patents are available from the PTO, which can do a patent search for you (for a reasonable fee) if you can provide the name of the inventor, approximate date of the invention, or years you wish to

A Solution to the
Partnership Checkbook Problem

Having only one bank account does not limit you to working out of a single checkbook. Here is a suggestion on how to keep track of business expenses coming out of two different locations when there is just one checkbook.

Years ago when I managed the office of a direct mail advertising firm, it was my responsibility to write all the checks for routine business bills, but because the owners didn't want me knowing their salaries and other private financial transactions, they kept one checkbook (the "master checkbook" into which all deposits were made) and I kept the other. As I needed money, my boss would simply say, "Put $10,000 in your checkbook," at which time he would deduct the same amount from his checkbook. Two checkbooks—one account. It worked like a charm.

Of course this system is dependent on one partner being responsible for the master checkbook and balancing bank statements each month, and each partner must have his or her own series of check numbers. (Banks don't care if you use two sets of check numbers for a single account.) The easiest way to accomplish this is to order the second checkbook from a mail-order check supplier, specifying the numbers you desire. (See *Checking Account* for the name of a supplier.)

See also Petty Cash.

search, and the title or subject matter of the invention. If any numbers are found, you would be provided with a list of them and could then order copies of any of interest for a nominal sum.

See also Trademark *and illustration of a patent.*

Three Partnership Tips

1. At the time you form a partnership, plan how you will eventually end it. Ask what you would do if either partner died, wanted out of the business, or wanted to buy out the other partner. In dissolving a partnership, it would be wise to hire an accountant to help determine the fair net worth of the business.

2. Protect yourself with partnership insurance. By law, at the death of a partner, a business is dissolved and can no longer operate until it is either liquidated or reorganized. For this reason, partners generally buy term insurance against each partner's illness, incapacity, or death so they will have a way to pay off a deceased partner's interest. They may also have an attorney prepare a Buy-Sell Agreement funded by life insurance. This establishes the price the survivor will pay for his or her share of the business and the amount the heirs will sell for, and the insurance provides the money to complete the transfer. In dissolving their partnership, two women worked out an agreement whereby one would make payments to the other over a three-year period and the buyer covered the contract with a declining life insurance policy in case anything happened to her before her financial obligations were complete.

3. Before signing a partnership dissolution contract, make sure the tax obligations of your partners are current. The IRS (and any other creditor) can levy any partner's account for uncollected funds, even the account of the partner who did pay his or her share. One couple reported that, two years after they dissolved a partnership with another person, the IRS levied their bank account because their former partner had not paid his income taxes for two years.

Pattern Publishing

See Break-Even Point; *all* Copyright *listings; and* Patterns, Commercial Use of.

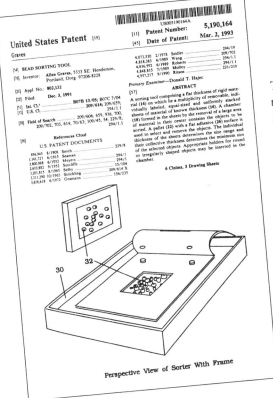

United States Patent [19]

Graves

US005190164A

[11] Patent Number: 5,190,164

[45] Date of Patent: Mar. 2, 1993

[54] BEAD SORTING TOOL

[76] Inventor: Allen Graves, 5333 SE. Henderson, Portland, Oreg. 97206-8228

[21] Appl. No.: 802,132

[22] Filed: Dec. 3, 1991

[51] Int. Cl.⁵ B07B 13/05; B07C 7/04
[52] U.S. Cl. 209/614; 209/659;
                                            294/1.1
[58] Field of Search 209/606, 659, 936, 700,
        209/702, 703, 614, 70/63; 109/45, 54; 229/8;
                                            294/1.1

[56] References Cited

U.S. PATENT DOCUMENTS

896,945	8/1908	Smith	229/8
1,141,727	6/1915	Seaman	294/1
2,600,068	6/1952	Meyers	294/1
2,610,882	9/1952	Sutcliffe	15/104
3,201,815	8/1965	Selby	209/614 X
3,211,290	10/1965	Strickling	156/235
3,658,618	4/1972	Gramann	
4,073,530	2/1978	Seidler	294/19
4,818,383	4/1989	Wang	209/702
4,836,592	6/1989	Roberts	294/1.1
4,848,815	7/1989	Molloy	221/210
4,957,217	9/1990	Ritson	294/1.1

Primary Examiner—Donald T. Hajec

[57]   ABSTRACT

A sorting tool comprising a flat thickness of rigid material (14) on which lie a multiplicity of removable, individually labeled, equal-sized and uniformly stacked sheets of material of known thickness (16). A chamber (18) formed in the sheets by the removal of a large area of material in their center contains the objects to be sorted. A pallet (22) with a flat adhesive (26) surface is used to select and remove the objects. The individual thickness of the sheets determines the size range and their collective thickness determines the minimum size of the selected objects. Appropriate holders for round or irregularly shaped objects may be inserted in the chamber.

6 Claims, 3 Drawing Sheets

30
32

Perspective View of Sorter With Frame

This is one of several pages of the registered patent document Allen Graves received from the United States Patent Office. Allen had an initial search done and did the patent application himself.

"My first application was rejected," he said, "but since I had no representation and the Patent Examiner found that the tool was patentable, he wrote claims that he would accept and that would overcome his objections. According to the book I used to prepare the application, this is the rule, not the exception, for individual unrepresented applicants. The claims that the Examiner wrote were extremely broad and appeared completely satisfactory, but I decided to consult an attorney at this point to make sure I really understood what was being said. This attorney suggested writing process claims. This would provide comprehensive protection, he explained, as not only would I be able to stop the illegal manufacture and sale and importation of the tool, but it would be illegal to import beads sized with the process the tool uses.

"I'm glad I spent the extra money. I amended the application to include the claims the Examiner wrote, and the attorney's process claims, and the application was approved."

Patterns, Commercial Use of

Q: *Is it okay to make items for sale from patterns found in magazines or commercial patterns purchased in a fabric store?*

The general rule of thumb is that you should not offer in the *wholesale marketplace* any item made from any design or pattern in a consumer crafts magazine or book, or from any pattern purchased from any other source. (With few exceptions, these patterns are intended for personal use only and, if you look closely, you may find a note on the pattern to this effect.) The fact that you can buy a pattern for a Raggedy Ann doll in your local fabric store does not give you the right to profit from the sale of Raggedy Ann dolls. Only the original creator of this doll has that right, and anyone who plans to sell such dolls commercially must enter into a licensing agreement with the copyright owner.)

This is not to say you cannot sell anything you have made from a pattern. It depends entirely on whose pattern you are using. The copyright to designs and projects appearing in craft and needlework magazines belong either to the creator or the magazine, depending on what rights an editor has purchased. Different magazines have different policies about the projects appearing in their publications or the patterns they sell separately. For example, patterns sold by *Woman's Day* bear a lengthy statement that basically says reproductions of the designs may not be sold, bartered, or traded. On the other hand, *Good Housekeeping* magazine indicates their patterns may be used for income-producing activities. *Crafts Magazine* also allows readers to use their patterns to make for-sale items at bazaars, craft fairs and boutiques, but prohibits the sale of such items in any outlet where profit will be realized by someone other than the crafter. The rule is, *when in doubt, ask*.

People often ask me about using garment patterns such as Simplicity or McCall's they have purchased in a fabric store. Although countless crafters do use such patterns to make items for sale at craft fairs, holiday boutiques, or craft malls, readers should remember that these patterns, like others mentioned above, are designed for individual use by consumers. They were never intended for commercial use. In my opinion, however, commercial use of such patterns is not as likely to create legal copyright problems as the use of designs and patterns in magazines because the pattern companies aren't going around looking for violators the way individual designers are doing. In addition, many people who sew modify commercial patterns to a considerable degree, making them virtually unrecognizable from the original pattern. Thus, if you use commercial patterns for generic items of clothing such as vests, aprons, shirts, etc. and sell them only in limited quantity at the retail level, I don't think there is much cause for alarm. However, *the only way to be sure about this is to write to the individual pattern companies and ask them if it's okay to make a limited number of items for sale from one of their patterns.*

Individual "designer patterns" that might be sold through fabric shops are something else entirely. Janet Burgess, owner of Amazon Drygoods in Davenport, Iowa, sells historic reproductions of clothing and household items as well as copyrighted patterns for Victorian and other period costumes. She says only a couple of the more than fifty pattern companies she represents include a notation on their patterns that "Reproduction for commercial purposes is expressly forbidden." From lengthy conversations with her two largest pattern suppliers, Janet has learned that one company is not much concerned about re-productions being sold on a small scale, but they really go after anyone who uses any of their charming drawings and graphics on business cards and other printed materials. "The other company is very firm in regard to any use at all of their patterns and graphics for any reason other than personal use," she reports. "If asked for permission to re-produce their patterns as ready-made garments for commercial sale, they will always say no, even if full credit and royalties are offered. Their main concern is that someone will manufacture some of their designs off shore and bring them into the United States for large-scale sale. Pirating is common today because it's difficult to catch compa-nies before they get their merchandise through Customs."

Janet adds that other pattern companies aren't likely to be concerned about the seamstress who sews a few of their skirts each year and sells them on consignment to a small boutique. She emphasizes, however, that "one must be exceedingly careful not to use the illustrations or the name of the garment as named by the pattern company."

See also Copyrights of Others *and* First Rights/All Rights Sales.

Tip

Many designers publish patterns and how-to projects but retain the right to sell finished products. You can always write to a designer in care of the magazine in which you found their pattern or project, or connect with over two hundred of them in the *Pattern Designer Directory* published by Front Room Publishers (see resource chapter for address). Some of the designers in this directory are agreeable to having their patterns used commercially while others are not. Some have set a limit on the number of items that can be made from any one pattern or require crafters to add a label or tag that shows the designer's name and copyright. There are many gray areas to this topic, so when in doubt, always go directly to the creator of the pattern and ask for permission to sell items made from that pattern.

Payment Methods

See COD Shipments; Checks Taken at Shows; Credit Card Sales; *and* Invoicing Policies.

Permits

See Licenses and Permits.

Personal Liability Insurance

Q: *If I start a business in my home, will the personal liability insurance I have on my homeowner's policy cover me in case one of my customers is injured while on my property?*

No. Personal liability insurance protects you against claims made by individuals who suffer bodily injury while on your property, but your homeowners policy does not cover any *business* activities on the premises. In the event of a lawsuit, one thing that will be considered is why the injured person was on your property in the first place. For example, a person might fall in your home while attending a holiday boutique or party plan presentation, or the UPS delivery person might slip on your icy walk while delivering a business package.

You need to discuss this problem with your insurance agent. Ask if you can extend your personal liability coverage with a business rider or an "umbrella policy" of some kind. (There are both personal and business umbrella policies.) Also check out the in-home business insurance packages now available to home business owners. They generally offer at least a million dollars worth of product and personal liability insurance.

See also Corporation *and* Home Business Insurance Policies.

Personal Loans

Q: *How do most people raise the cash they need to launch a small business at home if they can't qualify for a bank loan?*

Most people in homebased businesses today got started with some kind of personal loan, either by tapping a savings account, credit union account, life insurance policy, or the equity in their home.

If you have an insurance policy with cash value, you may be able to borrow on it at rates as low as five percent. If you have a Certificate of Deposit, you don't need to cash it in to get money. Instead, consider using the certificate as collateral for a temporary loan. Generally, you can borrow up to eighty-five percent of the amount of the certificate at an interest rate of perhaps three percent over what the account is earning. Since your account will continue to earn interest, that means your actual loan cost would be only three percent.

Although interest rates are generally very high on cash advances on a credit card (21 percent or more) many small-business people take comfort in knowing that in an emergency, they have access to immediate cash up to the limit set on the card.

See also Loans.

Tip

If you have a friend or relative who has money in a savings account, their passbook can be used as collateral for a bank loan. Although your friend or relative could not withdraw the amount outstanding on your loan, the savings account would lose no interest and as you paid back the loan, you would free up that amount of funds in the savings account.

Personal Property Used for Business

When you start a business that utilizes personal property already paid for (such as a typewriter, computer, desk, or other office furnishings), you can gain a tax deduction by transferring this property over to your business. Estimate the value of each item being transferred (the IRS seldom questions any reasonable amount) and make up a bill of sale. Then write a check on your business account to you or your spouse. (Yes, you can write a check to yourself, endorse it, and deposit it in another account.) Once the property has been purchased by your business, it can be depreciated or expensed like any other purchase of equipment or furnishings.

See also Business Expenses, Tax-Deductible.

Petty Cash

Q: *What's the easiest way to keep track of miscellaneous cash purchases made each month for my business?*

You can either keep a petty cash box (which I think is a pain in the neck), or you can simply spindle all your receipts for things you've paid cash for. Tally them at the end of each month and reimburse your personal outlay of cash with a check written to you on your business account. Either cash this check or deposit it to your personal account. (All you're doing is moving money from one pocket to another, but this is necessary if you wish to deduct these cash expenditures on your income tax return.)

Photo Kits

Here is an idea that would work well for many readers who want to break into wholesaling but cannot yet afford to buy color flyers. Select half a dozen of your best products and photograph each of them as artistically as possible. Take the original photographs to a bulk photo service center and get as many copies of each as needed for a mailing to your best customers and newest prospects. (Estimate cost at about twenty cents each.) Then make up "photo kits" by punching a hole in the upper left-hand corner of the pictures, adding an attractive protective cover that includes your business name, logo (if you have one), and your telephone number. Tie this little bundle together with a piece of leather thong or gold cording (depending on the type of handcrafts you sell). Send the photo kit with a cover letter and your wholesale price list. A couple of weeks later, follow up this mailing with a phone call to everyone who has not yet placed an order.

P.O. Box Address

Q: *I plan to offer products for sale by mail. Should I do business from my home address or rent a post office box? Are people as likely to order from a P.O. Box number as a street address?*

I've used a P.O. Box address since 1971 and have never seen any indication of concern from buyers. Although the U.S. Postal Service will deliver business mail to a home address, there are some advantages to using a post office box address.

First, it enables you to keep a low profile in the community if you don't want your neighbors to know what you're doing. Second, it deters your customers from dropping by to see your workshop or studio. More important, if local zoning laws prohibit or limit the activities of a homebased business, doing business out of a post office box can be a good way to get around this problem. One of my readers reported his local license bureau told him to obtain a post office box number for his business address because the post office was in a commercial zone and that would eliminate the need for any special use permit that zoning officials might ordinarily require.

NOTE: Some states require the inclusion of a street address along with a post office box address on business stationery and other printed materials, so check to see if this applies to you.

See also Sole Proprietorship *and* Zoning Laws.

Tip

To find the owner of a company operating out of a post office box address, request a copy of the company's registration form from the secretary of state in the state capital where the organization does business.

Poetry, Use of

See Copyrights of Others.

Postage Meter

If you plan to send a lot of mail, you might want to get information from Pitney Bowes about its postage meters. They offer a variety of systems, some of which have been designed for small mailers. These machines are available on a lease basis and are generally offered alone or with an electronic scale. (I do not recommend leasing an electronic scale because you can buy a scale for what you would probably pay for a year's lease of one.) For more information, call Pitney Bowes at 1-800-672-6937.

Postal Regulations

Q: *What postal rules and regulations might affect my homebased business?*

If you use the mail to sell products or services, be aware the U.S. Postal Service is the watchdog of the mail order industry. They work in close conjunction with the FTC, which is especially concerned about truth in advertising and false representation of products. You aren't likely to have any problems here if you are always careful to accurately represent yourself and your products to your mail order customers.

Other areas of concern to the Postal Service are chain letters and small business scams. Postal authorities are constantly pursuing promoters of chain letters and pyramid schemes as well as anyone else who runs a scam that involves the mail. Don't get involved with any of these people because doing so could put your name on a list being investigated by the U.S. Postal Inspection Service.

See also Nature Items *and* Scams.

Post Office

See Certified Mail; COD Shipments; Mail, Classes of; Mail Lists, Rental of; Mail, Size Regulations; Nature Items; P.O. Box Address; Postage Meter; Priority Mail; ZIP Code; *and article, "A Lost Mail Horror Story."*

Pottery

See Lead Testing.

PPD

When you see this abbreviation after a price—and it's always written in lower case immediately following a price—it means that shipping and handling costs have been included in the price. Example: $16.95 ppd.

See also Shipping and Handling Charges.

Premiums

Are promotional premiums something the average crafts marketer should use?

If you're talking about commercial premium items, I would say no. If you're talking about inexpensive premiums you can create yourself, yes. A promotional premium is something you give away to build customer good will, draw attention to your products, or encourage prospects to order from you. They are generally used by service providers who print their name and address on some item in hopes that customers and prospects won't forget them. You probably have several premiums in your home, from emery boards, pens, and yardsticks to refrigerator magnets, key chains, and calendars. While such commercial items aren't likely to work for a craft seller, you might experiment with some "freebie" items that express your creativity.

See also Freebies *and* Premium Sales.

Premium Sales

Premiums are items used by some companies to entice buyers into purchasing some product or service, and such sales are often made when a bright entrepreneur sees a product on the market that can be tied to one of his or own products.

As you know, banks may use premiums to entice people to open savings accounts while manufacturers use premiums to lure consumers into their dealer outlets to look at the newest model now being offered. Publishers may use books as premiums to entice new subscribers or get expired subscribers back again. Although few craft sellers can deliver the thousands of units a premium buyer is likely to want, small publishers in this field should definitely explore their marketing opportunities here.

Prepaid Legal Services

Q: *What's the least expensive way for me to get legal help for my business on a regular basis?*

If you've ever wished you had a lawyer "on tap" you could call occasionally for quick questions and small legal jobs, it would pay to join an organization that offers its members affordable prepaid legal services. As a member of a prepaid legal plan, you are likely to get (1) unlimited calls to an attorney about either personal or business matters; (2) one letter or phone call per topic discussed; (3) review of legal documents; (4) preparation of a will; (5) representation against moving traffic violations or traffic tickets and so on.

A prepaid legal services plan will give you the most attorney representation at the lowest possible cost. One home business organization that has a good plan is the American Association of Home Based Businesses in Bethesda, MD. For less than $200 a year (which is less than many lawyers today charge for an hour's worth of time), you can buy the "family package" of services, which this organization says is good for homebased businesses. (The business plan runs about $600/year.)

See also Lawyer.

Preprinted Papers

If you have a computer and laser printer, you can create full-color business cards, stationery, brochures, flyers, and other printed materials by using colorful preprinted papers available from suppliers such as Paper Direct (1-800-A-PAPERS) and Queblo (1-800-523-9080). These papers are not inexpensive (generally about twenty dollars for a box of one hundred sheets), but when you really want to make an impression on a few prospective buyers or customers, they do the job beautifully. For the names of other suppliers who offer designer papers for your laser printer, read computer magazines.

See also Presentation Folders and Table Signs *and* Office Supply Catalogs.

Prepublication Offer

This is a special money-saving offer made to a selected list of customers. A few weeks before a new product is scheduled for release, the seller offers it at a money-saving prepublication price (usually twenty percent off retail price). Book publishers often use this strategy to get a surge of orders to cover up-front printing costs of a new title, but other product makers have also used it successfully. You must be careful to explain to customers exactly when you will ship the new product and not make the prepublication offer until you are absolutely sure shipment will be made on the date you indicate. Otherwise you may be in violation of the FTC's Thirty-Day Mail Order Rule.

See also Federal Trade Commission Rules.

Presentation Folders and Table Signs

If you want to create an artistic presentation of your work—something that might include a cover letter, business card, photos, brochure, and price list—consider using the beautiful presentation folders and binders available from Paper Direct (1-800-A-PAPERS). These come in different patterns with precut slots for business cards. This company also offers attractive acrylic holders into which you can insert your printed signs or sales messages at a crafts fair or other exhibit of your work.

Price List

Q: *What information should be included on my price lists for individual buyers and wholesale accounts?*

You should have separate retail and wholesale price lists that can be adjusted and reprinted as necessary for insertion into your brochures or catalogs. (Don't include prices with the description of catalog items unless you expect those prices to remain good until your next catalog reprinting.) Your price list should include all the regular information, such as business name and logo (if you have one), address, telephone, fax number, and lines for all the information you need from customers who order.

Retail price lists (for consumers) should include information on how much sales tax and shipping charges must be added. If you don't expect to ship within thirty days, include a note about how long delivery will take so you don't violate the FTC's Thirty-day Mail Order Rule. Example: "Most items are shipped within a few days, but please allow three to six weeks in case of back order."

Wholesale price lists should include any special ordering instructions you may have about minimum order/reorder requirements, terms of payment, how and when orders will be shipped, shipping charge information, your cancellation or returns policy, any special ordering instructions or information about colors and sizes, plus your guarantee, if one is offered. Here is an example of how the House of Threads & Wood, Inc. in Rogers, Arkansas, presents their ordering instruction on the back of their Wholesale Price List/ Order Form:

- Item minimums as shown ($5 service charge for under minimum orders); $50 opening order minimum; $50 reorder minimum.
- Payment required with order or order will ship COD. No credit cards accepted on wholesale orders. Net fifteen day terms may be established with references. There will be a one percent penalty charge assessed on accounts over thirty days. Returned checks subject to $15 charge.
- In-stock items usually ship UPS next day. We ship UPS unless otherwise specified.
- Cancellations/Returns: Cancellations must be made fourteen days in advance of ship date. Refused or returned orders subject to all freight charges.

See also Federal Trade Commission Rules; Guaranty of Satisfaction; Order Policies; *and sample Wholesale Price List/Order Form.*

Pricing Guidelines

Q: *Pricing is my biggest problem. How can I tell if my prices are right for the special wholesale markets I'm trying to reach?*

A thorough discussion of how to price art and handcrafted products is beyond the scope of this book, but this book's companion volume, *Handmade for Profit*, includes a lengthy chapter on this topic. For our purposes here, I will provide only a few general pricing guidelines.

If you're selling directly to consumers at retail, anything goes where pricing is concerned. Strive always to get the highest price the market will bear. The general rule of thumb is that a good price is one low enough for the product to sell and high enough to yield a satisfactory profit to its maker.

The picture changes when one moves into wholesaling, however. Now industry markups must be taken into consideration. Unless both a product and its pricing structure are just right, it will be impossible to crack certain wholesale distribution channels. Whenever you have a

Name _____

Company _____

Shipping Address _____

Mailing Address _____
(required for bulk mailings)

City, State, Zip+4 _____

Phone _____

Social Security # or Driver's License # _____ Ship Date _____
(required on first order only)

HOUSE of Threads & WOOD INC.
10 Brooks Drive
Rogers, Arkansas 72756
(501) 631-1438

8 a.m. - 5 p.m. CST
Monday - Friday

Pat & Ed Endicott
10 Brooks Drive
Rogers, AR 72756

800 / 442-2130

FAX: 501-631-6964

WHOLESALE PRICE LIST / ORDER FORM

Qty	ITEM - Size/Color/Design/Combination	Code	Minimums	Price Each	Total
	Paw Print Placemat - Set of 4: BM__CB__NM__NCB__DG__RW__GB__A__	PPP	min 2	$28.50	
	Coordinating Napkins: Country Blue__ Navy__ Dark Green__	NAP	min 8	1.50	
	Scented Coasters: BM__CB__NM__NCB__DG__RW__GB__A__	SC	min 12	1.75	
	Unscented Coasters - Set of 4: BM__CB__NM__NCB__DG__RW__GB__A__	USC	min 6	6.25	
	Panhandlers, PAIR: BM__CB__NM__NCB__DG__RW__GB__A__	PH	min 6	4.00	
	Log Cabin Potholder: BM__CB__NM__NCB__DG__RW__GB__	LCP	min 6	3.00	
	Bun Warmer: Assorted prints	BW	min 6	3.75	
	Tea Cozy: BM__CB__NM__NCB__DG__RW__GB__	TC	min 4	9.00	
	Toaster Cover: BM__CB__NM__NCB__DG__RW__GB__	TC2	min 4	12.00	
	Seasonal Tablerunner: Assorted prints (swatches available)	TR	min 3	11.50	
	Seasonal Mantle Scarf: Assorted prints (swatches available)	MS	min 3	11.50	
	Colors available for Trivets are dictated by center prints				
	Potpourri Trivets		can assort		
	Cottage/Bird House Series: MX4 only				
	Homespun Series: MX only	T-C	Qty 6-23	5.25 or	
	Garden Series: MX2 only	T-H	Qty 24+	5.00	
	School/Quilt Series: BM__NM__RW__	T-G		↓	
	Apple Series: MX3 only	T-SQ		↓	
	16" Split Heart Wire Hanger	T-A		↓	
	7 1/2" Heart Wire Hanger w/dowel	16HH	min 3	2.00	
	3 Pocket Hanging: BM__CB__NM__NCB__DG__RW__GB__A__	3WHH	min 3	1.75	
	Ohio Star Wallhanging: BM__CB__NM__NCB__DG__RW__GB__A__	3WH	min 3	10.00	
	Cute as a Button Hanging with dowel: Assorted scenes	OHWH	min 3	10.50	
	Mini Cute as a Button Hanging: School__Americana__	CAB	min 6	7.00	
	Quilted Pillow 12": BM__CB__NM__NCB__DG__RW__GB__A__	MCAB	min 6	4.50	
	Quilted Pillow 16": BM__CB__NM__NCB__DG__RW__GB__A__ Log Cabin__Split Rail__	SPIL	min 3	12.50	
	Armchair Caddy: BM__CB__NM__NCB__DG__RW__GB__A__ Log Cabin__Split Rail__	LPIL	min 3	15.00	
	Keychain: BM__CB__NM__NCB__DG__RW__GB__A__	AC	min 6	8.25	
	Card Carrying Keychain: BM__CB__NM__NCB__DG__RW__GB__A__	KC	min 12	1.85	
	Oak Display Rack can be used for both size Keychains or Thing on a String. $14.00 value offset with product as described below	CCKC	min 12	3.00	
	12KC, 12CCKC + 4 KC free	Plan A1			
	12KC, 12CCKC + 3CCKC free	Plan A2			
	24KC +4KC free	Plan B		72.20	
	24CCKC + 3CCKC free	Plan C		72.20	
	18TS + 2TS free	Plan D		58.40	
				86.00	
				77.00	
			Total Side 1		
			Total Side 2		
			Shipping		
		TOTAL ORDER			

★ ★ **Thank you for your order!** ★ ★

(OVER)

★ ★ **A COMPLETE ORDER FORM WILL BE ENCLOSED WITH YOUR SHIPMENT** ★ ★

Call 1-800-442-2130 today to place your order

Effective 1/19/97

product you think would sell in a special market (floral or garden shop, hardware store, fabric shop, chain store, etc.) you'll have to read trade journals or visit trade shows to learn what the standard markups are for each industry of interest. Unlike craft and gift shops that normally double a seller's wholesale price to get the retail price, other buyers, such as mail order catalog houses, may triple or quadruple a seller's wholesale price, resulting in a retail price that's too high to sell.

See also Break-Even Point; Catalog Houses, Selling to; Discounts; Mark-ups; Overhead; Price List; Shipping and Handling Charges; Supplies, Buying Wholesale; Trade Shows; *and article, "Pricing Formulas for Handcraft Sellers."*

Printed Materials

Q: *Which printed materials are most important to artists and craft sellers?*

It depends on what and to whom you are trying to sell. If you sell primarily at art or craft fairs, a business card, brochure, and price list may be all you really need to stimulate follow-up mail order sales after a show. If you are interested in actively promoting to your craft fair buyers after a show, you will need promotional postcards that announce your next craft fair appearance and follow-up mailings of a brochure or catalog.

If you are trying to wholesale products to shops and stores, you may not get the response you are seeking without good stationery and a full-color presentation of your products. If you cannot yet afford color flyers, see the *Photo Kits* listing for an affordable idea that may work for you in the interim.

It is beyond the scope of this book to provide detailed guidelines on how to design professional-looking printed materials and use them to increase sales, but you will find a whole chapter on this topic in my book *Handmade for Profit* (M. Evans), along with eighty-four illustrations of letterheads, business cards, brochures, postcards, catalogs, hang tags, and labels used by professional artists and craft sellers.

See also Brochure; Hang Tags and Labels; Mail, Size Regulations; Office Supply Catalogs; Preprinted Papers; Presentation Folders; Printing Terms; Self-Mailers; Stationery; *and article, "How to Cut Printing Costs."*

Pricing Formulas for Handcraft Sellers

Without identifying the object we are making, let's assume that our materials cost is going to be $1.50, we can make three units an hour, and we want $10/hour for our labor. (Labor cost per unit, then, will be $3.33.) In the last formula, we also will add $.20 for overhead and a twenty percent profit based on the whole-sale price.

A. Materials x 3 + Labor = Wholesale price x 2 = Retail price
$1.50 x 3 = $4.50 + $3.33 = $7.83 x 2 = $15.66

B. Materials + Labor x 3 = Wholesale price x 2 = Retail price
$1.50 + $3.33 x 3 = $14.49 x 2 = $28.98

C. Materials + Labor + Overhead + Profit =
Wholesale Price x 2 = Retail Price
$1.50 + $3.33 + $.20 + $1.01 = $6.04 x 2 = $12.08
($1.20 + $3.33 + $.20 = $5.03 x 20% = $1.01)

Interesting, isn't it? Now if the item we were making happened to be a piece of jewelry, all three prices would be realistic, since jewelry runs the gamut in both price and style. However, if the item happened to be a Christmas ornament or a ceramic coffee mug, all prices would be high, although certain mugs and ornaments might sell for twelve to sixteen dollars in exclusive shops. The point I'm trying to make is that formulas are fun, but they often are impractical, and the retail price still has to be adjusted to whatever consumer market one is trying to reach.

— An excerpt from the revised fifth edition of Homemade Money *by Barbara Brabec (1997, Betterway Books)*

Tip

Before you order stationery or brochures imprinted with your name and address, register your business name locally to make sure no one else is using the name you've selected. (See also *Business or Trade Name Registration/Protection.*)

Printing Terms

When ordering stationery, business forms, brochures, and other printing, communication with the printer will be easier if you are familiar with the following printing terms:

- Bleed—is when the printed image or a color screen extends to the trim edge of the page.
- Color Proof—is something you should get before authorizing a large print run of a brochure. (This costs a little extra, but it gives you a chance to spot any errors before the job is printed.)
- Color Separation—is the process of separating full color illustrations into the primary printing colors in negative or positive form.
- Matte Finish—is dull paper finish without a gloss, often used on photographs.
- Mechanical—is a term for artwork that is all pasted up and camera-ready. (All type, photos, line art, etc. are positioned on one piece of artboard.)
- Ream—500 sheets of paper. (Stationery is often ordered by the ream.)

See also Preprinted Papers *and article, "How to Cut Printing Costs."*

Priority Mail

Q: *Is there any advantage to using Priority Mail for small shipments of art or handcrafts instead of Insured Fourth-Class Mail or United Parcel Service?*

Yes. In many cases, Priority Mail costs only a nickel more than parcel post and it gets preferential treatment with delivery anywhere in the country usually within two or three days. If you regularly ship small packages weighing eleven ounces or more, the use of Priority Mail (which receives first-class handling) not only speeds delivery but saves you money. The post office will provide all the free Priority Mail envelopes and boxes you need, and there is quite a variety of sizes and shapes. Currently, you can ship a Priority envelope or box weighing up to two pounds anyplace in the country for just three dollars. The same package shipped by UPS could cost nearly two dollars more, depending on the delivery zone. The one big advantage UPS has over Priority Mail is that each shipment is automatically covered for one hundred dollars worth of insurance, and UPS has the ability to track shipments while the postal service does not.

See also United Parcel Service.

Tip

Anything you can fit into one of the standard Priority Mail Envelopes will go at the two-pound rate even if the package weighs more than two pounds.

Product Labeling

See Hang Tags and Labels *and* Labels or Tags Required by Law.

Product Liability Insurance

Q: *My business is small, my products are safe, and I sell only through craft malls or at fairs. Do I really need product liability insurance?*

The purchase of insurance is always an individual choice, but most craft sellers today operate without product liability insurance because they can't afford it.

What product liability insurance does is protect you against lawsuits by consumers who are injured while using one of your products. Theoretically, everyone who makes and sells a product to the public is at risk, but most handmade items are so safe that the risk of the average crafter being sued is quite small. Your need for this kind of insurance has much to do with the kind of products you make and the size of your homebased business. Your financial risk will increase in direct proportion to the volume of business you do annually and the number of individual products you put into the marketplace. The cost of product liability insurance varies greatly from state to state and is also based on annual gross (or anticipated) sales, the number of products you sell, and the possible risks associated with each of them. If you find you cannot afford an individual product liability policy, check out the in-home business insurance packages, most of which offer a minimal amount of product liability insurance.

Once you enter the wholesale marketplace with a line of craft products, you may find that some buyers—particularly national mail order catalog houses and buyers of children's products— won't deal with you unless you have product liability insurance. Products for children naturally fall into a higher-risk category. (For an example of weird things that can happen where children's products are concerned, we need only recall the national news stories during the 1996 Christmas season about the dolls that were "eating" children's hair.)

In discussing this topic with my American Family Insurance agent, he said product liability insurance is "an individual thing. So much depends on the size of the business, the degree of risk inherent in that particular area and the number of such claims that have been received in the past." He then recounted the story of how coverage had been refused to a woman who was launching a needlework kit because there was a chance children could get hold of the needles. "This is a perfect illustration of how insurance companies think," he added.

See also Consumer Safety Laws; Guarantees and Warranties; Home Business Insurance Policies; and Lead Testing.

How to Cut Printing Costs

Look for a printer who will listen to your needs and work within the budget you have. You may find it necessary to develop relationships with two or more printers, since each may specialize in a particular type of printing such as book printing, envelopes, catalogs, booklets, or newsletters. (A list of such printers will be found in Marie Kiefer's *Directory of Printers*. See Ad-Lib Publications in the resource chapter.)

Once you've found a good printer or two, give them your loyalty. The more work you have printed, the more attention your jobs will receive. As a valuable customer for the printer, you may find yourself receiving special customer discounts or Net thirty-day terms instead of payment up front. (This is a great boon to your cash flow as it enables you to print something, get it in the mail, and have money coming back from that mailing before you have to pay the printer's bill.)

Prior to printing any job, get paper samples and cost estimates so there won't be surprises later. Always ask for recommendations on how you might cut costs without lowering quality. Color is expensive, but by substituting duotones or screens, you can create different shades of the same color and dramatically cut printing costs.

Tip

To lower your risk of a lawsuit due to a defective product, never make express warranties (claims) about how a product will perform. With or without insurance, it's a good idea to make your products as safe as possible. Also take a sharp look at everything you are presently selling and try to imagine the dumbest thing anyone could do to hurt themselves with your products. Create special hang tags if buyers need to be alerted in any way. (Examples: "This doll is intended for adult collectors and should be kept out of children's hands" or, "To avoid breakage, do not subject this item to extreme heat or cold.")

Profit and Loss (P&L) Statement

See Financial Statements *and sample P&L form nearby.*

Pro Forma

Shipping *pro forma* means you will send your customer an invoice for the merchandise they have ordered and ship it as soon as payment as been received. (If they send a check, wait until it clears the bank.) *Pro forma* shipments aren't without problems, however. As one crafter told me, "Half the time we pack the shipment, send the invoice and then we wait and wait, and sometimes they cancel the order and we have to restock all the merchandise."

See also COD Shipments.

Purchase Order

In the typical homebased business, purchase orders generally come in, rather than go out. However, you might consider using a purchase order form each time you order office supplies or raw materials of any kind. This will not only give you a handy record of who you're doing business with but will serve as a reminder of incoming supplies and invoices that need to be paid.

Tip

Your use of a purchase order may change the way you are perceived by manufacturers, distributors, or wholesalers who are often reluctant to give wholesale prices to craftspeople. Since only businesses generally use such forms, your use of them might make the difference in whether a supplier will sell to you at wholesale or not.

Raw Materials

See Bones, Claws, and Ivory; Fabrics; Feathers; Found Objects; Fur Products; Nature Items; Paints, Varnishes, and Other Finishes; Wool and Other Textiles; *and* Supplies, Buying Wholesale.

PROFIT AND LOSS WORKSHEET

_____ (name of business) _____

PROFIT AND LOSS STATEMENT
For Period Ending _____

1. SALES [1] $_____

2. COST OF GOODS SOLD [2] $_____
3. GROSS PROFIT MARGIN [3] $_____

4. ADMINISTRATIVE & GENERAL EXPENSE [4] $_____

5. NET PROFIT BEFORE TAXES [5] $_____

_Explanatory Note: The figures needed for this financial statement
will be lifted from your more detailed Income Statement as follows:_

      (1) Total Income figure
      (2) Total Cost of Goods Sold figure
      (3) Trading Profit figure
      (4) Total Administrative Expenses figure
      (5) Net Operating Profit Before Taxes figure

Record-keeping

Memory fails, but records endure. The longer you are in business, the more records you will find yourself needing or simply wanting to keep for curiosity's sake. Since there are no rules for keeping records, you can have fun creating those you want or need. Doing them manually or on computer will be your choice.

See also Business Records, Protection of; Financial and Tax Records; *and* Inventory.

Refunds

If a customer returns a product or publication in undamaged condition because you have guaranteed satisfaction, you must send a refund promptly. If the price the customer paid included shipping charges, you should keep the shipping charges and refund only the actual cost of the product unless the product was defective to begin with. (This is standard procedure with all mail order catalog houses.)

When you receive a check from a customer who has accidentally overpaid on an order (generally because of an error in addition) or one who has sent money for two products when only one is currently available, it is prudent to wait until the check clears (usually within ten days) before sending the refund. If you refund immediately and the check happens to bounce, you would lose twice. If the amount is only a couple of dollars, you might prefer to send your customer a credit memo that can be applied to any future order for any item in your catalog, or returned for cash refund.

Registered Mail

This type of mail offers secured delivery for items of significant value, such as jewelry or stock certificates. It travels safely locked and delivery is recorded on signed receipts by postal authorities.

Rent-a-Space Shops

Q: *What's the difference between craft malls and rent-a-space shops?*

Rent-a-space shops are similar to craft malls in that they both rent space to individual sellers, but they are generally smaller than craft malls. Some are laid out like a mall with one display area after another while others are set up like a gift or craft shop with display controlled by the shop owner or manager. Some shops simply rent shelf space, wall space, or a corner nook while also taking handcrafts on consignment or selling a line of commercial goods. In some shops, crafters must either work in the shop for a little while each week or pay a higher commission on sales.

Treasure Caché, a chain of franchise retail craft outlets in selected shopping malls and tourist areas operates on a rent-a-space basis but charges a hefty commission on sales as well. Although professional crafters may be able to get much higher retail prices in these exclusive handcraft shops, they must produce in volume to do well here. For more information, look for Treasure Caché on the Internet or write to the address given in the resource chapter.

See also Craft Mall Selling.

Resale Tax Number

See Tax Exemption Certificate.

Retirement Plans

See IRA *and* Keogh Plan.

Return Receipt Mail

When you want proof that a piece of mail has been delivered, return receipt mail gives you a postcard in the mail that indicates the date the mail was received and who signed for it.

Returns Policy

Q: *How do I deal with the problem of customers wanting to return merchandise they have ordered?*

To avoid unauthorized returns from customers, you must establish a returns policy and include on your price list, order form, and invoice the terms under which returned merchandise will be accepted. If you allow returns, realize that a certain amount of returned merchandise will be returned in unsalable condition because it has been improperly packed for shipment or has been excessively handled prior to return. Also, many sellers have told me that merchandise is often returned without the hang tags they went out with, or they come back with price stickers you can't get off. What the restocking fee does, then, is help you salvage some of your loss. Below are some examples of returns notations I've found on craft sellers' printed literature:

- Notify within five days of damage or shortage. Ten percent restocking fee on all returned merchandise. No returns accepted after thirty days.
- All returns must be made within thirty days. Merchandise must be in the same condition as when it left our shop. Returned merchandise subject to shipping fee and fifteen percent restocking fee.
- Cancellations must be made fourteen days in advance of ship date. Refused or returned orders subject to all freight charges.

I like the personal touch one seller used: "I take a great deal of pride in my work, and if you're unhappy, I'll probably take it personally, but that's allright. Please just repack the doll carefully, include the packing slip or enclose a note with your comments and the adjustment you would like. Ship prepaid and insured. The exception is personalized items, which are nonreturnable."

See also Invoice; Invoicing Policies; Minimum/Maximum Order Policy; Price List; *and* Refunds.

Royalties on Books

Q: *What kind of royalties are offered by book publishers, and do I need an attorney's help with the contract?*

Book royalties vary considerably, depending on current industry standards and what individual publishers can afford or are willing to pay. As for hiring an attorney to check a royalties contract, you aren't likely to gain much unless the attorney routinely works with author/publisher contracts. (See *Author/Publisher Contract.*)

• **Trade Books**. Trade book publishers are those who sell primarily to bookstores, libraries, schools, etc. They work only on a royalty basis and royalties generally start at five percent on paperback editions and ten percent on hardcover editions (on either retail or net price). Royalties higher than a publisher's "norm" must be negotiated. If a publisher insists on a low royalty, however, try to get an escalation clause stipulating that royalties will increase after a certain number of books have been sold (10,000, 25,000, 50,000, etc.) This may not be difficult to get since the average trade book today may never sell in such large quantities. (Aggressive marketing on an author's part will make a big difference in book sales and total royalties.)

Since publishers often wholesale books at discounts greater than fifty percent, royalty arrangements based on net receipts are not particularly desirable, especially when a contract has a clause that stipulates royalties will diminish (or be halved) on books sold at discounts greater than this. In this case, you might be envisioning royalties much greater than what you'll actually receive. Although professional writers with a track record may be able to demand and get more contract considerations from a publisher than a novice writer, beginners may get better royalties if they can find a book agent who will represent them. (To find book agents, see *Literary Market Place* directory in your library.)

• **Art/Craft "Floppy Books" and Leaflets**. Within the crafts and needlecrafts industries are publishers who produce "floppy books." I'm sure you've seen examples of these full-color books (twelve to twenty-four pages) in craft and needlework shops. According to reports my readers have sent through the years, payments for books of this kind vary considerably. Some publishers work on a royalty basis while others buy material outright. Here are a few examples:

- five percent royalty on a book that sold only 5,000 copies
- $375 for material in the book, plus four cents per book after the first 10,000 copies had been printed, with a stipulation that royalties would terminate after $19,600 had been paid to the author
- three percent cash advance on an initial printing of 50,000 copies of a needlework leaflet. Her royalty (not disclosed) was based on the net (wholesale) price.
- six cent royalty on the wholesale price of a booklet retailing for $2.25 in shops
- $1750 for all rights to several patterns and designs for stuffed animals and pillows from a publisher that often buys material outright. This same publisher had paid as little as $500 to other designers. (The difference has much to do with a designer's reputation, how many other books of a similar nature a publisher already has in its line and how sales of such books are faring.)

See also Licensing Arrangements *and* Royalty Arrangements, Other.

Tip

In negotiating a publisher contract, one author who has worked with publishers on both an outright sale and royalty basis says you need to consider (1) how many books will be printed and (2) how long most of the publisher's books are kept in print. Another points out that designers who do not do their own artwork or written instructions are likely to receive lower royalties than those who are skilled in this area. Developing these skills now could translate to extra dollars in the future.

Royalty Arrangements, Other

In addition to the discussions given to royalties in other parts of this book, here are a few "royalty tidbits" that might be helpful to some readers:

- **Clothing Designs.** "Royalties vary from company to company," reports a manufacturer of ski-wear. "A flat fee plus a percentage is common practice. An example might be a flat fee of $1500–$2000, plus six percent for the first year, five percent the second year, four percent the third and so on. Some clothing manufacturers just pay a flat fee of from $100–$300."

• **Greeting Cards.** Generally, outright payments of between $125–$300 per card are made until one has an established reputation and some experience with a particular company. Royalties are usually paid only to artists with substantial reputations and talents.

• **Embroidery Kits.** When one of my readers wrote to the one company in the United States that makes Bunka embroidery kits (all others come from Japan), she was told that a kit that retailed for about $30 would pay only a 25-cent royalty to the designer, and after three years the design would become theirs. Don't ever sell your creativity for so little money. You could make and sell your own needlework kits or designs for much greater profit.

See also Designer Fabrics, Commercial Use of; Licensing Arrangements; Patent; Patterns, Commercial Use of; *and* Royalties on Books.

Rubber Stamps, Commercial Use of

See Copyrights of Others.

Safety Deposit Box

One of the best ways to protect a homebased business is to rent a safety deposit box to hold irreplaceable records, papers, and computer back-up disks or tapes. Do consider, however, that while a safety deposit box may be water- and fire-resistant, it is not waterproof or fireproof. This could make a big difference if you happen to live in an area that is prone to floods or earthquakes.

Tip

Before renting a safety deposit box with someone else, be sure to ask the bank's policy about sealing the box in the event of the other person's death. You would not want to lose access to your most valuable business records.

Sales Commissions

Q: *I know I have to pay a sales commission to anyone who helps me sell my work, but what percentage is standard?*

Commissions are a percentage of sales you pay to someone for selling your work, and they run the gamut from ten to fifty percent depending on who you are working with. For example, you might:

- consign your work to an art gallery or consignment shop where the commission could range between thirty and fifty percent of the retail price
- consign your work to a local holiday boutique where the sales commission may vary from twenty-five to forty percent
- occupy space in a rent-a-space shop that charges a monthly fee and may also take a sales commission of sixteen to twenty percent of the retail price
- make an arrangement with the local beauty shop or some merchant to display and sell some of your products, for which you might offer a twenty-five percent sales commission and increase it if that isn't acceptable
- work with a literary agent whose commission will generally be fifteen percent of your royalties
- hire a sales representative or agency that will typically take fifteen to twenty percent of net sales

See also Author/Publisher Contract; Consignment Selling; Rent-a-Space Shops; Sales Representatives; *and* Toy and Game Brokers.

Sales Representatives

Q: *I need help in reaching new wholesale outlets. How can I find a good sales rep and what will this cost?*

Many sales rep organizations have teams of individual reps who cover specific regions or the whole country. Because artists and craft sellers cannot produce in sufficient quantity to interest most sales rep organizations, most will do better if they work with only one or two individual reps. Sales reps can be found by reading trade magazines, visiting trade shows or gift showrooms, or networking with other craft sellers. One of the best sources of such information, however, is the *Directory of Wholesale Reps for Craft Professionals* published by Northwoods Trading Company (listed in resource chapter). It includes listings for over a hundred companies interested in hearing from craft sellers with wholesale lines.

Crafts manufacturer Dodie Eisenhauer has found it profitable to work with a few individual reps. Her contract with them does not specify particular territories, but Dodie has agreed not to sign up other reps who are representing her at certain trade shows. One rep displays her work in a permanent showroom and receives a twenty percent commission on sales (wholesale price). Dodie also has a couple of "road reps" who show her products to various shops and stores. These reps receive a fifteen percent commission because their overhead costs are lower than that of the showroom rep. The sales reps receive their commissions as soon as Dodie receives payment for her invoice, and at year's end, she sends them a 1099 form showing total earnings.

Some rep contracts stipulate that the sales commission must be sent as soon as they have made a sale, but this is not standard practice in the industry and you should never agree to do this. The primary concern of a sales rep is to make a sale; they are not concerned about your getting paid. If they sell to a questionable account who doesn't pay your invoice, you lose the value of your merchandise, but if the rep doesn't get paid, he or she has lost only the time it took to make that one call.

Professional sales representatives will have their own contract, probably filled with fine print you need to read very carefully. But if you should decide to hire a friend or some other entrepreneurial individual to rep for you, you may have to draft your own sales rep agreement.

See also Trade Shows; *sample agreement; and article, "Sales Rep Agreement."*

Tip

If an individual sales rep works for you and only you, that person cannot legally be called an independent contractor but could be considered a statutory employee for tax purposes. Individuals who work for you and other companies as well, however, can qualify as independent contractors. Both types of workers need to receive 1099 tax forms at year's end. (For more information on this topic, see *Statutory Employees*.)

A Sales Rep Agreement

In addition to the basic points covered in the nearby sample, craft sellers should include clauses about:

1. Product Samples. Display room samples are generally provided free of charge while road samples may be charged to the rep's account at half the wholesale price. Make sure there is a provision for getting back your showroom samples if the agreement is cancelled.

2. Printed Materials. Clarify what printed materials are required by the rep and the quantities that will be needed of each.

3. House Accounts. Try to retain your six best accounts (the ones that reorder automatically) as "house accounts" and stipulate in your contract that the rep is not to call on these accounts nor will any sales commission be paid on orders received from them.

4. Mail Order Promotions. If you normally make mail order promotions to all your accounts, orders that result from accounts in the sales rep's territory would earn a commission for the rep even though you have generated the order by mail. Just make sure the rep understands you will be making such promotions. Otherwise it may look as though you're trying to compete for sales and deny the rep's commission. This is a touchy area that needs to be clarified in your agreement.

5. Terms of Exclusivity. Specify the territory to be covered by the rep and the trade shows or showrooms in which your products will be displayed. This will leave you free to hire reps in other areas or exhibit in other showrooms or trade shows. A crafter who makes one-of-a-kind art creations puts it this way: "Stay clear of any representative who wants you to sign a contract that makes your product his sole property, hemming you in so you cannot take advantage of any other offers."

6. Extra Fees. Sales reps normally pay all their own expenses, but if your products are to be displayed in a showroom or at a trade show, you will probably be asked either for extra money to pay exhibiting costs or a higher sales commission on these sales. Just make sure you understand what those fees will be and try to set a maximum on how much you will be asked to pay in any given year.

See also Trade Shows.

MEMORANDUM OF AGREEMENT

Made _____(date)_____ between _____*(name of sales representative or organization)*_____
(hereinafter referred to as the Associates), of ___*(address of sales representative or organization)*___
_____ and ___*(your business name and address)*___
_____ .

This agreement shall be in force for the period of one year and shall continue thereafter for one-year periods unless either party gives notice to the other in writing six months in advance of the renewal date or on that date for a date six months hence.

The Associates shall be our exclusive representative to the _____ *(specify trade area or industry)*___
_, both retail and jobber, in the following states or parts thereof:

(list states or territory here)

We expect the Associates to give this territory diligent and intensive coverage for which a commission of_____ % will be paid on all invoices of sales made by the Associates. Commission payments will be sent to you on the 15th of each month, accompanied by copies of invoices for all the billing to trade accounts in your territory that have been collected to that date. All expenses of travel and maintenance will be paid by the Associates. You will call on major accounts ___*specify how often,*___
___*based on discussion with rep)*___ .

We grant the right of access at all times to our files of copies of all invoices to enable you to ascertain the correctness of our commission payments to you.

We agree that your services to this company are not exclusive (meaning that the Associates will continue to represent other companies).

Please indicate your acceptance to this agreement by signing and returning the attached copy of this agreement.

Sincerely,

___*(your signature)*_____
for _*(your business name)*_____

Accepted:

_____*signature of sales rep)*_____ Date: _____ *(date signed)*_____

Sales Tax

Q: *I'm just starting to sell my handmade products for extra income. Since this is more of a hobby than a business, do I have to collect sales tax on my sales?*

Yes. With the exception of Alaska, Delaware, Montana, New Hampshire, and Oregon, all states have sales taxes, and anyone who sells merchandise direct to consumers must collect and remit sales taxes accordingly. All sellers—even hobby businesses—are required by law to register with the Department of Revenue (Sales Tax Division) in their state. If you are a seller of merchandise, then you're subject to tax, even if you sell only a couple of times a year. Most retailers file monthly sales tax reports, but if your income is low, you may only have to file quarterly or annually. Here are some special sales tax situations you may be wondering about:

• **Craft Fairs**. Craft sellers must always collect sales tax at a fair, but how and when it's paid can vary. Sometimes a show promoter will get an umbrella sales tax certificate for their event and sellers will either report their sales to management at the show's end or actually give management a check for sales tax that will be picked up by a state sales tax agent. In most cases, however, individual sellers are required to get a temporary sales tax certificate for the run of the show and the information on how to do this is always provided by show promoters. Each state has its own rules about when sales tax must be paid, but when you're selling in a state other than your own, you will generally have to pay the sales tax within thirty days after a show.

Many beginning sellers ignore the sales tax law completely and sell their wares at small fairs without collecting sales tax. Don't try this at a large show, however, because lawbreakers could be subject to severe financial penalties. In my state, anyone caught violating the sales tax law would be subject to a penalty of twenty percent over and above any normal tax obligation, and could receive for each offense (each return not filed) from one to six months in prison and a fine of up to $5,000. Don't mess around here because it's easy to get caught. Tax people generally attend craft fairs with tax forms in hand and they turn up at small business conferences too whenever merchandise is being sold. On more than one occasion while selling my books at a home business conference, I've had a tax man standing by to pick up my sales tax check at the end of the day. Adds Richard Edwards, publisher of the *Mid-Atlantic Craft Show List*: "According to recent reports, more and more shows are being visited by state income tax people to make sure that crafters have tax resale numbers. For many of the larger shows, six to eight tax inspectors arrive at a show together so they can sweep through quickly and move on to the next one. We have even gotten reports of displays being confiscated."

• **Holiday Boutiques**. If you participate in an annual holiday boutique with several other craft sellers, the cashier may collect the sales tax on all purchases but each individual seller is responsible for collecting and reporting his or her own taxable sales. When the profits are doled out at the end of the sale, each craft seller should get back all sales tax collected on his or her sales so it can be reported and forwarded to the state when the next sales tax return is due.

• **Charitable Events**. Someone once asked me who was responsible for collecting the tax if merchandise has been consigned to a charitable organization on a 70/30 percentage basis. The answer is, the organization. Always remember the rule is *the party who makes the sale to the consumer is the one who must collect and pay sales tax to the state in question*.

• **Sales through Other Shops and Stores**. The only time you don't need to collect sales tax is when you consign or wholesale your products or when you sell them through craft malls or rent-a-space shops. In this case, the individual shops, stores, and malls are responsible for collecting sales tax. You must keep track of all these sales, however, since such income is exempt from state sales taxes and must be itemized and deducted accordingly on your tax return.

See also Online Sales *and* Tax Exemption Certificate.

Tip

Even when you don't have to collect sales tax, a tax exemption certificate may still be required by your state for other reasons. You will need it, too, in order to buy raw materials without paying sales tax. When selling to buyers at wholesale, you also need to get their resale tax number as proof that your sales to them are tax exempt.

Samples

 In trying to sell to wholesale buyers, should I send sample products for evaluation?

This is something you will have to decide on your own, but here are three tips:

1. Don't send a sample product to a shop or store buyer until you are asked to do so or at least until you know you have the buyer's attention. For example, if you send a promotional mailing to a prospective buyer and get any kind of interest, you could follow up with a telephone call to ask for the order, and if there is any resistance, then ask if a small sample would help in making a buying decision. As one crafts producer told me, "I don't send a sample until I know I'm dealing with a large shop with buying volume. In that case I might send one item that costs me less than fifteen dollars, or a couple of smaller items. It depends on the size of the shop. Most small shops don't even ask for samples."

2. If you are trying to sell a product to a catalog company, a sample may be required. But call the company to get the name of the buyer who should receive the sales literature and product sample or it may be a waste of your time and money.

3. Don't expect sample products to be returned by anyone.

See also Sales Representatives.

Tip

Instead of offering dealer samples, consider offering first-time buyers a special "get acquainted" sampling of products at a lower-than-usual-price—something you could afford to do if this was a standard order that could be prepacked in advance. Depending on what you sell, the suggested price of a get-acquainted sampler might be in the range of fifty to one hundred dollars.

SASE

Q: *In my classified ads, is it a good idea to ask people to send money for my catalog or at least a self-addressed stamped envelope?*

Advertisers use the SASE abbreviation (sometimes with periods between the letters) when they are offering free information in a classified ad or news release but don't want to stand the expense of the postage and envelope to mail it. This is common practice in the home business and crafts community as well as in the publishing industry, where book and magazine publishers expect all writers to send an SASE if they want Writer's Guidelines or a response to a query letter.

Before you ask people to send fifty cents or an SASE to receive your advertising material, however, consider that this may decrease by twenty-five to thirty-five percent the total number of responses you will receive. By asking for money or an SASE, you are making it more difficult for people to respond. Not everyone will take the time to tape coins to a card or dig up the right size envelope. Given the number of people I see standing in line at the post office with unstamped letters in their hands, I conclude that many homes don't keep a supply of stamps on hand. Also, the average individual may not know what you mean if you ask for an LSASE (large SASE). You may want a #10 business envelope, but people reading the ad might think they have to send a 9 x 12-inch envelope. (Asking for a "business-size SASE" might make it clearer to some.)

Finally, when you ask for an SASE, expect that about five percent of the total who respond will forget to include the envelope. Of course you must also respond to these people because they are as likely to order from you as the ones who send the SASE.

SBA Loans

Q: *My husband and I would like to expand our business but we need more capital than we can raise on our own. Is it difficult to get a small business loan from the U.S. Small Business Administration?*

The SBA offers a microloan program that offers loans of from $200 to $25,000 to budding entrepreneurs through selected private nonprofit lenders. One couple told me they found the SBA easy to work with when they wanted a loan to set up a crafts shop in their home.

"We learned the SBA will offer up to $10,000, basically unsecured, except that they will not loan money for intellectual property, nor will they underwrite a computer programming business," they reported. "There is a monthly judging process where the plans are reviewed by a committee of ten or so who decide who's worthy of a loan. The interest rate is comparable to what banks would give, and we were offered a repayment schedule from one to six years. We paid a loan closing fee of $300."

To get an SBA loan, you will need a good credit rating and will have to provide a business/financial plan with figures for the past year and projections for the coming year. Guaranty Loans are available to certain new/young businesses when a local bank will not provide a loan without additional backing. Some Direct Loans are also available to handicapped persons and disabled Vietnam-era vets. More information about SBA loans can be obtained from an SBA or SCORE office near you or from this toll-free number: 1-800-827-5722.

See also Business Plan; Cash Flow Projection; *and* SCORE.

Scams

 Is it my imagination, or are there more con artists at work today than ever before?

It's not your imagination—con artists are running rampant today and this problem will only get worse as the Internet grows. (See article, "Scams on the Internet.") A growing number of home business owners are now being targeted as victims so it's more important than ever to not let your ego get in the way of clear thinking when something comes along that seems too good to be true. These days, it probably is. Here are some scams currently being targeted to homebased business owners:

• **COD Shipments**. A con artist places a large order for several thousand dollars worth of merchandise and is most agreeable when you say you will have to ship COD. However, they pay with a company check and send a letter a couple days later to say they made an error and the check may bounce. Just redeposit it, they advise, knowing full well it will bounce again. Since you can run a check through only twice, your only option then will be to notify the police or District Attorney's office. The best way to avoid this scam is to insist on a certified check or money order as payment of the COD delivery. Don't be surprised if the con artist says he or she can't do business that way.

• **Simplified Payment Methods.** Be wary of companies that sell you something and then urge you to authorize a monthly automatic withdrawal from your checking account. They say all you have to do is give your bank's name and address as well as your checking account number. The fraud occurs when counterfeit checks or phony "demand drafts" are used to make unauthorized cash withdrawals from your account.

• **Shops with Multiple Outlets.** A buyer may place a large wholesale order with terms of net thirty days, saying they will be placing merchandise in several shops in other cities. As soon as the order is received, the buyer disappears with the merchandise.

• **Office Supply Scams.** Con artists in this field are bilking small business owners out of millions of dollars annually. They gain entrance to your business via the telephone, and they may try to sell you everything from inferior office supplies at reduced prices to cheap laser toner cartridges that could ruin your printer. Any time you are approached on the telephone with an offer that sounds too good to be true, ask that information be sent to you in the mail. If you are told this can't be done, it's probably a scam. Because fraudulent sales pitches made by mail run the risk of investigation by the U.S. Postal Service, many con artists limit their promotions to the telephone or the Internet. Although you can call the Better Business Bureau for a report on a company, by law this agency cannot release information on how long a customer has had phone service. This, of course, gives con artists a perfect shield. Be especially wary of anyone who says you've got to buy right now to get the savings, and *never* give a credit card number to someone who has called you out of the blue and suggests you put the charge on a credit card. For more information on this topic, contact the Federal Trade Commission's Public Distribution Center (see resource chapter) to request the booklet, "Office Supply Scams."

• **Phone-Card Scams**. This is now an international problem. Be careful when you use your long-distance calling card in any public place, particularly when other people are standing nearby. Any one of them could be a con artist who is trying to see the numbers on your card, or monitor the numbers you punch when you make calls. Thieves are even using binoculars in airports to get such information. Once they have your number, of course, it will be sold and you could end up with hundreds of calls on your bill.

• **Invention Hucksters**. The Federal Trade Commission reports that thousands of amateur inventors regularly pay millions of dollars a year to invention promotion firms who just take money from unsuspecting people (fees of up to $5,000 or more) and provide no worthwhile services for it. Although such firms may be able to offer evidence of their success in marketing an invention by giving you the names of one or two clients, FTC investigations of such firms have often shown that a company may have only a handful of success stories out of thousands of clients registered with them. (See also *Inventor's Clubs and Associations* and *Patent*.)

• **Homework Scams**. I've saved the most common scam for last. Avoid classified advertisements for home sewing and craft assembly work that promise good money for making simple products like aprons, baby bibs, or jewelry. Promoters promise to buy all the products you make, but they never do and their reason will be that your work doesn't "meet their standards" even when it's perfectly made. That's because they are interested only in selling their product kits to unsuspecting consumers. (For more information on this topic from victims of this scam, see my home business bible, *Homemade Money*.)

The U.S. Postal Service says two of the five biggest lies regularly fed to consumers are "This chain letter is perfectly legal," and "You can stuff envelopes at home and earn BIG $$$." Chain letters are not only one of life's biggest losers, they say, but any chain letter asking for money is a type of lottery that is illegal when sent through the U.S. Mail. As for stuffing envelopes, these ads are simply lures to try to get you to set up your own business to conduct the same scheme as the advertiser's. When you continue a fraud by getting other victims involved, you're setting yourself up for investigation by the U.S. Postal Inspection Service, whose penalties for mail order fraud are severe.

- Other consumer scams likely to continue for years are (1) "You are a guaranteed winner of one of five valuable prizes" (you fork over big bucks for worthless products); (2) "Your humble assistance is highly solicited in transferring millions of dollars—all we need is your bank account number" (good way to lose all the money in your account); and (3) "You have been selected to receive a fabulous vacation" (a traveler's nightmare). If you receive solicitations like any of those above, turn them over to your local postmaster for forwarding to the Postal Inspection Service.

See also Cellular Phones; COD Shipments; Credit/Trade References; *and* article, *"Scams on the Internet."*

Tip

If you have been targeted by a con artist, that individual has probably hired others to give phony credit references. If you become suspicious, call Information for the telephone number of all companies named as trade references. If different from the numbers you have been given, it's a scam. Be especially wary if the bank reference you have been given gives a glowing report on the company because banks never give out such information to callers.

Schedule C Form

If you are a sole proprietor, you must report your income and expenses from your business or profession on Schedule C or Schedule C-EZ (Form 1040) and file it with your Form 1040. The amount of net profit (or loss) from Schedule C is reported on the appropriate line on page one of your tax return. If you operate more than one business, you must prepare a separate Schedule C or Schedule C-EZ for each business.

NOTE: You may be able to use Schedule C-EZ if you have gross receipts from your nonfarm business of $25,000 or less and business expenses of $2,000 or less. Other requirements that must be met are listed on Schedule C-EZ.

See also Business Expenses, Tax-Deductible; Employees, Family; Hobby Income; Home Office Deduction; Inventory; *and* Social Security Taxes.

SCHEDULE C
(Form 1040)

Department of the Treasury
Internal Revenue Service   (O)

Profit or Loss From Business
(Sole Proprietorship)

▶ Partnerships, joint ventures, etc., must file Form 1065.

▶ Attach to Form 1040 or Form 1041.   ▶ See Instructions for Schedule C (Form 1040).

OMB No. 1545-0074

1996

Attachment
Sequence No. **09**

Name of proprietor | Social security number (SSN)

| A | Principal business or profession, including product or service (see page C-1) | B Enter principal business code (see page C-6) ▶ | | | | |

| C | Business name. If no separate business name, leave blank. | D Employer ID number (EIN), if any | | | | | | | |

E   Business address (including suite or room no.) ▶
    City, town or post office, state, and ZIP code

F   Accounting method.   (1) ☐ Cash   (2) ☐ Accrual   (3) ☐ Other (specify) ▶
G   Did you "materially participate" in the operation of this business during 1996? If "No," see page C-2 for limit on losses. ☐ Yes ☐ No
H   If you started or acquired this business during 1996, check here . . . . ▶ ☐

Part I   Income

1	Gross receipts or sales. **Caution:** If this income was reported to you on Form W-2 and the "Statutory employee" box on that form was checked, see page C-2 and check here . . . . . . ▶ ☐	1	
2	Returns and allowances	2	
3	Subtract line 2 from line 1	3	
4	Cost of goods sold (from line 42 on page 2)	4	
5	**Gross profit.** Subtract line 4 from line 3	5	
6	Other income, including Federal and state gasoline or fuel tax credit or refund (see page C-2) . .	6	
7	**Gross income.** Add lines 5 and 6 . . . . ▶	7	

Part II   Expenses. Enter expenses for business use of your home **only** on line 30.

8	Advertising	8		19	Pension and profit sharing plans	19	
9	Bad debts from sales or services (see page C-3) . .	9		20	Rent or lease (see page C-4):		
				a	Vehicles, machinery, and equipment .	20a	
10	Car and truck expenses (see page C-3)	10		b	Other business property . .	20b	
11	Commissions and fees . .	11		21	Repairs and maintenance . .	21	
12	Depletion	12		22	Supplies (not included in Part III) .	22	
13	Depreciation and section 179 expense deduction (not included in Part III) (see page C-3)	13		23	Taxes and licenses	23	
				24	Travel, meals, and entertainment:		
				a	Travel	24a	
14	Employee benefit programs (other than on line 19) . . .	14		b	Meals and entertainment		
15	Insurance (other than health) .	15		c	Enter 50% of line 24b subject to limitations (see page C-4) .		
16	Interest:						
a	Mortgage (paid to banks, etc.) .	16a		d	Subtract line 24c from line 24b .	24d	
b	Other	16b		25	Utilities	25	
17	Legal and professional services	17		26	Wages (less employment credits) .	26	
18	Office expense	18		27	Other expenses (from line 48 on page 2)	27	

28	**Total expenses** before expenses for business use of home. Add lines 8 through 27 in columns . ▶	28	
29	Tentative profit (loss). Subtract line 28 from line 7	29	
30	Expenses for business use of your home. Attach **Form 8829**	30	
31	**Net profit or (loss).** Subtract line 30 from line 29		
	• If a profit, enter on **Form 1040, line 12,** and ALSO on **Schedule SE, line 2** (statutory employees, see page C-5). Estates and trusts, enter on Form 1041, line 3.	31	
	• If a loss, you MUST go on to line 32.		
32	If you have a loss, check the box that describes your investment in this activity (see page C-5).		
	• If you checked 32a, enter the loss on **Form 1040, line 12,** and ALSO on **Schedule SE, line 2** (statutory employees, see page C-5). Estates and trusts, enter on Form 1041, line 3.	32a ☐ All investment is at risk.	
	• If you checked 32b, you MUST attach **Form 6198.**	32b ☐ Some investment is not at risk.	

For Paperwork Reduction Act Notice, see Form 1040 Instructions.   Cat. No. 11334P   Schedule C (Form 1040) 1996

How SCORE Helped One Craft Business

Back in the late 1980s, at a time when Sue Brown was feeling depressed about her business, she called SCORE to arrange for a free counseling session. After just two meetings, she reported this was the smartest move she ever made. Through the years, Sue's Wood Cellar Graphics business has grown to include a large line of originally-designed rubber-stamps and related paper products such as hang tags and note papers. In looking back to her session with SCORE, Sue recalls that the SCORE counselor was impressed with her progress to that point and confirmed she had products with money-making potential.

"This naturally boosted my ego," says Sue. "Some of the things we discussed were the importance of how a mail order business like mine should best be presented, and this led to a discussion of creating a catalog. The counselor talked about the importance of making a commitment to the business and having enough faith in my products to get together whatever funds were necessary to do some healthy advertising. More than anything, my session with SCORE lit a fire under me. The advice and encouragement I received was invaluable, so I can't imagine anyone not taking advantage of this free service."

Tip

If you're looking for an inexpensive and easy-to-learn software program that will not only do your accounting but will also create your Schedule C tax form in the process, contact Bette Laswell at BDL Homeware (see resource chapter) and ask for information about her BDL.SCHED-C software.

SCORE

The Service Corps of Retired Executives (SCORE) is a nonprofit organization sponsored by the U.S. Small Business Administration. It exists solely to provide free business information and advice. SCORE counselors are retired men and women who have had successful business careers as company executives or owners of their own businesses. When you need help, a counselor will be assigned to your case. He or she will offer suggestions, advice, and recommendations for a solution to your problem but will not perform any of the actual work required, such as writing a business or marketing plan. To find a SCORE counselor, see your local telephone directory under SCORE, U.S. Government or call 1-800-634-0245 to get an information packet and a connection to your nearest SBA or SCORE office.

Tip

Many fields and professions are represented by SCORE counselors. For best results, ask for someone who is familiar with your particular type of business. If you need help in launching a design business, for example, it won't do you much good to be counseled by a successful grocer.

S Corporation

See Corporation.

Self-Mailers

A self-mailer is any mail piece placed in the mail stream without an envelope. Generally, such pieces measure 11 x 22 inches. They are usually folded in half, then in half again to create a mailer that measures 5½ x 8½ inches, but other sizes of paper and types of folds may also be used. The most important consideration here is the weight of the paper. You should strive to keep the weight of a self-mailer to an ounce or less, but if you use anything lighter than sixty or seventy pound weight paper, your mail piece is likely to be chewed up by mail processing machines. Ask your printer for suggestions.

Self-Publishing

See Desktop Publishing.

Selling Terms

See Terms of Sale.

Sewing

See Copyrights in Public Domain; Designer Fabrics, Commercial Use of; Flammability Standards; Garment Manufacturing; Patterns, Commercial Use of; Maintenance Agreements; *and* Scams: Homework Scams.

Sheltered Workshops

When you need help in producing craft items but don't want to hire employees, check to see if there is a sheltered workshop in your area such as Veterans Industries. This organization and various others hire disabled workers who excel at doing tedious, routine work you may not have the time or patience for. Through the years, several readers have reported their satisfaction with the work done by such organizations. Examples of work that could be done for a reasonable price by a sheltered workshop might include tying on tags or affixing labels, packaging kits or pattern packages, stuffing envelopes, doing routine fabric cutting or hand-painting, and so on.

Shipping and Handling Charges

Q: *How do I figure what to charge customers for shipping and handling of their orders when each order weighs a different amount and cost may vary depending on how they want delivery to be made?*

A note found on the order form of one seller indicates that some crafters don't understand the importance of including "handling charges" to their prices. It read, "I haven't figured out what handling means, but whatever it is, I still don't charge for it." "Handling charges" are your total cost of packing and shipping an order, including the cost of shipping cartons, sealing tape, address labels, packing lists, and something to cover your labor costs in doing this work. You shouldn't charge buyers extra for these costs, but they need to be taken into consideration when you set your retail and wholesale prices.

Shipping costs, however, are to be passed along to customers unless a special offer of free freight has been made. (Sometimes to encourage orders at a trade show, sellers will offer free freight with prepaid orders.) Some sellers charge the actual postage or shipping costs incurred while others work on a certain percentage of the order—usually between seven and ten percent—which few buyers will ever question. It's easy enough to figure shipping charges on a wholesale order you are invoicing, but difficult to figure out what to charge when customers are expected to send payment with order. Here's how one craft seller has handled this problem in her retail catalog:

"Regular ground-service domestic U.S. shipping is included in all the prices. For faster delivery via UPS Second Day Air, add $5 to your order. Canadian and overseas orders, see enclosed chart."

Most mail order sellers figure out some kind of shipping chart that will work for their products. For example a pattern seller might set up a shipping chart based on how many patterns have been ordered (i.e., "1 pattern, $1; 2–4 patterns, $1.50; 5 or more, $2") while a product seller might work with dollar amounts. Julie Peterson, who sells Minnesota Naturals by mail, uses the following shipping and handling chart for her birch bark products:

Total price of Items	Add
$1.00 – $20.00	$4.95
$20.01 – $30.00	$5.95
$30.01 – $40.00	$6.95
$40.01 – $60.00	$7.95
$60.01 –$100.00	$8.95
Over $100.00	$9.95

It's difficult to work up a chart like this and you'll have to do some experimenting to find the right rate structure for your products. Julie said she studied several mail order catalogs and found there was a pattern to what others were charging. "After setting up my shipping and handling chart," says Julie, "I monitored all my shipments for a month to see if I was charging too little or too much. I found I had to raise all my prices by a dollar. Sometimes I come out a little ahead, other times I come out losing a bit, but it all works out in the end."

See also Packing Materials *and* Shipping Methods.

Tip

If you're selling only a few items, you might want to build shipping charges into the price of each item. In that case, you would list the price on your order form as $16.95 ppd. ("ppd." means "postage paid.") This is the method I have used for years to sell my books, each of which has a different weight. If you're selling to Canada, ask for an extra dollar per item to cover the higher postage rates to this country.

Shipping Methods

See Air Courier Services; COD Shipments; FOB; Priority Mail; *and* United Parcel Service.

Shop Failures

Q: *How can I get my merchandise out of a craft shop or mall that has gone out of business but hasn't returned goods to its consignors or renters?*

This is one reason why you always need to get the name and telephone number of a shop's owner or manager. Sometimes a shady owner will strip a place bare before they leave town; other times, they just sneak away and leave to others the problem of what to do with all the merchandise. If a shop closes and you don't have the name of the owner, call the Better Business Bureau in the city where the shop is located and explain what has happened. One crafter who did this not only got the owner's name and address but a report that an investigation had already been started. In return for this information, she was asked to fill out a legal complaint form.

Problems with shops that close owing you money or the return of your merchandise should also be reported to the Consumer Fraud Division of the District Attorney of the county in which the shop was located. Reporting your loss to the proper authorities may make you feel better, but don't expect to get back the money you've lost. The kind of people who close up shop and disappear usually owe not only all the crafters in their store, but state sales tax and other taxes as well. If there is any money to be recovered, you can be sure the government will get its share first.

See also Consignment Laws.

Show Listings

Q: *I'd like to enter craft fairs and shows outside my area but don't know how to get information about them in advance. Is there a good source for this information?*

Yes, many show listing calendars and periodicals are available by subscription from publishers in the crafts industry. Some that list events nationwide are *Arts 'N Crafts ShowGuide, The Crafts Report, Neighbors & Friends, SAC Newsmonthly,* and *Sunshine Artists Magazine* (all listed in the resource chapter). Many craft show listings are also posted on the Internet now. Search art and craft web sites to locate this kind of information.

Signs

Q: What kind of advertising signs can I put on my property?

It depends entirely on the zoning laws in your community. Call your city or county clerk to get the answer to this question.

See also Zoning Laws.

Small Claims Court

Q: Is it difficult to sue someone in Small Claims Court, and is this a practical way to collect on a bad check or unpaid invoice?

Small Claims Courts are designed to resolve small monetary disputes, and many small business owners have had success in collecting money owed to them by individuals or companies who gave them bad checks or refused to pay an invoice. Sometimes the mere threat of a suit in Small Claims Court will convince a person to pay up; others may hold out until a judgment has been entered against them and finally pay when they learn that the Sheriff can walk into their place of business, make a list of property advertised for sale, and sell enough of it at auction to pay their debt. For the few who ignore a judgment altogether, collection strategies such as garnishing wages, seizing money from a bank account, or filing a lien against real estate may need to be employed.

Generally speaking, however, small claims court procedures are simple, inexpensive, quick, informal, and effective. Filing fees are nominal and paperwork (generally a one-page form that states your grievance in general terms) is kept to a minimum. Each state has a statute of limitation (usually at least one year) that limits the time you can wait to sue after an event occurs. The amount of the dispute and the maximum amount that can be claimed varies from state to state, but in some states, you can sue for $5,000 or more.

Something you need to check initially is whether you can sue the defendant in your state; that is, do your state courts have jurisdiction over the defendant? If the defendant does not reside in your state or do business there, you might have to sue in the defendant's home state, which might be more trouble than the bad check or unpaid invoice is worth. Also find out if you can file a claim by mail, or whether you must appear in person to present your case. If the defendant fails to show up, you will probably get a judgment by default.

Small claims court offices are listed in your local telephone book under municipal, county, or state government headings. For more information on this topic, see the book, *Everybody's Guide to Small Claims Court* by Ralph Warner (Nolo Press).

See also Collection Strategies.

Social Security Earnings

Q: *How much can I earn from a part-time business before I begin to lose my Social Security Earnings?*

The amount you can earn changes every year, so you should call your local Social Security office to get the exact figures each year. For the year 1997, if you are under the age of sixty-five, that amount is $8,640, and for every two dollars earned over this amount you would lose one dollar. If you are over sixty-five, the maximum amount you can earn without losing benefits in 1997 is $13,500 (and this is *net income,* by the way). For every three dollars earned over this amount, you would lose one dollar.

Maybe some day the government will remove these earning restrictions and stop penalizing America's senior citizens. In the meantime, you can look forward to turning seventy because at that point you will be allowed to earn as much as you're able to make without losing a dollar of your social security benefits. For answers to any questions you may have about Social Security, call this toll-free number: 1-800-772-1213.

See also Corporation *and* Social Security Taxes.

Tip

Check your social security earnings periodically to make sure your annual payments are being credited to your account. To do this, send a letter to the Department of Health and Human Services, Social Security Administration, Baltimore, MD 21235 and ask for "Summary Statement of Earnings." Include your name as it appears on your card, your address, social security number, and date of birth.

Social Security Taxes

As a self-employed individual, you must pay into your personal Social Security account by filing a Self-Employment Tax form when the profit on your Schedule C tax report reaches $400 or more. The amount of tax you will pay, and the amount of earnings on which social security taxes will be due continues to increase. Check with the IRS or an accountant each year to get this information.

If you hire employees—even your spouse—you will have to withhold social security and Medicare taxes on wages paid to employees, report to the employees the amount withheld (W-2 Form), remit quarterly tax payments to the IRS (Form 941) and send an annual report to the Social Security Administration (W-3 form and copy of employees' W-2 forms). An accountant can give you details about how to do this.

See also Social Security Earnings.

Sole Proprietorship

A Sole Proprietorship is the easiest kind of business to start and operate. It has no existence apart from the owner and its liabilities are the owner's personal liabilities. Advantages are that the business is controlled by the owner, all profits go directly to the owner, there is little regulation, and earnings are personally taxed.

Although there are no legal formalities involved in ending a sole proprietorship beyond simply stopping the business activity, there are ethical considerations involved, particularly in a mail order or publishing business that is likely to generate orders long after all advertising and promotions have ceased. If you open such mail, and it includes a check or money order, you are obligated to return it. Some people have told me they just tear up the checks, but this is an unethical thing to do because the people who sent these orders won't know what you've done. If you can't afford to answer mail to a dead business, simply order a rubber stamp that reads "Out of business— return to sender." By stamping and returning all mail unopened, it won't cost you anything and you will have fulfilled your ethical obligation to customers. If you've been using a P.O. Box address, mail will automatically be returned to sender if you close the box.

See also Legal Forms of Business.

Sports Logos, Commercial Use of

Q: *I'd like to sell sweatshirts or novelty items that promote local sports organizations. How do I get permission to do this?*

In talking with a business owner who sells merchandise with famous sports logos on them, I learned it is not difficult to get permission to use such logos for commercial purposes. Sports organizations like publicity for their teams, she told me, so their licensing rules and regulations are relatively easy for small business owners to comply with.

For example, if you wanted to make an item that incorporates the logo of your favorite sports team, you might only have to pay a small licensing fee and percentage of your sales for this privilege. The bigger the organization, of course, the higher the licensing fee. For more information, contact a sports organization of interest and ask to speak to its Licensing Department.

State Laws

See Bad Check Law; Bedding and Upholstered Furniture Law; Business or Trade Name Registration/Protection; Celebrity Rights Act; Consignment Laws; Employees, Family; Employees, Nonfamily; Endangered Species; Homework Laws; Independent Contractors; Kitchen Laws; Labor Laws; Licenses and Permits; Nature Items; *and* Taxes.

Statement

Statements are generally used when a company regularly ships to customers who have a charge account. They need monthly reminders of their current indebtedness to you and a statement serves this purpose. Small businesses normally send statements on the last day or first day of each month.

While an invoice includes details about a customer's purchase, a statement merely recaps the date and total of all invoices still unpaid at the end of the month. Since some accounts are likely to ignore the first statement, you might want to create a standard STATEMENT form as well as a PAST DUE STATEMENT form that includes a note that the account is past due and should be paid immediately to avoid collection costs.

See also Invoice *and* Invoices Not Paid.

Stationery

See Printed Materials; P.O. Box Address; Supplies, Buying Wholesale; *and* Telephone.

Statutory Employees

Q: *What's the difference between an independent contractor and a statutory employee? Are there tax advantages to hiring statutory employees?*

Many people hire help on an independent contractor basis, which, as I have explained elsewhere, is a dangerous thing to do these days. A solution used by many small craft manufacturers is to hire statutory employees. Although it costs a business more to hire statutory employees than independent contractors (because you must pay social security and Medicare taxes), it is the perfect solution for small manufacturers who want to operate legally. On the other hand, statutory employees are less expensive to hire than employees because there are no unemployment taxes on statutory employees. (Like independent contractors, statutory employees can deduct their trade or business expenses from their W-2 earnings.)

According to the IRS's *Tax Guide for Small Businesses,* "If an individual who works for you is not an employee under the common law rules, you do not have to withhold federal income tax from that individual's pay. However, for social security and Medicare taxes, the term *employee* includes any individual who works for you for pay in one of the following two categories (two additional categories are excluded here because they are not applicable to this book's readers):

1. An individual who works at home on materials or goods you supply and that must be returned to you or to a person you name, if you also furnish specifications for the work to be done;
2. A full-time traveling or city salesperson who works on your behalf and turns in orders to you from wholesalers, retailers, contractors (etc.). The goods sold must be merchandise for resale or supplies for use in the buyers' business operations. (You might not think this category is applicable to a small business, but if you were to hire a sales rep who worked only for you and no other companies, that person could be considered a statutory employee for tax purposes but could not legally be called an independent contractor.)

Dodie Eisenhauer, owner of Village Designs in Daisy, Missouri, uses a combination of regular employees who work in her workshop and statutory employees who work for her out of their own homes. She says it was a big step for her to switch over from independent contractors to employees but it wasn't as painful a process as she had been led to believe and the benefits have been enormous. "I encourage people who are still using independent contractors to reclassify their workers as soon as possible," says Dodie. "You immediately gain peace of mind from knowing you're operating on a 100 percent legal basis and you no longer have to worry about the IRS or Department of Labor putting you out of business."

See also Employees, Nonfamily; Sales Representatives; *and article, "How One Manufacturer Solved Her Independent Contractor Problem."*

A Lost-Mail Horror Story

"Early in April, after mailing a dozen checks to creditors on March 26, I began to get calls from creditors who had not received my payments yet," one of my readers reported. "They didn't care that the mail might have been lost; they just wanted payment without delay. On April 20, I filed twelve Mail Loss/Riffling Reports (tracer forms) with the post office, and was told that each tracer "would take its own routine length of time."

"As the weeks passed, the creditors continued to call, day and night. I explained again and again the necessity of waiting for notification from the post office. Finally, tired of it all, I told each creditor that I would send a replacement check, but if the post office delivered the first check, they would either have to destroy it or send it back to me. They all agreed to this request. I told each creditor that only one check would clear my bank. At the end of June, I sent each of them a new check. You can guess what happened next. My lost mail finally got delivered and every creditor deposited both checks.

"During the second week of July, I received twelve insufficient funds notices from my bank at fifteen dollars per returned check. And when the March 26th checks didn't clear the bank, several of the creditors sent me an invoice for returned check fees (twenty-five dollars per invoice). With explanations to the creditors (again), they withdrew these invoices. I then called our main branch postmaster, related this situation to her, and requested a reimbursement from their loss of my bills. The postmaster's reply: "Sorry, we give no reimbursements for lost mail."

This story certainly illustrates the importance of putting a stop payment order on any check for more than twenty-five dollars that you believe has been lost in the mail.

Tip

Dodie says it used to take hours to do her weekly payroll, figure the monthly tax deposits, and do the quarterly employee tax forms. Now that she has a good computer payroll program, however, she can do this job in about half an hour a week. She uses and recommends *Quickbooks* by Intuit because it is inexpensive and easy to learn.

Stop Payment Order

Q: *It's expensive to stop payment on a check. When is this really necessary?*

A stop payment order makes sense if (1) you have ordered goods or services that prove to be unsatisfactory (which gives you some leverage to get a job done over or merchandise replaced); or (2) a bill payment appears to have been lost in the mail. If you happen to lose your checkbook, notify your bank immediately. (It is their responsibility to verify the signature on a check against the one they have on file for the account holder.) Instead of putting a stop payment on all the checks in your checkbook, it makes more sense to close out the account as quickly as possible. (The bank can tell you which checks haven't yet cleared.) Remember, if one of your checks falls into the hands of a con artist, it will be child's play to modify the name and address information on one of your blank checks and order a new supply of checks from a mail order check-printing company.

See also article, "A Lost-Mail Horror Story."

Sub-Chapter S Corporation

See Corporation.

Supplies, Buying Wholesale

Q: *I would like to buy my supplies and materials at wholesale prices, but many companies won't sell to me, and others have minimum quantities that are too high. What's the solution to this problem?*

If you can't buy supplies at wholesale, it's almost impossible to make a good profit on handcrafts sold at the retail level, and wholesaling them is out of the question. The first thing you need to understand is that there are two types of craft suppliers: those who will sell to homebased business owners and those who won't. For nearly thirty years (that I know of) most wholesalers and manufacturers in the craft supply industry refused to sell to craftspeople who ran businesses out of their homes. In recent years, however, sponsors of the Hobby Industry Association (HIA) shows have finally acknowledged that craft designers and "converters of craft materials for the gift market" comprise a legitimate market that must be recognized. Now professional crafters can gain entry to HIA trade shows to search for supply sources, but it's still up to individual exhibitors as to whether or not wholesale orders will be accepted from them.

The Association of Crafts & Creative Industries (ACCI) also works to put professional crafters in touch with suppliers through their *Professional Crafters Trade Shows,* and the National Craft Association (NCA) offers the *MEGA Arts & Craft Supply Directory* that lists products available from nearly 2,000 suppliers (see resource chapter).

Companies interested in selling to homebased craft businesses advertise in trade magazines such as *Craft Supply Magazine.* In addition to the craft industry suppliers, there are thousands of other manufacturers and wholesalers in this country who welcome your orders. These suppliers advertise in various trade journals, or you can track them down by studying the *Thomas Register of American Manufacturers,* a directory available in most libraries. Its several volumes include a listing of products in alphabetical order with the names and addresses of companies who make them. In some cases, you may be able to buy directly from manufacturers; in others, you will be referred to a nearby distributor or dealer.

If you can't qualify to buy at wholesale prices, strive to find suppliers who will sell to you at bulk discounts. A good source for this kind of information is *The Crafts Supply Sourcebook* by Margaret Boyd (Betterway). Regularly updated, this directory includes over 2,500 product listings in the categories of general arts, crafts, hobbies, needlecrafts, sewing, and fiber arts. Although designed primarily for use by individuals who need mail order supply sources, this directory also lists companies who sell at wholesale or bulk prices. (Check bookstores or order directly from the publisher by calling 1-800-289-0963.)

See also Discounts *and* Purchase Order.

A Humorous Tax Audit

Two years after filing her annual tax return, The IRS questioned Beverly Durant about her miscellaneous business deductions which they said seemed higher than they should be. They said she had to come into their office and bring with her all her tax receipts for that year. At that time, Beverly didn't have all her receipts beautifully organized and filed in monthly envelopes as she does now, but had just dumped them loose into a file drawer. Naturally irritated that her small homebased business was being audited in the first place, she just pulled all those receipts out of the drawer and dumped them into a big brown box. When she was called into the IRS agent's office, she plunked the box down in the center of his desk.

"With the box between us, I couldn't see him and he couldn't see me," Beverly said. "He opened the box, looked in, and said 'Them's your records?' I said, 'Yep, that's them.' And then he sat back down, filled out a bunch of forms, handed them to me and said, 'sign here.' And that was that. I'll never be afraid of the IRS again," she concluded.

NOTE: This might not work for everyone. It's possible that Beverly had a little Divine Intervention. You must consider that in the crafts industry she is known as "The Angel Lady."

Tip

Manufacturers and wholesalers are most likely to deal with craft businesses that appear to be professional. In addition to having a sales tax number and the ability to meet supplier minimums, craft sellers should have a business name and telephone number printed on their stationery and cards. One signal that you may be a hobbyist trying to buy at wholesale prices is the way you ask about minimum order requirements. One craft professional suggest that, instead of using the word "minimum," ask instead about the supplier's *opening* order and re-order minimum.

Surge Suppressor

A surge suppressor measures the amount of voltage that can pass through after clamping has occurred. The less voltage that gets through, the more effective the protection. The Underwriters Laboratories standard is 400 volts, which means you shouldn't buy any surge suppressor that allows more than 400 volts to pass through before clamping occurs. A typical household receives a hundred power surges of as much as 1,000 volts a month from electrical storms and the usual on-and-off switching of appliances, so don't take this problem lightly. These sudden voltage increases could damage or destroy your computer, fax machine, laser printer, and other electronic equipment unless it is protected by a surge suppressor.

Tip

Lightning zaps nearly 100,000 computers a year and computer losses have increased in recent years because more people with a fax/modem now leave their system on all the time. When you do this, however, you only double your chances for loss because now you have two paths for potential lightning strikes. Since a surge suppressor won't save your computer system in the event of a direct lightning strike, the only sensible thing to do is unplug it during storms.

Tax Audits

Q: *What can I do to keep my chances of being audited as low as possible?*

To reduce your risk of being audited, attach an explanation if you think the IRS might question a large deduction. Make your return as neat as possible, be sure to sign and date it and attach necessary W-2 forms as instructed.

Some people assume they will automatically be audited if they take the Home Office Deduction on their Schedule C, but that is not true. Anything you do to attract undue attention to your return, however, such as filing an amended return, will increase your chances for an audit. If you are ever audited, don't volunteer any information, records, or files. Wait until the IRS tells you what is being questioned and give them only what they specifically request. For detailed guidelines on how to defend yourself in an audit, see the book *Stand Up to the IRS* by Tax Attorney Frederick W. Daily (Nolo Press).

NOTE: There is a statute of limitations that keeps the IRS from auditing returns after three years have passed. (For example, a return with a filing deadline of April 15, 1998 (for tax year 1997) would remain subject to an audit until April of 1999.) However, there is no time limit to when the IRS can begin an audit if you fail to file a return or file one that is fraudulent.

See also Home Office Deduction *and article, "A Humorous Tax Audit."*

Tax Deductions

See Business Expenses, Tax-Deductible.

Taxes: Local, State, and Federal

President Herbert Hoover was the first President to give his salary back to the government. Now the government would like everybody to do it. "When it comes to taxes," a comic has quipped, "most of us would be willing to pay as we go if we could only catch up on where we've been."

"Some folks feel the government owes them a living," adds another, "but the rest of us would gladly settle for a small tax refund." We may joke about taxes, but we can't afford to ignore them. Here is a brief summary of the various taxes applicable to small businesses:

- **Local taxes.** Local sales taxes are calculated together with state sales taxes and paid to the state on a regular basis. In addition, your state or local government may impose an inventory or property tax on business equipment and inventory. Check local officials for more information about this.
- **State taxes.** Most states have an income tax that is calculated on your net income or profit and payable at the time you file your annual federal tax return. Businesses that have employees will also have to pay unemployment tax.

- **Federal Taxes**. These include (1) owner-manager's income tax or corporation income tax; (2) employee income tax and unemployment tax (if you have employees); and (3) estimated tax payments (due from self-employed individuals).

See also Sales Tax *and* Social Security Taxes.

Tax Exemption Certificate

Also called a "resale tax number" or "Retailer's Occupation Tax Registration Number," this is a document that bears a special number identifying you as one who is qualified to buy goods in the wholesale market without paying sales tax. All sellers of goods must obtain a resale tax number from their state's Sales Tax Bureau, Department of Taxation and Finance. Having a resale tax number means you also have to collect sales tax on everything you sell directly to consumers. Always take your tax certificate with you when you exhibit and sell in any show since a tax agent may ask to see it.

Your resale (or sales) tax number doesn't entitle you to avoid sales tax on small purchases of supplies at the local hardware store or craft shop, but it does enable you to avoid paying sales tax on wholesale purchases of supplies that will be used to make products for sale. When considering whether to sell to you or not, your resale tax number is the first thing a wholesaler will want from you.

See also Supplies, Buying Wholesale *and* Sales Tax.

Tax Preparer

See Accountant *and* Enrolled Agents.

Tax Return

See Accountant; Certified Mail; Financial and Tax Records; *and* Legal Forms of Business.

Teaching

See Copyright "Fair Use" Doctrine; Copyrights of Others; Health Hazards; Lead Testing; *and* Newsletter Publishing

Telephone

Q: *I can't afford a separate line for business. I don't plan to run any ads with my home phone number, but is it okay to list it on my business cards and stationery?*

Legally, you can receive business phone calls on a residential line and make outgoing business calls, but *advertising* your residential phone number on your business card or stationery is likely to be a violation of local telephone company regulations. (Each state has a separate commission that determines the usage of a residential phone, so you need to call your local telephone company for more information.) In some states you could be fined for improper use of a residential phone or simply told that you will have to pay business rates in the future. (I suspect only a few states are as easy-going as Missouri. Once, when I lived in Springfield and called the telephone company to ask what they did when they discovered people who were advertising their home phone for business, a friendly, down-home operator said, "Why, we'd just ask them to stop doing it.")

Telephone companies are savvy about homebased businesses and many now publish newsletters to educate small business owners about the availability of extra lines for business, special phone equipment, toll-free numbers, and so on. An extra line for business may be less expensive than you think. Ask your local telephone company if they offer any "Remote Relay Services" or "phantom phones" that allow calls to your business number to be relayed through your personal phone line and charged separately. Such approved business numbers can then be legally advertised. If you've delayed getting a fax machine because you don't want the expense of a separate telephone line, ask if any kind of "flex line service" is available. (See *Fax Machine* for more information on this topic.)

See also Cellular Phones; Directory Assistance; Fax Machine; Long Distance Carriers; Telephone Messages for Callers; Toll-Free Number; Voice Mail vs. Answering Machine; *and article, "Fax Installation Tips."*

Tip

If you happen to operate two or more small businesses from your home, you don't have to get two or three different telephone lines. Instead, ask your telephone company about their "custom ringing" options. This service enables one to have three phone numbers ringing on one line, each with a different sound so you'll know how to answer it.

Telephone Messages for Callers

Poor telephone messages are a pet peeve of mine. If you're still trying to run a business on your personal telephone line, at least answer with your full name, and if your spouse is a partner in your business, mention his or her name, too. Often when I try to call a woman who has a homebased business (and has listed her number on her business stationery), I get a message on the machine that goes something like this: "Hi, this is Jim. I can't take your call now, so leave a message at the tone." *Jim WHO?* If I'm trying to reach Susan Jones of SewSmart Services, I don't even know whether I've reached the Jones residence or not.

Although I believe all business owners should have a line dedicated to the business, until such time as you can justify the cost of doing this, here is a solution to the problem of how to take business calls on a residential line. Although I have a separate business line, I continually get business calls on my personal phone because people ask Directory Assistance for "Barbara Brabec" not realizing that my business name is "Barbara Brabec Productions." When we take calls personally on this line, Harry and I both answer with our full name. Callers who get the answering machine that's attached to this line hear this message, which you may wish to adapt to your own needs:

We both cheerfully say "Hello" together, then I say, "This is Barbara Brabec," and Harry says, "This is Harry Brabec. Please direct your message to either one of us with your name and phone number, and we'll return your call as soon as possible." Then I say, "If you wish information about my books and reports, leave your complete address to receive my free brochure." Harry then closes with,

"Listen for the tone and then start your message," and we close by saying "Thank you!" together.

See also Voice Mail vs. Answering Machine.

1099 Form

You must issue a 1099 form any time you pay more than $600 to someone for services rendered. By the same token, you should receive a 1099 form from anyone for whom you have provided services worth $600 or more. For example, writers, teachers, speakers, and consultants would generally receive 1099 forms from publishers, organizations, and businesses with whom they have worked during the year.

Terms of Sale

Q: *I know I will have to invoice my wholesale accounts, but what about large sales to individual buyers? Are there any particular invoicing pitfalls I might avoid?*

When selling at retail, always collect payment from individual buyers at the time of sale, unless that individual buyer happens to represent a business or corporation that needs to be invoiced (i.e., an order for a hundred items for use as Christmas or employee gifts). Another exception would be taking custom orders for later delivery, in which case you might prefer to ask only for a deposit up front (see *Custom Orders*).

In establishing your terms of sale, decide whether you will offer (1) *Net Thirty Days* (full payment within thirty days from date of invoice); (2) *Net Ten Days* (full payment within ten days); or (3) *Two Percent Ten Days* or *2/10/30* (two percent discount if payment is made within ten days). Most sellers request full payment within thirty days, but some do offer the two percent discount in an attempt to get their money in hand as quickly as possible. If you do this, however, be aware that some buyers may pay the invoice a month later and still take the discount. If they do, invoice them for the difference and remind them of your terms of sale.

Although your terms may be Net Thirty, you will find that larger buyers who routinely get sixty- to ninety-day terms from others may ignore your thirty-day terms. You'll have to stay on their heels to train them to pay you promptly. In researching this topic, I noticed that Pat Endicott at House of Threads & Wood offers terms of Net Fifteen Days. This is unusual, so I wondered why she worked this way. "When I offered terms of Net Thirty Days, I was lucky to get payment within sixty days," she said, "but when I switched to Net Fifteen, people began to pay me generally between twenty-five and thirty days, which is what I really wanted in the first place. No one has ever given me a hard time about my payment terms."

See also Invoicing Policies; Order Policies; *and* Price List.

Testimonials

Q: *How important are customer testimonials to the sale of my products, and what's the best way to get them?*

Sales are likely to increase when you use testimonials about your products in your brochure or catalog because they build buyer confidence in your offer. If your customers or clients don't send you written comments after purchasing your work, be aggressive in getting them yourself. For example, when a buyer says something great about one of your products, jot down the remark, rewording it to your advantage. Then send the customer a copy and ask if you can use their comments in your brochure, quoting them by name and listing their city and state with the quote. Try to find something in what your buyer has said that can be translated into a benefit someone else would pick up on.

For example, if someone at a crafts fair said at the time of purchase, "I just love your work! This monogrammed pillow will make a wonderful gift for my mother's birthday," jot down the remark right away, rewriting it just a bit so it sounds like a buyer benefit. Your "edited copy" might read: "I was delighted to find that you offer custom-design services. The monogrammed pillow you made for me solved the problem of what to give my mother for her birthday!" Most people will be glad to let you use a remark like this in your printed advertising, even if those weren't the exact words they said. Never quote anyone without getting permission in writing, however, as some people would consider this an invasion of their privacy.

NOTE: If you happen to publish a periodical, The FTC requires reader testimonials used in printed advertising material to be from current (not expired) subscribers.

Tip

"Don't be sheepish about prompting your customers for testimonials," advises Jeffrey Lant, author of *Money Making Marketing*. "Ask them about particular aspects of your product or service, write down what they say, and then ask for their permission (which you must always have) to use it. The meek do not do well at marketing."

Textile Fiber Products Identification Act

Q: *I've read that textile items are required by law to have some kind of hang tag or label, but what kind of tag is needed, and which craft products are considered "textiles?"*

The Bureau of Consumer Protection requires a label or hang tag on all textile wearing apparel and household furnishings, with the exception of textile wall hangings which, curiously, do not have to be labeled under this Act. "Textiles" include any material that is woven, which means all fibers, yarns, and fabrics. "Textile household furnishings" would include such items as quilts, pillows, placemats, stuffed toys, and rugs. To all such items, product makers must attach a tag or label that includes the following information:

a) the name of the manufacturer or other person marketing the textile fiber product

b) the generic names and percentages of all fibers in the product in amounts of five percent or more, listed in order of predominance by weight. Examples: "one hundred percent combed cotton" or "ninety-two percent cotton, eight percent other fibers." (For other examples of such tags, just open your closet door and check the labels on your various items of clothing.)

Deadlines Were Made to Be Broken

Brabec's Law is that all home business deadlines fall (1) before some important holiday you were hoping to have off; (2) the week before you planned to leave on vacation; or (3) the day before company is arriving for the weekend. If you're lucky enough to miss any of the above, you're likely to be delayed by an unanticipated medical emergency, a home maintenance crisis, or a family situation that requires your immediate attention. This book is a perfect example.

When I agreed to deliver it to the publisher by a certain date, I figured I had given myself plenty of time. What I hadn't counted on was that my husband would have a heart attack in the interim and that I would lose more than three months' writing time because of his bypass surgery and all the time and help he needed from me during his long recovery. I also didn't count on the fact that, during this same period, our area would experience a "storm of the century" and subsequent rains that would cause our basement to flood not once but four times before we could identify and fix the problem.

Harry is fine now, and in finishing this book I was once again reminded that no matter how far away a deadline date may be, nor how hard I work to do what needs to be done in the interim, something *always* comes along to delay me. I cannot recall a single instance when I have not found myself wishing for just one more hour, day, week, or month to finish some particular task by the stipulated deadline date. We need deadlines to spur us onward but sometimes it's impossible to meet them. When this happens, we must ask for (or give ourselves) an extension of time. If in the future you find yourself unable to meet a deadline, just do the best you can and lower your stress by forgiving yourself. Sometimes the only way to get it all done without going to pieces it *to get it done late.*

A.J. WISCHMEYER, QUILTMAKER

COTTON AND/OR BLENDS
COTTON BATTING & BACKING
MACHINE WASH GENTLE
DRY FLAT OR ON LINE

A.J. WISCHMEYER
20118 West Ray Rd.
Buckeye, AZ 85326
(602) 386-3295

In designing the required label for her quilts, Ardith Wischmeyer simply sent a copy of her business card to the printer and they reproduced it as a fabric label she could stitch to her products. (Note that iron-on labels are also available from some label manufacturers.)

All garments must also have care labels to meet the labeling requirements of the FTC, which also requires an additional label on any garment containing fur, any product made from wool, or any textile product that uses imported fibers. Products with concealed stuffing, such as pillows, dolls or soft sculpture, may require another label under your state's bedding law. (See below for references to information about each of these label laws.) Note that the various tags and labels required by law do not need to be fancy. You can create your own or obtain them at reasonable cost from commercial suppliers.

See also Bedding and Upholstered Furniture Law; Care Labels; Fur Products; Hang Tags and Labels; *and* Wool and Other Textiles.

Time Management

Q: *I have a hard time meeting deadlines. What can I do to become more efficient in managing my time?*

It's too bad that the time we save on one day can't be placed in storage for use the next day. And just think of all the time we'd save if we stopped showing up in doctors' offices on time. Many books have been written on the topic of time management and organization, and I've recommended a couple of my favorites in the resource chapter. Here's a trick I've learned from years of experience in pushing myself ever onward: *To get ahead, work backwards.*

For every major job or task I undertake that has any kind of deadline attached to it, I make a written plan that starts at the point where I must be finished and works backward to the beginning. When there is no automatic deadline, I set one myself to keep me on target. Then I outline all the work involved in the project, estimate the amount of time each phase will take and plot it to a calendar. This gives me a starting date I automatically push back one week more, for good measure. (Although I try to build in extra time for "life's little interruptions," as an eternal optimist I rarely add enough.) As I work, I keep tabs on whether I'm still on schedule or running behind. When I find myself running behind schedule—almost always the case—I begin looking for ways to find the extra time I'll need to finish on time.

I have always related to this saying popular on plaques and sweatshirts and I'm sure you do, too: "God put me on Earth to accomplish a certain number of things. Right now I'm so far behind I will never die."

See also article, "Deadlines Were Made to Be Broken."

Toll-Free Number

Now that toll-free numbers are so affordable, even small homebased businesses are using them to draw prospect inquiries and orders resulting from advertising or publicity. For example, AT&T advises that a homebased business can add a toll-free number that will come in on its regular line with no on-site hookups required. There is a one-time installation charge and a small, fixed monthly fee, plus the cost of calls, of course. Check your local phone company for more information.

If you do decide to get a toll-free number for your business, be sure to keep a record of all your incoming calls. If not, you may be losing a tidy sum of money every month, says Bette Laswell. "When you have a toll-free number, you get a list of the date and time people call, along with their phone number and city. A lot of people dial the wrong number and then hang up. Although I am always billed for such calls, I don't have to pay for them, but the only way to know which calls are invalid is to keep a daily log of everyone who calls. Each month when I get my phone bill, I check each call billed against calls on my log sheet. By being able to identify invalid calls, I have saved as much as forty dollars a month on my phone bill. Companies that don't keep records like this have no idea how much money they're losing to invalid calls," Bette emphasizes.

Tip

The number of 800 numbers is finite (9,999,999) so when the supply ran out in 1996, it was necessary to introduce a new prefix (888) so another ten million numbers could be offered. The fact that there are no new 800 numbers left means that every number that may become available in the future has belonged to one or more users in the past. When you take an 800 number, you are automatically assuming the liability for calls coming into the old 800 number, so it might be better to get a new 888 number that has never been assigned before than an old 800 number that may still be generating calls from one or more companies' earlier advertising.

Toy and Game Brokers

An industry insider who prefers anonymity offers these tips to anyone trying to market a toy or game to a manufacturer: "Novice inventors don't realize that most companies refuse outside idea submissions, preferring to work with toy and game *brokers* instead. Milton Bradley alone reportedly receives in excess of 8500 unsolicited submissions a year which are usually returned without being reviewed. Fraudulent invention marketing firms charge outrageous fees up to $5,000, but a reputable agent (broker) normally charges between $100 and $200 for a product evaluation. If they agree to market the product, however, they will expect between forty and fifty percent of all profits."

See also Toymaking.

Toymaking

See Bedding and Upholstered Furniture Law; Consumer Safety Laws; Flammability Standards; Homework Laws; Labels or Tags Required by Law; Paints, Varnishes, and Other Finishes; Patterns, Commercial Use of; *and* Toy and Game Brokers.

Trade Associations/Publications

Each trade association (or organization) represents a particular industry and generally publishes a magazine or newsletter for its members. Trade publications or magazines are not found on newsstands but are available only by subscription or in libraries. Some associations sponsor trade shows, gift fairs, or expositions, offering members an opportunity to exhibit and sell their wares, but membership is not a requirement if you merely wish to visit a trade show to get the lay of the land or check out the competition. See the resource chapter for addresses of selected trade organizations (Association of Crafts and Creative Industries, Hobby Industry Association, and the National Needlework Association). Selected trade magazines (*Craft and Needlework Age, Craftrends/Sew Business,* and *Gifts & Decorative Accessories*) are also listed.

See also Home Business Organizations *and* Trade Shows.

Trade Magazines

See Trade Associations/Publications.

Trademark

 What does a trademark do and at what point would it be practical to invest in one?

Much depends on how grand your plans are for the future and how strongly you feel about protecting your creativity. What a registered trademark does is prevent one individual or company from trading

Common Law Trademarks

The longer you use any kind of mark in interstate commerce, the stronger your claim to it whether it is ever formally registered or not. This is called a "common law" trademark, and from experience, I have learned it carries considerable power. It had never occurred to me to trademark the name of my *Homemade Money* book, so I was naturally upset when someone lifted this book's title and attached it to a magazine of questionable quality, thereby suggesting that I was somehow connected to this publication or the company behind it. With the help of an attorney who sent several strongly-worded letters for me, I was able to stop a powerful multi-level-marketing company from using the words "Homemade Money" as the title of their magazine or MLM business. The attorney said my case had strength because, by that time, my home business "bible" had been in print for almost ten years and its title was closely identified with my name and personal reputation. "In building a trademark case," my attorney said, "much depends on the nature of the two products or publications in question, and whether it is likely that people would confuse one with the other."

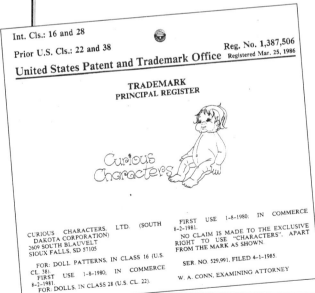

This is an example of the document the Trademark Office sends when a trademark has been officially registered.

on the good name and reputation of another. It may include any word, name, symbol, device, or any combination thereof that a manufacturer or merchant uses to identify his products and distinguish them from the products of others. You cannot trademark generic and descriptive names in the public domain, but you can protect your business logo, your company name, the names of new products, the artistic way you write your name, or even collections of colors and designs.

For example, the inventors of a tool for turning fabric tubes from wrong- to right-side out have named their product FASTURN®, and protected it by trademark. (The *R* in a circle tells us that the trademark has been officially registered.) Designer Patricia Kutza uses the name WHATKNOT™ as the name of her line of fashion accessories. Until this mark is officially trademarked, she can use the initials TM to indicate she has laid claim to this descriptive word. (See TIP below.)

Since you cannot adopt any trademark that is so similar to another that it is likely to confuse buyers, you may need to do a trademark search. This is expensive when done by an attorney, but you can do your own research by using the annual *Trademark Register of the U.S.* Available in large city libraries, this reference book contains every trademark (nearly 800,000) currently registered with the U.S. Patent & Trademark Office. Many libraries also subscribe to an online computer service such as *Trademark Scan* or *Thomsen and Thomsen.* Ask your library for more information since they may be able to help you make an economical trademark search. (There will be a per-minute charge for this service.)

Although the basic fee for a trademark is low, an application can be rejected for a variety of reasons and the whole process could take as long as two years to complete. If you plan to file an application without an attorney's help, be sure to read a couple of self-help books first to increase your chances for success. One you might look for is *Trademark: How to Name a Business & Product* by McGrath & Elias (Nolo Press).

Call the Patent & Trademark Office's toll-free number to hear recorded messages on this topic: 1-800-786-9199. You can also order a U.S. Trademark Search from The Trademark Register in Washington, D.C. for around $100 (price goes up about five dollars every year). This service provider will do an online computer search of all currently registered and renewed trademarks in the U.S. Patent & Trademark Office and send you a report (by fax if you wish). Their toll-free number for more information is 1-800-888-8062.

See also Business or Trade Name Registration/Protection; Copyright Categories of Protection; Patent and Trademark Searches; *and article, "Common Law Trademarks."*

Tip

Whether you plan to register your trademark or not, add the letters TM to any mark you wish to protect. Although this gives you no legal protection and does not obligate you to file a formal trademark application, it does give notice to others that you've claimed a mark and may discourage use by others as a result. If you later decide to register your trademark in Washington, these letters would be replaced with the trademark sign, ®, after every use of the trademark word or symbol. You may also use the words, "Registered in U.S. Patent and Trademark Office" or "Reg. U.S. Pat. and Tm. Off.")

Trade Name

See Business Name.

Trade Practice Rules

Certain industries must follow established trade practice rules set down by the Federal Trade Commission (FTC). If you are wholesaling products that fall into any of the following categories, contact the FTC and request information about rules relating to that industry:

- jewelry making
- leather or ladies' handbags
- feathers and down
- the catalog jewelry and giftware industry
- millinery
- furniture making
- mail order

If you violate an FTC rule and the FTC learns of it, they may order you to cease the illegal practice. Penalties generally occur only if a cease-and-desist order is ignored.

See also Federal Trade Commission Rules.

Trade References

See Credit/Trade References.

Trade Secret

According to the Department of Labor, the legal definition of a trade secret is: "Any confidential formula, pattern, process, device, information, or compilation of information that is used in an employer's business, and that gives the employer an advantage over competitors who do not know or use it." Common trade secrets are colors, flavors, perfumes, and formulas for soft drinks. In the crafts industry, a trade secret might be the glaze formula used for ceramics or the recipe that makes bread dough creations unique. It could also be the way in which a product is constructed. As one product maker told me, "I've put my doll together in such a way the average crafter can't figure out how to copy it and sell it herself."

In summary, trade secrets protect all kinds of business know-how as long as they do not become a matter of public knowledge. Since common law trade secret protection exists, you might have grounds for a lawsuit if someone steals your trade secret.

Trade Shows

 How can I find trade shows through which to market my handcrafts and gifts?

The type or kind of trade show you will exhibit in depends on what you're selling and the kind of buyer you want to reach. Professional artists, craft sellers, and makers of toys, gifts, and decorative accessories can choose from many different shows. Publications in the field of art and crafts, sewing, and needlework that regularly announce wholesale gift and trade shows include *The Crafts Report, Craft Supply Magazine, Craft and Needlework Age,* and *Gifts & Decorative Accessories.* Some organizations that regularly produce trade shows include the American Craft Association, Hobby Industry Association, and the National Needlework Association. (All are listed in the resource chapter.)

Small producers who cannot afford the high cost of exhibiting in a trade show can reach this market through sales representatives who regularly exhibit in trade shows or have a presence in one or more gift marts. If you just want to browse a trade show to get the lay of the land, be prepared to prove you are in business and not just a hobbyist. (Prior to registering to attend a show, ask what kind of identification you will need to bring with you.)

See also Sales Representatives; Trade Associations/Publications; *and* Wholesaling.

Trunk Shows

A trunk show is a marketing strategy used by designers and craft sellers who are trying to interest particular shops or stores into carrying a large inventory of their work. It's similar to what bookstores do when the author of a new book comes in for the day to personally autograph all books sold and answer questions from his or her fans.

Sellers offer to bring a supply of products to the store that they will sell in person over a period of days, giving the store owner an agreed-upon percentage of total sales. Stores will generally send postcards to their customer list about such an event or run special ads. (It's helpful to give them artwork accordingly.) Stores benefit financially from such a promotion, and the designer or craftsperson also benefits from personal contact with so many new customers who may prompt ideas for new products.

Two-Step Advertising

In one-step advertising, the goal is to get a direct sale. While this can be done in a display advertisement or direct mailing, it is almost impossible to do in a classified advertisement. The two-step method is commonly used here because advertisers understand that people generally need more information to make a buying decision. Generally, a catalog, brochure, or other information is offered (free or at a small fee) in the hope that the more detailed information will generate a sale. Since only a small percentage of people will order in any event, it is always necessary to do follow-up mailings to all prospects who have responded to your two-step ads.

United Parcel Service

Did you know that UPS will pick up packages at your home? You call one day and they pick up the next. In addition to the shipping charge, you will be charged a modest weekly pickup fee that applies to the first pickup of the week and covers all other packages and pickups in that same week. You will find a toll-free number for UPS in your phone book. When you call for a pickup, the operator will want to know:

a) where the package is going
b) its weight and measurements
c) whether you want it insured for more than the normal amount of $100.

You will be instructed to give the UPS driver a check in the right amount. Although UPS rates are more expensive than shipping by mail, the advantage of using UPS is that packages can be tracked and they are rarely lost or damaged. Delivery anywhere in the country takes only a few days. If you plan to use UPS regularly, ask for information about their "Ready Customer Pickup Service."

See also Canadian Sales *and* Priority Mail.

Tip

Always check with your Canadian customers before shipping anything by UPS. Such shipments must go through Customs, which causes delays and extra charges to customers who must pick up packages themselves. When possible, ship small packages to Canada by first-class or priority mail. Larger packages can be sent by fourth-class mail (what the U.S. Postal Service now calls Standard Mail). This is free from Customs inspection and is delivered right to the customer's door.

UPC Bar Codes

Q: *Which products must have UPC Codes on them?*

A UPC (Universal Product Code) is a set of numbers that identifies a company and a product it sells. The first six digits (which are assigned by the Uniform Code Council) identify the company, while the next five digits (which are assigned by the manufacturer) indicate the product. A last "check digit" provides additional identity information. Bar codes must be computer-generated through special software programs or handled by a printing company. UPC registration is currently $300 and is good for the lifetime of the manufacturer. (The Uniform Code Council offers a free brochure on this topic titled "About the Universal Product Code.")

The good news is that most artists and craftspeople don't have to worry about bar coding because bar codes are not common to the gift industry (gift shops, craft shops, craft malls, etc.). However, bar coding is likely to be required on products wholesaled to large retailers, chain stores, and bookstores who use a computerized inventory system. (When bar codes are scanned at the checkout counter, the retailer's inventory figures are automatically adjusted.)

U.S. Postal Service

See Mail, Classes of *and* Postal Regulations.

Vehicle Used for Business

The IRS allows self-employed individuals to deduct expenses for the part-time business use of a personal vehicle. You are not required by law to keep a travel diary, but you must keep some kind of records to prove your deductions to the IRS. If your daily travel is routine (to places where the mileage doesn't change, such as the bank, post office, printer, etc.), a simple calendar notation should suffice. At month's end it's easy to multiply number of trips times distance to each place to get total business mileage. If you travel to many different locations, it would be wise to log beginning and ending odometer readings to your calendar for each trip. Don't forget to make a note of the odometer reading at the end or beginning of each year.

See also Car Insurance *and* Labor Laws: OSHA Act of 1970.

Tip

The older your vehicle, the more advantageous it may be to figure your vehicle deductions on the basis of total operating costs instead of mileage. How you start figuring deductions in your first year of business is important, says the IRS. If you begin by figuring expenses on total operating costs, you will be locked into using this method forever; however, if you begin by calculating vehicle expenses on the basis of mileage, in following years you may choose whichever method is most tax-advantageous for you.

Voice Mail vs. Answering Machine

Q: *What's the difference between using an answering machine and a voice mail service?*

An answering machine can provide callers with a standard greeting and take only one call at a time while voice mail allows a business to leave a variety of messages for callers while taking several calls at once. With voice mail, you can either create a personal greeting or choose the standard greeting. Changing the greeting is just a matter of punching a few buttons to record a new message and listen to it before saving it.

Voice mail records messages when your phone goes unanswered as well as when you're on the phone. Because several calls can be taken simultaneously, voice mail is terrific for those times when you're expecting many customers to call to place orders. For example, my voice mail message tells callers I will be happy to return their call, but if they just want to place an order on a credit card, they should give me information accordingly. This is especially handy when I'm traveling, and particularly when I'm on vacation because my customers can still place orders for my books. (During vacation periods, I simply change the voice mail message to indicate exactly when calls will be returned.)

Another benefit of voice mail is its ease in retrieving messages when you're away from your home office. You simply call your service, listen to messages, and punch a button to repeat, delete, or save each message for later handling. My voice mail system allows me to save as many as thirty messages for up to sixteen days.

See also Fax Machine *and* Telephone Messages for Callers.

Tip

Many people hate voice mail because it sounds cold and indifferent and gives too many instructions on buttons to push, so the shorter and friendlier you can make your voice mail message, the better.

Wholesaling

See Accounts Receivable; Advertising; Brochure; Catalog Houses, Selling to; Checks; COD Shipments; Collection Strategies; Copyrights of Others; Credit Card Sales; Credit/Trade References; Designer Fabrics, Commercial Use of; Distributor/Jobber; Fax Machine; Flammability Standards; Invoices Not Paid; Invoicing Policies; Markups; Packing List; Patterns, Commercial Use of; Photo Kits; Price List; Pricing Guidelines; Printed Materials; Product Liability Insurance; Pro Forma; Purchase Order; Sales Representatives; Supplies, Buying Wholesale; UPC Bar Codes; *and article, "Pricing Formulas for Handcraft Sellers."*

Windows Software

You should know that all new PC-based computers today are shipping with this software installed. It may seem wonderful to get this program as part of a computer purchase, but this is not "user-friendly" software, and it will take time to learn. Long-time computer users who have grown up with DOS-based software and now use it to run their homebased businesses may not want Windows software on their next computer, but they're going to get it anyway because Microsoft, the maker of this software, is reportedly penalizing computer manufacturers if they ship any computer without this software installed. (When I called Gateway Computers to confirm this, they refused to comment but did tell me I would have to take Windows with any computer I ordered from them in the future, whether I wanted it or not. I was assured, however, that once I got the computer, I could call their support system and they would walk me through the uninstallation procedure to get this software off the hard disk.)

As one of my business friends has learned, however, some brands of computers will not allow Windows software to be uninstalled (or erased). She reported that when she bought a new Pentium computer with Windows 95 software on it, she was assured that she could run WordPerfect 6.0 for DOS on that machine. Although that software program installed okay, it would not run and the whole system locked up every time she tried to use WordPerfect. She had to shut off the computer to get out of the lockup. Then, when she tried to uninstall Windows 95, the machine would not allow her to do this; worse, when she tried to get rid of it by formatting the hard disk, she got an "access denied" message. Now she's stuck with a computer she can't really use because it won't accept the software she prefers.

Unlike Windows 3.1 (the older version of this program that is compatible with all DOS-based software), Windows 95 appears to have something embedded in its programming that not only makes it impossible to erase, but also makes it impossible to run certain DOS-based software on the same system. Currently, some DOS software will run with Windows 95, but a computer techie tells me that one day soon, neither Windows software or new computer hardware will work with DOS at all, and long-time DOS users like myself will suddenly find themselves up the creek without a paddle when their old system dies. Although new versions of all leading software programs have been designed to operate with the latest versions of Windows software, I resent the fact that individual computer users like myself are literally being forced to learn new software programs we neither need nor have time to learn.

Wool and Other Textiles

In addition to the textile labeling requirements of the Bureau of Consumer Protection (discussed under *Labels or Tags Required by Law*), the FTC requires certain labels on all textile wearing apparel, household furnishings, garments containing fur (see discus-

Sample labels provided by Charm Woven Labels. Note how Carolyn's Creative Stitchery has included the "where crafted" information on her regular fabric label.

sions elsewhere), and all items made of wool. The FTC's *Wool Products Labeling Act* requires that all wool or textile products bear a label that clearly indicates where the product has been made, and when imported ingredients are used. Thus the label for a shawl woven in the United States from imported fibers would read, "Made in the USA from imported products." Items that originate entirely in this country need only state "Made in the USA," "Crafted in USA," or words to that effect. (These regulations are also applicable to the descriptions of such products in mail order catalogs sent to consumers.)

If you happen to be shearing your own wool for textile products or yarns you sell, your products must also meet certain fabric flammability standards of The Consumer Product Safety Commission. The agency will send you more information on request.

See also Flammability Standards *and* Labels or Tags Required by Law.

Workers' Compensation Insurance

Workers' Compensation Insurance protects business owners against lawsuits from employees who are injured on the job. Each state has its own law about when such insurance is necessary, so you should contact your state capitol for more information on this topic. Generally speaking, however, it is required only for craft businesses with four or more part- or full-time employees who are *not* family members, independent contractors, or statutory employees who work for you out of their own homes. (Be sure your independent contractors meet the necessary legal requirements.)

See also Independent Contractors.

Writing

See Author/Publisher Contract; Book Copyright; Contracts; Copyright Categories of Protection; Copyrights in Public Domain; Copyrights of Others; Desktop Publishing; *and* First Rights/All Rights Sales.

ZIP Code

ZIP stands for Zone Improvement Plan. Our system of 5-digit codes was established in 1963. Large volume mailers can lower the cost of their mailings by the use of ZIP+4 (additional digits that identify a specific range of delivery addresses). Your postmaster will be happy to provide details on how to do this. If you plan to do regular mailings or handle any volume of mail inquiries, consider purchasing the *National Five-Digit Zip Code and Post Office Directory* (about fifteen dollars) from your local post office.

Zoning Laws

Q: *I'm afraid I may be violating local zoning laws. What should I do about this?*

To accommodate the large number of home office workers throughout the country, many communities have changed their zoning laws in recent years. Some have eased the restrictions while others have only made them worse by limiting the amount of square footage a homebased business can occupy or the number of employees a business can hire. Some communities still haven't done a thing about badly outdated zoning laws written in horse-and-buggy days. You need to find out where you stand so you can take appropriate action.

Either call your city or county clerk or visit the library to get a copy of your community's zoning regulations. Find out what zone you're in and read the section that pertains to home occupations.

If you learn you are currently violating a zoning ordinance, don't panic. Thousands of others who work at home have learned that what zoning officials don't know about a business can often remain a secret that harms no one. The most important thing to do is keep a low profile by not advertising locally, discussing your homebased business with neighbors, or doing anything to annoy them. Zoning officials aren't likely to check on a business or discover a zoning violation unless a business owner has attracted media attention locally or a neighbor has registered a complaint. Things most likely to cause problems in any neighborhood are loud noises, strong odors, obvious customer traffic, the tying up of parking places, use of a business sign when one is prohibited, or anything else that disturbs the serenity of a neighborhood.

• **Home Parties and Other Product Sales.** If you plan to present home parties or sell products of any kind to people who come to your home for a sales demonstration, be aware that zoning regulations in some areas prohibit one from using the home to transfer the sale of merchandise. To avoid breaking the law, accept payment for all orders at the time of the sale but deliver products the next day instead of letting customers walk out the door with them.

• **Holiday Boutiques.** Zoning officials generally view one- and two-day home boutiques in the same light as garage sales, but it's always a good idea to check with authorities before planning such an event. Advertising signs are normally taboo in a residential neighborhood but temporary boutique or sale signs may be approved by city officials upon request. To make sure your neighbors don't give you problems about the lack of parking spaces during the sale, offer them a sneak preview the night before and perhaps a ten percent discount on merchandise as well.

Although there have been exceptions, there is usually no financial penalty for violation of U.S. zoning laws beyond immediate cessation of the business activity. Violating the cease and desist order, however, would probably trigger a fine.

See also Licenses and Permits *and* P.O. Box Address.

Tip

Some businesses have been successful in obtaining a zoning variance (also called a special use, conditional use, or special exemption permit) that gives permission to use one's home for any reason that is clearly secondary to its use as a dwelling. Generally, people who apply for a special use permit must post a sign announcing their application to the local Board of Appeals, then attend a formal meeting to obtain the necessary permission. Having the support of neighbors can make a big difference here.

Resources

NOTE: All listings in this chapter appear in alphabetical order by business name within the individual categories.

Business and Trade Periodicals

This is a selected list of publications in the art, craft, and home business industries believed to be of special interest to this book's readers. For the names of other periodicals, check library directories such as *The Standard Periodical Directory*, *Ulrich's International Periodicals Directory*, *Hudson's Subscription Newsletter Directory*, and the *Oxbridge Directory of Newsletters*.

Most of these publications have been discussed or mentioned in the text. For more information, check the index to find page references.

- *The Art Calendar—The Business Magazine for Visual Artists, P.O. Box 199, Upper Fairmount, MD 21867*
- *Arts 'N Crafts ShowGuide,* P.O. Box 25, Jefferson City, MO 65102
- *Craft and Needlework Age,* 225 Gordons Corner Plaza, Box 420, Manalapan, NJ 07726
- *Crafts Magazine,* Box 1790, Peoria, IL 61656 (This newsstand monthly includes author's "Selling What You Make" column.)
- *The Crafts Report—The Business Journal for the Crafts Industry,* Box 1992, Wilmington, DE 19899, 1-800-777-7098
- *Craftrends/Sew Business,* Box 1790, Peoria, IL 61656

- *Craft Supply Magazine—The Industry Journal for the Professional Crafter,* 225 Gordons Corner Rd., Manalapan, NJ 07726 (Subscription includes annual Trade Directory.)
- *The Dream Merchant—How to Make Money from Good Ideas,* 2309 Torrance Blvd., Suite 201, Torrance, CA 90501
- *The Fiberfest Magazine,* P.O. Box 112, Hastings, MI 49058
- *Gift Basket Review, Festivities Publications, Inc.,* 815 Haines St., Jacksonville, FL 32206
- *Gifts & Decorative Accessories,* Geyer-McAllister Pub., Inc., 51 Madison St., New York, NY 10010 (Subscription includes annual *Buyer's Guide.*)
- *Mid-Atlantic Craft Show List,* P.O. Box 161, Catasauqua, PA 18032
- *Neighbors and Friends—The Art & Crafts Market Guide,* 3410 Black Champ Rd., Midlothian, TX 76065 (This magazine is also available online.)
- *The Professional Quilter,* 104 Bramblewood Lane, Lewisberry, PA 17339
- *SAC Newsmonthly,* P.O. Box 159, Bogalusa, LA 70429, 1-800-TAKE-SAC
- *Sew News—The Fashion Magazine for People Who Sew,* PJS Publications, Inc., Box 1790, Peoria, IL 61656
- *Sunshine Artists—America's Premier Show and Festival Publications,* 2600 Temple Dr., Winter Park, FL 32789

Organizations

This is a selected list of art, craft, and home business organizations likely to be helpful to readers of this book. Check the Index to find page number references to organizations mentioned in the text. Some of these organizations sponsor trade shows and most offer a newsletter or magazine as part of their membership benefits. Organizations that offer merchant bank card services or group medical insurance programs have a reference in parentheses after the listing.

To find names and addresses of other organizations, check library directories such as the *Encyclopedia of Associations* or *National Trade and Professional Associations of the U.S.*

- American Association of Home-Based Businesses, P.O. Box 10023, Rockville, MD 20849, 1-800-447-9710 (Offers bank card services and group health insurance plan. Members receive *AAHBB Connector* newsletter.)
- American Craft Association, 21 S. Eltings Corner Rd., Highland, NY 12528, 1-800-724-0859
- American Craft Council, Membership Dept., P.O. Box 3000, Denville, NJ 07834 (Offers group health insurance plan. Members receive *American Craft* magazine.)
- American Society of Artists, Inc., P.O. Box 1326, Palatine, IL 60078
- Arts and Crafts Business Solutions, 2804 Bishop Gate Dr., Raleigh, NC 27613, 1-800-873-1192
- Association of Crafts and Creative Industries, P.O. Box 2188, Zanesville, OH 43702
- Hobby Industry Association (HIA), 319 E. 54th St., Elmwood Park, NJ 07407
- Home Business Institute Inc., P.O. Box 301, White Plains, NY 10605, 1-888-DIAL-HBI (Offers bank card services and group health insurance plan. Members receive *Inside Home Business* newsletter.)
- Inventors Workshop International, 1029 Castillo St., Santa Barbara, CA 93101 (Members receive *Invent!* magazine.)
- The National Association of Fine Artists, P.O. Box 4189, Ft. Lauderdale, FL 33338, 1-800-996-NAFA (Offers bank card services and group health insurance plan. Members receive *ArtTalk* newsletter.)
- National Craft Association, 1945 East Ridge Rd., Suite 5178, Rochester, NY 14622, 1-800-318-9410 (Membership includes free listing in *National Directory of Artisans*.)
- National Mail Order Association, 2807 Polk St. N.E., Minneapolis, MN 55418 (Members receive *Mail Order Digest* newsletter.)
- The National Needlework Association, Inc., P.O. Box 2188, Zanesville, OH 43702
- Small Publishers Association of North America (SPAN), P.O. Box 1306, Buena Vista, CA 81211 (Members receive *SPAN* newsletter.)
- Society of Craft Designers, P.O. Box 2188, Zanesville, OH 43702
- Volunteer Lawyers for the Arts, 1 East 53rd St., New York, NY 10022, Legal Hotline: 1-212-319-2910

Government Agencies

Your tax money is paying for all the free business information available from government agencies, so be sure to obtain needed information. Check the index to find text references to the following agencies and a reminder of why you need to contact them.

- Bureau of Consumer Protection, Division of Special Statutes, 6th & Pennsylvania Ave. NW, Washington, DC 20580
- Consumer Product Safety Commission, Bureau of Compliance, 5401 Westbard Ave., Bethesda, MD 20207, 1-800-638-2772
- The Copyright Office, Register of Copyrights, Library of Congress, Washington, DC 20559, (202) 707-3000
- Department of Commerce, Office of Consumer Affairs, Washington, DC 20233
- Federal Trade Commission, 6th St. & Pennsylvania Ave. N.W., Washington, DC 20580 (For *Office Supply Scams* booklet, direct request to the attention of the Public Distribution Center, Room B-3 at above address.)
- Internal Revenue Service (Check your telephone book for the nearest IRS office and request all free booklets related to running a business at home.)
- Patent & Trademark Office, U. S. Department of Commerce, Washington, DC 20231, 1-800-786-9199
- SCORE, 1-800-634-0245
- Social Security Administration, Department of Health and Human Services, Baltimore, MD 21235, 1-800-772-1213
- The Trademark Register, National Press Bldg., Suite 1297, Washington, DC 20045, 1-800-888-8062
- U. S. Fish & Wildlife Service, Department of the Interior, Washington, DC 20240
- U. S. Small Business Administration, 1-800-827-5722 (To receive a listing of all the low-cost management and assistance publications and bibliographies available from the SBA, write to SBA Publications, P.O. Box 30, Denver, CO 80201-0030. Ask for *SBA Form 115A*.)

Suppliers and Service Providers

The following suppliers and service providers have been mentioned in the text. For additional information about their offerings, check the index for page number references.

- The Art & Creative Materials Institute, Inc., 100 Boylston St., Suite 1050, Boston, MA 02116
- BDL Homeware, 2509 N. Campbell Ave., Tucson, AZ 85719
- Charm Woven Labels, 2400 W. Magnolia Blvd., Burbank, CA 91506, 1-800-843-1111
- Checks In The Mail, 2435 Goodwin Lane, New Braunfels, TX 78135, 1-800-733-4443
- Connect America, 1-800-745-9650
- Coomers, Inc., 6012 Reef Point Lane, Fort Worth, TX 76135
- Dover Publications *Pictorial Archive Books*, 31 E. 2nd St., Mineola, NY 11501
- E & S Creations, P.O. Box 68, Rexburg, ID 83440
- Equifax, Credit Information Services, Wildwood Plaza, 7200 Windy Hill, Suite 500, Marietta, GA 30067
- GraphComm Services, P.O. Box 220, Freeland, WA 98249, 1-800-488-7436
- Grayarc, 1-800-243-5250
- Great Papers, 1-800-287-8163
- Independent Insurance Agents of America, 1-800-221-7917
- ISBN Agency, R. R. Bowker, 121 Chanlon Rd., New Providence, NJ 07974
- Novus Services, Inc., 1-800-347-2000
- Office Depot, 1-800-685-8800
- OfficeMax, 1-800-788-8080
- Paper Direct, 1-800-A-PAPERS
- Pitney Bowes, 1-800-MR-BOWES
- Queblo, 1-800-523-9080
- Quill, 1-800-789-1331
- Safeware, The Insurance Agency, Inc., 1-800-848-3469
- Trans Union, National Consumer Disclosure Center, 25249 Country Club Blvd., P.O. Box 7000, North Olmsted, OH 44070

- Treasure Caché, 33 Walt Whitman Rd., Suite 110, Huntington Station, NY 11746
- TRW Consumer Assistance Center, P.O. Box 749029, Dallas, TX 75374
- Uniform Code Council, Inc., 8163 Old Yankee Rd., Suite J, Dayton, OH 45458
- Viking, 1-800-421-1222
- Widby Enterprises, 4321 Crestfield, Knoxville, TN 37921
- Wood Cellar Graphics, 87180 563rd Ave., Coleridge, NE 68727

Recommended Books, Booklets, and Directories

Books published by leading trade publishers can be found in any bookstore or library. Many of the titles on the following list, however, have been self-published by authors who generally sell only by mail. On the address list immediately following this list of books, you will find contact information for publishers who will send you additional information about a title upon request.

NOTE: When checking your library for any of these books, pay close attention to the latest edition referenced for each. Libraries do not always replace old editions on their shelves with the latest editions in print, so for the most up-to-date information on any topic, obtain the latest edition of any book of interest.

- *Art Marketing 101: A Handbook for the Fine Artist* by Constance Smith (ArtNetwork)
- *The Basic Guide to Selling Arts & Crafts* by James Dillehay (Warm Snow Publishers)
- *Business Forms and Contracts (in Plain English) for Crafts People* by Leonard D. DuBoff (Interweave Press)
- *The Business of Sewing—How to Start, Maintain, and Achieve Success* by Barbara Wright Sykes (Collins Publications)
- *The Complete Guide to Self-Publishing—Everything You Need to Know to Write, Publish, Promote, and Sell Your Own Book* by Marilyn and Tom Ross (3rd. ed., Writer's Digest Books)

- *The Copyright Handbook—How to Protect and Use Written Works* by Attorney Stephen Fishman (3rd ed., Nolo Press)
- *Crafting as a Business—The Do-It-Yourself Guide to a Successful Crafts Business* by Wendy Rosen (Chilton)
- *Crafting for Dollars—How to Establish & Profit from a Career in Crafts* by Sylvia Landman (Prima)
- *Craft Malls—The Basics of How-to-Do-It* by Barbara Massie (Magnolia Press)
- *The Crafts Supply Sourcebook* by Margaret Boyd (Betterway Books)
- *Creative Cash—How to Sell Your Crafts, Needlework, Designs & Know-How* by Barbara Brabec (5th ed., Barbara Brabec Productions)
- *Directory of Craft Shops & Galleries* by Adele Patti (11th ed., Front Room Publishers)
- *Directory of Craft Malls & Rent-a-Space Shops* by Adele Patti (2nd ed., Front Room Publishers)
- *Directory of Printers* by Marie Kiefer (Ad-Lib Publications)
- *Directory of Wholesale Reps for Craft Professionals* by Sharon Olson (Northwoods Trading Co.)
- *Don't Get Zapped by Your Computer* by Don Sellers (Peachpit Press)
- *Everybody's Guide to Small Claims Court* by Attorney Ralph Warner (6th ed., Nolo Press)
- *Getting Organized* by Stephanie Winston (Warner Books)
- *Handmade for Profit—Hundreds of Secrets to Success in Selling Arts & Crafts* by Barbara Brabec (M. Evans)
- *Homemade Money—How to Select, Start, Manage, Market, and Multiply the Profits of a Business at Home* by Barbara Brabec (rev. 5th ed., Betterway Books)
- *How to Be a Weekend Entrepreneur Making Money at Craft Fairs & Trade Shows* by Susan Ratliff (Marketing Methods Press)
- *How to Get Happily Published* by Judith Appelbaum (5th ed., HarperCollins)
- *How to Put On a Great Craft Show, First Time and Every Time* by Dianne and Lee Spiegel (FairCraft Publishing)
- *How to Start & Run a Successful Handcraft Co-Op in Your Own Community* by Catherine Gilleland (Front Room Publishers)
- *INC Yourself—How to Profit by Setting Up Your Own Corporation* by Judith H. McQuown (8th ed., HarperBusiness)

- *The Inventor's Handbook: How to Develop, Protect, and Market Your Invention* by Robert Park (2nd ed., Betterway Books)
- *Legal Forms for Starting & Running a Small Business* by Attorney Fred S. Steingold (Nolo Press)
- *The Legal Guide for Starting & Running a Small Business* by Attorney Fred S. Steingold (3rd ed., Nolo Press)
- *Marketing Online* by Marcia Yudkin (Plume)
- *Money Making Marketing—Finding the People Who Need What You're Selling* by Jeffrey Lant (JLA Publications)
- *The Needlecrafter's Computer Companion—Hundreds of Easy Ways to Use Your Computer for Sewing, Quilting, Cross-Stitch, Knitting & More!* by Judy Heim (No Starch Press)
- *Newsletters from the Desktop—Designing Effective Publications With Your Computer* by Roger C. Parker (Ventana Press)
- *Organizing Your Home Office for Success* by Lisa Kanarek (Plume)
- *Patent It Yourself* by Attorney David Pressman (3rd ed., Nolo Press)
- *Pattern Designer Directory* by Adele Patti (Front Room Publishers)
- *Professional Teaching Techniques: A Handbook for Teaching Adults Any Subject* by Elizabeth Nelson (WE Unlimited)
- *Publishing Newsletters* by Howard Penn Hudson (The Newsletter Clearinghouse)
- *The Self-Publishing Manual—How to Write, Print & Sell Your Own Book* by Dan Poynter (7th ed., Para Publishing)
- *Sell and Resell Your Photos* by Rohn Engh (Writer's Digest Books)
- *Selling in Craft Malls* by Patricia Krauss (Showplace Marketing)
- *Sew Up a Storm—How to Succeed in a Sewing-Related Business* by Karen L. Maslowski (SewStorm Publishing)
- *Small Time Operator—How to Start Your Own Business, Keep Your Books, Pay Your Taxes, and Stay Out of Trouble* by Bernard Kamoroff, CPA (Bell Springs Publishing)
- *Smart Tax Write-Offs: Hundreds of Tax Deduction Ideas, for Home Based Businesses, Independent Contractors, All Entrepreneurs* by Norm Ray (Rayve Productions)
- *Stand Alone, Inventor! And Make Money With Your New Product Ideas!* by Robert G. Merrick (Lee Publishing)
- *Stand Up to the IRS* by Attorney Fred Daily (3rd ed., Nolo Press)

- *Trademark: How to Name a Business & Product* by Attorneys Kate McGrath and Stephen Elias (Nolo Press)
- *Turning Your Great Idea Into a Great Success* by Judy Ryder (Peterson's)
- *The Woodworker's Guide to Pricing Your Work* by Dan Ramsey (Betterway Books)

Book Publishers

- Ad-Lib Publications, 51½ W. Adams, Fairfield, IA 52556
- ArtNetwork, P.O. Box 1268, Penn Valley, CA 95946
- Bell Springs Publishing, P.O. Box 640, Laytonville, CA 95454
- Betterway Books, 1507 Dana Ave., Cincinnati, OH 45207, 1-800-289-0963
- R. R. Bowker Co., 205 E. 42 St., New York, NY 10017
- Barbara Brabec Productions, P.O. Box 2137, Naperville, IL 60567
- Collins Publications, 3233 Grand Ave., Suite N-294, Chino Hills, CA 91709
- FairCraft Publishing, P.O. Box 5508, Mill Valley, CA 94942
- The Front Room Publishers, P.O. Box 1541, Clifton, NJ 07015
- Interweave Press, Inc., 201 E. Fourth St., Loveland, CO 80537
- JLA Publications, 50 Follen St., Suite 507, Cambridge, MA 02138
- Lee Publishing Co., 690 W. Fremont Ave., Suite 3, Sunnyvale, CA 94087
- Magnolia Press, 127 Flathead Drive, Cherokee Village, AR 72529
- Marketing Methods Press, 2811 N. 7th Ave., Phoenix, AZ 85007
- The Newsletter Clearinghouse, P.O. Box 311, Rhinebeck, NY 12572
- Nolo Press, 950 Parker St., Berkeley, CA 94710, 1-800-992-6656
- Northwoods Trading Co., 13451 Essex Ct., Eden Prairie, MN 55347
- No Starch Press, 401 China Basin St., Suite 108, San Francisco, CA 94107
- Para Publishing, P.O. Box 4232-175, Santa Barbara, CA 93140, 1-800-PARAPUB
- Rayve Productions, Box 726, Windsor, CA 95492, 1-800-852-4890
- SewStorm Publishing, 944 Sutton Rd., Cincinnati, OH 45230

- Showplace Marketing, 7046 Broadway #360, Lemon Grove, CA 91945
- Warm Snow Publishers, P.O. Box 75, Torreon, NM 87061
- WE Unlimited, P.O. Box 120633, St. Paul, MN 55112
- Writer's Digest Books, 1507 Dana Ave., Cincinnati, OH 45207, 1-800-289-0963

Index